Sisters in Sin

The prostitute and her sister in sin – the so-called "fallen" woman – were veritable obsessions of American Progressive Era culture. Their cumulative presence, in scores of controversial theatrical productions, demonstrates the repeated obsession with the prostitute figure in both highbrow and lowbrow entertainments. As the first extended examination of such dramas during the Progressive Era, *Sisters in Sin* recovers a slice of theatre history in demonstrating that the prostitute was central to the development of American realist theatre. Plays about prostitutes were so popular that they constituted a forgotten genre – the brothel drama. The brothel drama's stunning success reveals much about early twentieth-century American anxieties about sexuality, eugenics, contagion, women's rights, and urbanization. Introducing previously unexamined archival documents and unpublished play scripts, this original study argues that the body of the prostitute was a corporeal site upon which modernist desires and cultural imperatives were mapped.

KATIE N. JOHNSON specializes in theatre, film, and gender studies in the English Department at Miami University of Ohio where she is Associate Professor. In 2003, she was awarded the Gerald Kahan Award for best essay in the field of theatre studies by a younger scholar. Her work has appeared in *Theatre Journal, Theatre Survey*, the *Journal of American Drama and Research, American Drama*, the *Eugene O'Neill Review*, the *American Transcendental Quarterly*, and the *Encyclopedia of American Cultural and Intellectual History*.

CAMBRIDGE STUDIES IN AMERICAN THEATRE AND DRAMA

General Editor
Don B. Wilmeth, *Brown University*

Advisory Board
C. W. E. Bigsby, *University of East Anglia*
C. Lee Jenner, *Independent critic and dramaturge*
Bruce A. McConachie, *University of Pittsburgh*
Brenda Murphy, *University of Connecticut*
Laurence Senelick, *Tufts University*

The American theatre and its literature are attracting, after long neglect, the crucial attention of historians, theoreticians, and critics of the arts. Long a field for isolated research yet too frequently marginalized in the academy, the American theatre has always been a sensitive gauge of social pressures and public issues. Investigations into its myriad of shapes and manifestations are relevant to students of drama, theatre, literature, cultural experience, and political development.

The primary intent of this series is to set up a forum of important and original scholarship in and criticism of American theatre and drama in a cultural and social context. Inclusive by design, the series accommodates leading work in areas ranging from the study of drama as literature to theatre histories, theoretical explorations, production histories, and readings of more popular or paratheatrical forms. While maintaining a specific emphasis on theatre in the United States, the series welcomes work grounded broadly in cultural studies and narratives with interdisciplinary reach. Cambridge Studies in American Theatre and Drama thus provides a crossroads where historical, theoretical, literary, and biographical approaches meet and combine, promoting imaginative research in theatre and drama from a variety of new perspectives.

BOOKS IN THE SERIES

Sisters in Sin

Brothel Drama in America, *1900–1920*

KATIE N. JOHNSON

CAMBRIDGE
UNIVERSITY PRESS

CAMBRIDGE UNIVERSITY PRESS

Cambridge, New York, Melbourne, Madrid, Cape Town, Singapore, São Paulo

CAMBRIDGE UNIVERSITY PRESS

The Edinburgh Building, Cambridge CB2 2RU, UK

Published in the United States of America by Cambridge University Press, New York

www.cambridge.org
Information on this title: www.cambridge.org/9780521855051

First published 2006

Printed in the United Kingdom at the University Press, Cambridge

A catalogue record for this publication is available from the British Library

ISBN-13 978-0-521-85505-1 hardback
ISBN-10 0-521-85505-5 hardback

For Timothy and Liam
And for Ruby Gabler Fick

Through the countless ages, and on down into our own times, the scarlet woman has been looked upon as one who in sheer wantonness had chosen her evil mode of life. "Very well," said society, "she has made her bed, now let her lie in it."

Madeleine, a turn-of-the-century prostitute

Contents

Illustrations

Acknowledgments

As I often tell my students, any project worth its salt undergoes extensive revision. Their jaws usually fall open when I explain just how many drafts this project has gone through. Mine does as well. But it's true: *Sisters in Sin* has been read by numerous people who have given generously of their time and intellect; without their tireless efforts, this work would never have been possible.

I am grateful to the insightful comments from my Miami colleagues: Barry Chabott, Mary Jean Corbett, Frances Dolan, Stefanie Kyle Dunning, Susan Morgan, Kerry Powell, Dianne Sadoff, Jonathan A. Strauss, and Keith Tuma. A hearty thanks goes to Miami University for providing me with extraordinary institutional support, including an assigned research leave, a summer faculty research and travel grant, plus several publication grants.

Special thanks to series editor Don B. Wilmeth for his enormous help in shaping and editing the project and to Victoria Cooper, Rebecca Jones, James Woodhouse, Anna-Marie Lovett, and the readers at Cambridge University Press.

My mentors from the University of Washington were invaluable: Barry Witham, Jack Wolcott, Stephen Weeks, Sara Schneider, and Kate Cummings. In particular I'd like to thank Sarah Bryant-Bertail for her many insights into my work. In a most incalculable way, the generous spirit of the late Michael Quinn has guided me throughout this project. Fellow graduate students at the University of Washington Drama school – Shinya Inoe, Tina Redd, Rebecca Brown, Terry Donovan Smith, and, especially, Tamara Underiner – continue to sustain me.

I am grateful to those editors whose suggestions have improved my work that has appeared elsewhere in print: Rosemarie K. Bank, Noreen Barnes-McLain, Susan Bennett, Zander Brietzke, Harry J. Elam, Loren Kruger, Vera Mowry Roberts, and David Román. Thanks also to Laurence Senelick for sharing his clipping files with me and to David Savran and the American Society for Theatre Research Gerald Kahan Award Committee. I wish to also thank publishers for permission to reprint articles, all of which have been revised for this book. These articles include: "'*Anna Christie*': the Repentant Courtesan, Made Respectable," *Eugene O'Neill Review* 26 (June 2004): 87–104; "Rachel Crothers' *Ourselves*: Feminist Dramaturgy in the Brothel Drama," *Journal of American Drama & Theatre* 15.3 (Fall 2003): 101–121; "*Damaged Goods*: Sex Hysteria and the *Prostitute Fatale*," *Theatre Survey* 44 (May 2003): 43–67; "*Zaza*: That Obtruding Harlot of the Stage," *Theatre Journal* 54 (May 2002): 223–43; and "Censoring *Sapho*: Regulating the Fallen Woman and the Prostitute on the New York Stage," *ATQ: Nineteenth-Century American Literature and Culture* 10.3 (1996): 167–86.

Many people from various archives and libraries have assisted me in perusing their materials. Ed Via and Jim Bricker from Miami University Interlibrary Loans have spent endless hours finding documents all over the United States (and sending them to me at various locations). Thanks to Bill Wortman at Miami University's King Library; Marty Jacobs at the Museum of the City of New York; Marc Swartz at the Shubert Archive; Kevin Winkler and team at the New York Public Library for the Performing Arts; the staff at the Sherman Theatre Archive at Southern Illinois University, Carbondale; and to those at the Fales Library at New York University, University of Chicago Special Collections, and Harvard University. Thanks also to Jonathan Gray at the Theatre Museum in London and to Richard Mangan at the Mander and Mitchenson Archive in London.

Tom Lisanti and Jeremy McGraw at the New York Public Library Photo Services, and Marguerite Lavin at the Museum for the City of New York were helpful in securing visuals for this project.

There are several institutions to thank as well. This project was made possible through a National Endowment for the Humanities Summer Stipend. During my research leave in England I was graciously supported by Newnham and Selwyn Colleges at the University of Cambridge.

I am grateful to my students, who have taught me much about writing and critical reading. My parents, Lyle and Sally Johnson, have taught me to dream beyond the prairies of South Dakota. My former teachers – Rosie Blunk, Patrick Quade, Susan Cocalis, and Karen Warren – inspired me to study feminist theatre. And thanks go to Sinhaketu, who has guided me toward seeking equanimity and to trying to live my life with metta.

Finally, I am indebted to my partner Timothy D. Melley, whose critical eye has read these pages so many times. His insight, support, and love indelibly mark this work, as they do my life.

Introduction: The Brothel Drama

As a theatre historian, my fascination with the figure of the prostitute stemmed from my constant encounter with her. She was everywhere. Not just in the shadows of a doorway, or the shady side of the underworld. On the contrary, she was center stage.

The prostitute and her sister in sin – the so-called "fallen" woman – were veritable obsessions of Progressive Era (1900–1918) American culture.[1] Streetwalkers, courtesans, and other fallen women were the ubiquitous subjects of best-selling books, vice-commission reports, pornography, fashion, and, especially important for this study, theatrical hits. From John Sloan's paintings of prostitutes outside the Haymarket Theatre to the formation of the FBI, whose original charge was to monitor the traffic in women, Progressive Era culture invested enormously in the study, regulation, and portrayal of prostitution. Indeed, the prostitute became, as Rebecca Schneider has put it, "a quintessential object of modernist fascination."[2]

If the prostitute "exemplifie[d] the modern narratable," as Peter Brooks notes, then American theatre was a central locus of cultural interest in prostitution.[3] At the turn of the twentieth century, plays about prostitutes and fallen women were so popular that they may be said to constitute a genre – the brothel drama. Between 1898 and 1922, approximately fifty plays featuring prostitutes were produced in New York City. The Library of Congress and Robert Sherman's *Drama Cyclopedia* list approximately fifty more that were copyrighted during this time, although it is uncertain whether they were ever performed.[4] Prostitute dramas ranged from lowbrow popular entertainments to highbrow social-problem plays. In addition to the ubiquitous "girl" musicals and scores of "working girl" plays, which depicted the fall of ordinary shop girls into prostitution, there were also more serious offerings. In 1905, Arnold Daly ventured to stage Bernard

Shaw's account of prostitution, *Mrs Warren's Profession*, only to have it shut down on obscenity charges. In spite of *Mrs Warren's Profession*'s tumultuous performance history, a surprising number of prostitute-characters followed in Kitty Warren's dramaturgical wake. Just four years after that famous obscenity case, the Broadway season of 1909 featured David Belasco's smash-hit story of an actress-turned-prostitute, *The Easiest Way*. The drama not only escaped censorship, but also was embraced by mainstream audiences, running for over two years.

Obscure and well-known authors alike took their turn at writing prostitute dramas. Though American theatre historians remember Eugene Walter, Rachel Crothers, Owen Davis, and John Reed for a wide array of accomplishments, little has been said about their unpublished brothel plays (*The Knife*, *Ourselves*, *Sinners*, and *Moondown*, respectively). Scores of dramatic texts by lesser-known artists played on the stages scattered across the United States. Some of these plays dominated Broadway for over two years, whereas others had regional success, and some only a copyright date. Many, like *Queen of Chinatown* (1899) and *The Traffic* (1913), had short runs, obscure authors, and performance histories that are virtually lost to us. Yet, during their day, they were the subjects of extensive publicity and public discussion. Their cumulative presence, in scores of small productions, suggests a consistent feature of both highbrow and lowbrow entertainments: the repeated obsession with the prostitute figure. While fin-de-siècle drama was "slow to take up the challenge of portraying the sexual degenerate," as Laurence Senelick has written, one degenerate figure – the prostitute – stood at the center of Progressive Era drama.[5] What is notable, in fact, is the prostitute's profound dramaturgical *presence* amidst her fellow degenerates' absence. As the white slave scare reached its apex in 1913, there were so many plays about brothels on the New York stage that theatre critic Charles W. Collins wrote, "I for one, am sick of the talk of white slavery."[6] In short, the figure of the prostitute became central to the development of American realist theatre and what has loosely been called early twentieth-century modern drama.

In spite of this remarkable phenomenon, what is astonishing is the extent to which prostitution has been disavowed, or forgotten, in the history of American theatre. While important studies have mapped out the relation of modernity to antiprostitution, urbanization, consumer culture, and social hygiene, the scant theatrical scholarship regarding dramatic representations of prostitutes in the theatre either focuses on an earlier period or neglects a feminist perspective.[7] Despite "the most

INTRODUCTION 3

intensive campaign ever waged against the prostitution trade in American cities," to quote social historian Barbara Meil Hobson, modern theatre scholars have almost entirely neglected the vast body of Progressive Era prostitute plays.[8]

Commercialized vice might at first glance be an unseemly topic for a scholarly work. However, closer analysis reveals that prostitution is a vital subject because, as Ruth Rosen has convincingly argued, a culture's view of whoredom "can function as a kind of microscopic lens through which we gain a detailed magnification of a society's organization of class and gender: the power arrangements between men and women; women's economic and social status; [and] the prevailing sexual ideology."[9] Dramas about the sex trade were, in other words, not only part of an elaborate system for the construction and regulation of sexuality and gender, but also, at times, the site of occasional ruptures in that policing.

Such plays were also part of a new American realism that recast the relationship between bourgeois spectators and lower-class subjects on stage. Legitimate theatre, while at first glance an unlikely venue for the marginal subject of the underworld, was a crucial site wherein tensions between legitimacy and whoredom found articulation. Bourgeois and upper-class audiences were, in fact, seduced by the practice of slumming via the theatre. In fact, much of the new theatre in the early 1900s was a sort of "voyeur realism." While John Corbin of *Life Magazine* asked in 1909, "What is the purpose of this elaborate exploitation of the slums?," few critics or theatre-goers questioned the voyeuristic impulses of this new dramatic realism.[10] From David Belasco's famous reconstruction of a New York flophouse (*The Easiest Way*), to the ladies section of a portside dive (*"Anna Christie"*), Progressive Era plays offered viewers a supposed authentic picture of lower-class life. At the same time, brothel entertainments afforded an opportunity for an invasive, and often regulatory, gaze – portraying, as it did, lower-class, female interiors. Offering titillating encounters with those from the so-called "lower depths," such slum dramas constructed for bourgeois and business class audiences simulated representations of "how the other half lives," to borrow Jacob Riis's phrase.[11] As one author noted in 1913, "The American drama has evidently entered upon its most realistic period. Our playwrights attempt to reveal life as it is, but . . . they concentrate their attention upon its most unpleasant aspects . . . In at least five recent plays the crucial scene is laid in a bawdy house."[12] Indeed, more of realism's roots can be found in the bordello symbolic than has been previously acknowledged. In the pages that follow, we will see that high and low entertainments routinely bled into one another; New York upper-class and bourgeois subjects had specific stakes in the carefully controlled depiction of low spheres.[13]

As the first extended examination of such dramas during the Progressive Era, *Sisters in Sin* seeks to fill the gap between historical and theatrical studies of prostitution. Beginning with David Belasco's adaptation of *Zaza* (1899) and ending with Eugene O'Neill's *"Anna Christie"* (1921–22), this analysis intersects with both the rise of American theatrical realism and the flourishing of antiprostitution reform. The life of the brothel drama is bracketed by the formation of The Committee of Fifteen, the first vice commission in New York City in 1900, and the closing of many red light districts in 1920. It spanned the time between the inaugural obscenity case of the twentieth century and the first Pulitzer Prize for a brothel drama.

The term "brothel drama" was coined and used commonly in the 1910s to describe the persistent, and often scandalous, representation of prostitution on stage. During its day this term most often referred to the sensational white slave genre, an extraordinary run of plays about white women abducted into sexual slavery. It is used in this project to describe not only white slave dramas – surely the bulk of prostitute theatre – but also those plays that featured no brothel at all, but which included a prostitute or fallen woman character *perceived* to be a prostitute in the popular imagination. In fact, very few brothel dramas actually portrayed brothel interiors, due, in part, to fears of obscenity charges. While representations of prostitution held enormous cultural cachet, the brothel was a vexed mimetic space, proving both immensely popular and highly volatile. The brothel drama was a flourishing type of theatre whose settings occasionally included brothels and opium dens, but more often alluded to vice from a variety of more respectable settings, including drawing rooms, country estates, and department stores.

What remains consistent to the brothel drama – whether it actually depicted a brothel or not – is the centrality of the prostitute and various fallen woman characters who were understood by Progressive Era audiences to be fundamentally indistinguishable from prostitutes. The genre featured therefore not only madams and white slaves in bordellos, but also courtesans, mistresses, and women seduced by men. These fallen women and prostitute characters are collectively described throughout these pages as "sisters in sin," a rhetorical strategy to show the connectedness and constructedness of these figures. Female sexuality – particularly sexual transgression – signifies differently in the constantly shifting contexts and historical moments to which human society subjects itself. After all, a woman who in one decade is deemed a courtesan might, in another, be viewed as a savvy dater. It is crucial, therefore, to discuss prostitution in the context of other forms of sexuality in an effort to expose the cultural conflation of these characters and to document genealogies of cultural and sex performances.[14]

If the sexual female body was scrutinized and policed in certain contexts, it also signified ambiguously in performance, as actresses' performance choices both subverted and reinscribed normative gender roles and sexual scripts. Brothel productions were "ghosted," to use Marvin Carlson's formation, by actresses' public personae, politics, acting choices, and body types.[15] Performances of early twentieth-century American actresses are therefore contextualized not only by their prostitute or fallen woman roles, but also by how each performing woman signified in the public sphere. Each chapter considers what Michael Quinn has called "celebrity performance," examining to what extent actresses' public lives, especially their feminist politics, collided with, or underscored, the representation of prostitution.[16] From the sizzling eroticism of Olga Nethersole to the petite and "plain" Pauline Lord, the actress's body and acting style became an important signifier in the semiotics of the brothel drama.

Origins of the brothel drama

In examining the array of dramas that feature prostitute or courtesan figures, the challenge is not in locating these texts, but rather in limiting them. The task of defining women in the brothel drama is not as clear-cut as it may at first appear. We might all agree that Kitty Warren, Bernard Shaw's notorious madam, should be included, but what about the vast number of plays about the so-called fallen woman?

It is impossible to talk about prostitution without noting late nineteenth and turn-of-the-century American theatre's obsession with fallen women's sexuality. For without Camille, there would be no Anna Christie. As Sos Eltis has written, "The epithet 'fallen' could be applied to any woman who had indulged in sex outside the legal and moral bonds of marriage, whether as a seduced virgin, adulterous wife or professional prostitute."[17] Indeed, nineteenth-century and Progressive Era culture typically conflated the sexual behavior of the fallen woman with that of a prostitute.

The brothel drama emerged from the tradition of fallen women plays and within a context of what Amanda Anderson calls the "rhetoric of fallenness," in which prostitution and aberrant women's sexuality were conflated in dominant discourse.[18] In such plays, the action of the drama occurs long after the dreaded sexual fall. Often, the fallen woman has assumed the identity of a lady in society, whereupon her sexual past comes back to haunt her. Once her history is revealed, she renounces her fallen ways, adopts the normative gender role she has thus far ignored, and suffers the consequences of her sexual truancy. Lesley Ferris notes that this long-standing treatment of "the penitent whore" requires not only the whore's renouncement of her sexual sins, but also her (often severe) punishment.[19] One of the striking features of late nineteenth-century and Progressive Era plays is their insistence that all fallen women – from promiscuous women to courtesans, mistresses, and streetwalkers – be understood and punished as prostitutes. Such punishment might include consumption (*Camille*), a broken heart (*East Lynne, The House of Bondage*), suicide (*The Second Mrs. Tanqueray, The House of Mirth*), murder (*Olympe's Marriage*), attempted suicide (*Branded, Sapho*), self-sacrifice (*Zaza, Lulu Belle*), or abandonment (*Mrs. Dane's Defense, The Notorious Mrs. Ebbsmith, The Easiest Way*, and *Mrs Warren's Profession*). Early twentieth-century playwright Bronson Howard wrote about the punishment that inevitably befell "erring women" in the drama of the day:

> In England and America, the death of a pure woman on the stage is not "satisfactory," except when the play rises to the dignity of tragedy. The death, in an ordinary play, of a woman who is not pure . . . is purely satisfactory, for the reason that it is inevitable . . . The wife who has once taken the step from purity to impurity can never reinstate herself in the world of art on this side of the grave, and so an audience looks with complacent tears on the death of an erring woman.[20]

Deaths of "impure" women were staged night after night, on both legitimate and vaudeville stages, by virtually every actress of note.

These dramaturgical demises were not an invention of the Progressive Era. They were part of a long tradition of thinking in which fallen women and prostitutes were marked as degenerate and branded by their apparently unavoidable trajectories towards death. As George Ellington wrote in his *Women of New York, or the Under-World of the Great City* in 1869, prostitutes spiraled inevitably toward a pauper's death: "Ninety-nine out of every hundred of the women-about-the-town go through these very grades, become the victims of their so-called lovers, and end their trials, troubles, and pleasures in the same oblivion – a pauper's grave in Potter's Field."[21] More than sixty years later, George J. Kneeland, in his foundational study, *Commercialized Prostitution in New York City* (1913), came to a similar conclusion: "The life of the professional prostitute has been estimated at five years, on the ground that she dies[,] withdraws, or is incapacitated . . ."[22] Although Kneeland acknowledged there were other possibilities for the prostitute other than Potter's Field, death and incapacitation figured heavily. What is rather remarkable, then, is that in spite of this doomed path from sin to grave, which was sketched repeatedly by so-called sex experts, the prostitute figure in fact lived on – in the brothel drama.

Plays about fallen women's sexuality relied upon a distinctly gendered sexual paradigm: women's sexuality was defined as either virtuous or deviant. Trapped by this binary, women could only fall from or be elevated upon a moral pedestal; there were no in-betweens. The early American sex reformer William Sanger, chief resident physician on Blackwell's Island Hospital and author of *The History of Prostitution: Its Extent, Causes and Effects Throughout the World* (1858), followed in the wake of William Acton's *History of Prostitution*.[23] Sanger's study was wide in scope, outlining the history of prostitution in the world since ancient time, but he devoted six chapters to prostitution in New York. Sanger contrasted the fallen woman with her sexually moral counterpart this way: "the full force of sexual desire is seldom known to a virtuous woman."[24] Facilitating the double standard on sex that dominated the nineteenth century, Sanger continued: "In other words, man is the *aggressive* animal, so far as sexual desire is involved. Were it otherwise, and the passions in both sexes equal, illegitimacy and prostitution would be far more rife in our midst than at present" (original emphasis).[25] Such views were echoed throughout turn-of-the century American culture by sexologists, antiprostitution reformers, politicians, and, of course, theatre artists.

The theatre itself had provided ample opportunities to circulate this punitive, regulatory model of female sexuality. From the middle of the nineteenth century, no other character epitomized the demise of the good-hearted fallen woman better than Marguerite of *La Dame aux Camélias*, popularly known in the United States as *Camille*. Emblematizing the penitent whore model, *Camille* became the prototype on which the brothel drama would later be molded. Marguerite is a courtesan "rehabilitated" by love, expressing self-sacrifice for her lover Armand, even in her dying moments. Based on the life of a real French prostitute, Marie Duplessis, *Camille* articulated the prevailing sexual ideology even as it conjured sympathy for its central character. Camille soon became the iconic hooker-with-a-heart-of-gold whose story would seduce audiences every Broadway season. The Americanized *Camille* was first introduced under the title *Camille: or The Fate of a Coquette* in 1853, featuring Jean Davenport. Revived throughout the nineteenth century, the drama was never as popular as it was during the Progressive Era. Between 1900 and 1918, *Camille* was revived at least forty times on the New York stage, making it one of the most frequently performed plays of the period.[26]

Camille is an important precursor to the brothel drama not only because it made the fallen woman a central dramatic character, but also because it fueled one of the central myths of Progressive Era sexual ideology: the notion that performing women were themselves promiscuous women or prostitutes. There are many reasons for this mistaken assumption. One of them is while male actors had an array of exciting tragic roles beyond the Shakespearean canon, actresses found the strongest female characters in fallen women plays like *Camille*. Because *Camille* was a standard piece in many great actresses' repertoires, it constituted a crucial link between the depiction of prostitution and the advancement of actresses' careers. Matilda Heron, for example, popularized her own version of Camille and, according to Stephen Stanton, from 1855 to 1864 acted this adaptation "over 1,000 times in the major cities of the United States."[27] Eleanora Duse, Olga Nethersole, Mrs. Patrick Campbell, Clara Morris, Mme. Réjane, Ethel Barrymore, and Helena Modjeska, to name a few, all had their own try at portraying the lady of the camellias.[28] In the season of 1895–1896 alone, *Camille* was performed by virtually every great actress in New York: Modjeska, Nethersole, Bernhardt and Duse. So many actresses devoted themselves to performing *Camille* in the 1895 season that when Mrs. Fiske did not, she caught the attention of Chapman and Sherwood, who observed: "Mrs. Fiske eschewed *Camille* but managed *A Doll's House*."[29] A review from the *New York Spirit of the Times* in 1894 noted, "New York has seen all sorts of *Camilles*:"

> First there was Matilda Heron, who made the Parisian heroine an Irish washerwoman but still won the sympathy of the public. Then Jean Hosmer and Mrs. Lander, both cold and prim and virtuous. Then Clara Morris, so homely that she could not possibly have attracted any Armand except Charles Thorne, who could make love to anything. Then Bernhardt, who was too keen and calculating for Camille's love scenes. Then Duse, whose Camille was an Italian. The Camille of Miss Nethersole is like none of these. It is a Camille of costumes.[30]

Comparisons with "other and famous Marguerites, past and present" were inevitable, and subject to constant reinterpretation, like the renegotiation of all historical narratives. This review of Margaret Anglin's *Camille* in April 1904, for instance, remembered the play's previous leading ladies more positively: "[M]ost of us are familiar with the luxurious Marguerite of Bernhardt, the soulful Marguerite of Duse, the passionate Marguerite of Clara Morris, and the fine performances of Helena Modjeska, Olga Nethersole, and Jane Hading. Miss Anglin's interpretation can rank with none of these."[31] A concurrent production of *Camille* featuring Virginia Harned elicited this remark in *Theatre Magazine*: "*Camille* cannot be whistled down the wind. It has a history that cannot be denied, and in its existence of more than half a century, it has employed some of the best genius of the stage, and has wrought upon the sympathies of innumerable theatre-goers."[32] *Camille* was here to stay. As Hamilton Mason notes in his history of French theatre on the New York stage, "Over eighty years of coughing has not impaired her theatrical health,"[33] and if the recent blockbuster film *Moulin Rouge* (2001) demonstrates anything, it is that the story of the consumptive hooker-with-a-heart-of-gold is still compelling to modern audiences.

Bernhardt's performance of *Camille*, and other courtesan roles, deserves special attention, not only because of her devotion to reviving the role, but also for its uncanny literality: Bernhardt herself had once been a courtesan.[34] Camille was the first role Bernhardt ever performed in the United States. Moreover, as Leigh Woods notes, "Bernhardt made Camille, the only part she played on both her tours, her most durable attraction in vaudeville."[35] Significantly, all five of Bernhardt's "Farewell" American Tours included performances of *La Dame aux Camélias*.[36] *Camille* was Bernhardt's cash cow, a role she performed more than 3,000 times over nearly forty-five years.[37] In 1912, an article in *Current Opinion* remarked that in "*La Dame aux Camélias*, still, she [Bernhardt] shows herself as an actress, the greatest actress in the world."[38] Bernhardt's career was so associated with the role that, as Cornelia Otis Skinner remarks, " 'La Bernhardt's' final New York performance was a matinee of *La Dame*."[39] In sum, Bernhardt's entire acting career in New York was framed by her performance of Marguerite Gautier and was ghosted by her own brushes with prostitution.

By the beginning of the twentieth century, the popularity of *Camille* had made it a virtual requirement that great actresses portray fallen women. As Progressive Era culture became increasingly interested in the figure of the prostitute, many actresses built repertoires that were comprised almost exclusively of parts from fallen women plays, many of which were, at some moment, labeled obscene. For example, in 1902, Mrs. Patrick Campbell's repertory included: *Magda*, *The Second Mrs. Tanqueray*, and *The Notorious*

Mrs. Ebbsmith.[40] Likewise, Mme. Réjane's repertory of 1904 included: *Lolotte, La Dame aux Camélias, Sapho,* and *Zaza.* "*Camille, Carmen, Zaza,* and *Sapho,*" Mason observes, "have made four outstanding contributions to the stage by the actresses who played them and the audiences who supported them."[41] In short, by the Progressive Era, the fallen woman had become a quintessential figure on the American stage, as integral to the staging of American identity as the more familiar types noted by theatre scholars, such as "bullying businessmen, desperate slaves, emancipated women, and savages (both murderous and noble)."[42] *Camille* can be seen as the dramaturgical ancestor to the brothel drama, influencing the emergence of new prostitute characters during the early twentieth century.

What distinguished Progressive Era drama from its nineteenth-century predecessors was an increased emphasis on depicting the social conditions leading to, and the consequences of, prostitution, rather than the whore's repentance and punishment. Intersecting with the rise of antiprostitution reform, the brothel drama staged what vice commissions studied: how to remedy commercialized vice given the emerging problems of twentieth-century urban life. Just as social science began to clarify social ills, so too the drama of the period sought to portray various vices more scientifically (some with more success than others). Although scores of prostitute characters appeared in the brothel drama genre, seven new archetypes emerged in the wake of *Camille*'s repentant courtesan: the performing woman, the shop girl, the madam, the white slave, the *prostitute fatale*, the legitimate courtesan, and the lesbian prostitute. While the consumptive hooker would still be found coughing on the stage during the early twentieth century, prostitute characters in the brothel drama would also move beyond the penitent tragic end. Some of these characters appear to channel their fallen women predecessors, yet they also cover new ground. There were still lingering expectations for the penitent whore to suffer and perish, but most of these characters *survive* when the curtain is finally drawn. In the new landscape of the early twentieth century prostitute characters in the brothel drama had more opportunities – and, paradoxically, limitations – than their nineteenth-century sisters in sin as they confronted working life, non-normative sexuality, display culture, and leisure entertainments.

The modern prostitute-construct

The brothel drama's stunning success reveals much about early twentieth-century American anxieties about sexuality, contagion, eugenics, women's rights, and urbanization. The body of the prostitute was a corporeal site upon which these desires and cultural imperatives could be mapped. The prostitute was, in other words, a construct of an array of modern discourses, of which theatre was one. As Shannon Bell has argued: "'[T]he prostitute' was actively produced as a marginalized social-sexual identity, particularly during the latter half of the nineteenth century and the beginning of the twentieth century."[43] Imagined as an Other in juxtaposition to respectable bourgeois identity, the "prostitute-construct" fulfilled the function of segregating normative from deviant sexuality in the modern imagination. Of course, conceptualizing the prostitute as the figure who guides us through the chaotic labyrinth of modernity has old philosophical roots. In the mid-nineteenth century, Charles Baudelaire astutely observed that the prostitute was an allegory of modernity.[44] Baudelaire invested much intellectual (and libidinal) capital in the enterprise of prostitution, which he viewed, according to Walter Benjamin, as "the yeast which allows the metropolitan masses to rise."[45] The whore also assumed significance in Benjamin's dialectical treatises on modernity: "In the prostitution of the metropolis," he writes, "the woman herself becomes an article that is mass-produced."[46] Prostitution thus became a framework to analyze mass pro-duction, modern technology, and the entry of women into the urban workforce – the prostitute becoming the personification of these changes.

The modern fascination with prostitution serves as a departure point for reading the portrayal of the prostitute-figure, a figure that Rebecca Schneider has called "a prime dialectical image because of the ambivalence inherent in her status as both 'commodity and seller' in one."[47] According to Schneider, the prostitute engendered a "collapse of active and passive, subject and object, into a single entity."[48] As such a paradoxical figure, the prostitute provoked cultural anxiety, threatening to dissolve oppositions that had become central to early twentieth-century hegemonic order: commodity/seller, public/private, and so on. *Sisters in Sin* seeks to demys-tify and disentangle this collapse. Weaving together the historical material reality of prostitutes with cultural discourse on prostitution, this project turns ambivalence back upon itself, showing how the prostitute-construct serviced many cultural clients.

Neighbors in sin

Another important context for the brothel drama is the history of anti-prostitution reform. During the nineteenth century, prostitution was often viewed as an unavoidable reality, or "Necessary Evil." As Timothy Gilfoyle points out in his important study of prostitution in New York City, "By the midnineteenth century, commercial sex with its underground economy and subcultures of prostitutes and sporting men was not only a fact of everyday urban life but also a fixture of popular culture."[49] As a stable feature of society, however, prostitution also seemed to require management, giving birth to extensive reform movements. From the first wave of American antiprostitution reform, which created the Magdalene Societies in the 1830s, to the debates of the second wave of reformers in the 1870s, reformers divided simply into regulationists or abolitionists. In his classic prostitution study of 1858, William Sanger linked unregulated prostitution to the spread of venereal disease, a position then utilized by regulationists to support their views. At the turn of the century, however, regulationist strategies had failed in most large cities; soon commissions arose to study what was increasingly being described as a "social," rather than a "necessary," evil.

The first substantial study by an American vice commission, The Committee of Fifteen, was organized in New York City in 1900 to study "the spread of the Social Evil in certain districts, and … the extent of flagrant offenses against public morality and common decency."[50] Their report in 1902 pointed out the failures of regulation in Europe, particularly in containing venereal diseases, and advocated instead long-term measures furthering the "moral redemption of the human race from this degrading evil."[51] Their recommendations included the prevention of overcrowding in tenement houses, providing "purer and more elevating forms of amusement," improving the "material conditions of the wage-earning class and especially of young wage-earning women," better treatment of infected women (though stricter confinement for those who were "notoriously debauched"), and changing the law to characterize prostitution not as a crime, but rather as a sin.[52] A final plea for "the creation of a special body of morals police" no doubt reflected the reformers' views of themselves as such a force.[53]

Numerous vice commissions were created throughout the United States to study the prostitute and her supposed link to venereal disease. Virtually every city supported such an investigation, but New York's was the most comprehensive. Formed in 1911, the Committee of Fourteen (a later incarnation of the original Committee of Fifteen) conducted extensive studies of commercialized vice, lobbied successfully for legislation, and established Night Court (also known as the Women's Court) for prostitutes. Their enduring work over twenty-one years was, as Gilfoyle notes, "the most successful antiprostitution organization in New York City history, achieving an impressive array of reforms."[54] George Kneeland's important 1913 study, a product of Rockefeller's Bureau of Social Hygiene, was the next American effort to focus on prostitution in New York. Based on interviews with prostitutes in the New York Bedford State Reformatory for Women, Kneeland's book was in many ways sympathetic to prostitutes and working women, though it also advocated regulation. In short, dozens of agencies and organizations emerged in New York in the 1910s in response to prostitution, part of a long pattern of studying, legislating, and regulating the "Social Evil," a pattern which social historian Ruth Rosen has characterized as "one of Western society's most zealous and best-recorded campaigns against prostitution."[55]

Such campaigns were intimately related to theatrical representation. In part, the reason the theatre became a central site of regulation is that there had always been an intense symbiotic relationship between the theatre and commercialized vice. As Timothy Gilfoyle has shown, New York City theatres and houses of prostitution were literally neighbors in sin. "By the Civil War," he writes, "six of fourteen Broadway theaters were sharing the same block as a house of prostitution, often in the rear of the theater along Mercer or Crosby Street. Other theatrical establishments were never more than a block from a brothel."[56] The interdependent relationship between theatres and brothels became more explicit as they relocated uptown together in the early twentieth century as a building boom swallowed up valuable industrial property in lower Manhattan. This partner-like shift uptown proved the ineluctable power of urban capitalism in shaping prostitution.[57] As Allen Churchill recalled in The Great White Way, his memoir of the Broadway theatre, "From Twenty-third to Thirty-fourth Street, New York's celebrated theatres (many twenty or thirty years old) ran like a string of pearls through the blackhearted Tenderloin."[58] Marvin Carlson has noted that the unique sense of invisibility invoked by the façade theatres at the turn of the century in New York not only blended the theatres together, but also conflated them with other forms of entertainment. "This liminoid quality," writes Carlson, "gives to districts of this sort a special excitement, often with a distinctly raffish or risqué element."[59]

This overlapping of theatre buildings and brothels created an interstitial space in which identity, particularly female identity, became destabilized. The Great White Way in particular became an unstable semiotic space where it was often impossible to distinguish society women from prostitutes as both groups engaged in their Broadway promenades. One cultural response to this ambiguity was to interpret the entire space as a commercialized sex region. As Churchill put it, "a legion of streetwalkers plied their trade" through the two-mile-long theatre district, effectively "clogging the sidewalks along Broadway from Twenty-third to Thirty-fourth Street."[60] Such accounts undoubtedly mistook Broadway girls or society women for streetwalkers, giving a reductive reading not only of public space, but also of women's sexuality within that sphere. Similarly anxious interpretations of women moving through these spaces emerged in response to the urbanization of turn-of-the-century America, the boom of the theatre district, and the commodification of sex. These misreadings produced a regulatory surveillance of women in public space, dictating expectations for the "proper" performance of gender, race, class, and sexuality.

Censorship and the conspiracy of silence fallacy

Although brothel narratives were quite familiar to the stage – and to popular discourse in general – they were often viewed as having broken the so-called "conspiracy of silence" about prostitution and sexuality. Yet, while certain discursive powers represented the topic of sex as if it were a matter of silence or repression, Progressive Era society was intensely invested in studying, surveying, and policing prostitution. In spite of the long-standing existence of legal, medical, and juridical domains that took charge of constructing sexual discourse, commentators from the Progressive Era insisted that they had instigated new discussions of sex (Bernard Shaw repeatedly gave voice to this view). But these discussions were not new. Sexual scientists, religious leaders, and the courts had been generating sexual discourse for some time.

The brothel drama tapped into this existing sex discourse. As prevalent as the brothel drama genre was, it was marked by contradictions as perhaps no other. Just as the Mann and Page Acts of 1910 regulated the trafficking in women (in the hope of controlling venereal disease), so the conflicted performance histories of brothel plays demonstrate that prostitution needed to be discursively surveyed and contained – but performed nonetheless.[61] In the United States, even in the absence of an official censoring office (like the Lord Chamberlain in England), censorship played a determining, though uneven, role in Broadway productions.[62] Stormy obscenity trials racked the New York stage in the early twentieth century, reflecting the influence of the New York police and Anthony Comstock, founder of the Society for the Suppression of Vice. The very first obscenity case of the new century involved the sensational arrest and trial of Olga Nethersole in her provocative production of *Sapho*, and in 1905 Comstock halted Bernard Shaw's *Mrs Warren's Profession* in a notorious obscenity case heard by the New York State Supreme Court.

While Comstock's reach was extensive, it was not limitless. Prostitute dramas flourished in spite of (and, in some cases, because of) Comstock and other censoring forces. "[T]he play that attracts the attention of the police," noted James Sheldon Hamilton in his aptly titled article, "The Sex-Tangled Drama" of 1913, "is one that is sure to attract large patronage from amusement seekers."[63] Indeed, by the beginning of the 1913 season, white slave dramas were the prevailing genre. That same year, *Damaged Goods*, the first venereal disease play staged in America, which also featured a prostitute, was invited to appear as a command performance at the White House. In an article called "Sex Dramas To-Day and Yesterday," Olga Nethersole captured the irony of this erratic performance history: "I recall that not many years ago I was arrested for playing *Sapho*. The city in which I was taken to jail soon afterward applauded *The Easiest Way* and now applauds *The Lure*, *The Fight* and their kind."[64] Indeed, brothel dramas thrived throughout the 1910s and 1920s, in spite of occasional police intervention. One of the longest running shows of this period (with 680 performances) was the white slave, opium-den play, *East is West*, which was made into a film in 1922 and again in 1930. By 1921 the topic of prostitution was arguably legitimized when America's best-known playwright, Eugene O'Neill, captured a Pulitzer Prize with his tale of a prostitute reformed by love, *"Anna Christie."* O'Neill's prize-winner was followed by the all-black version of *The Easiest Way*, retitled *Goat Alley* (1921), as well as the revival of the Yiddish prostitute drama *The God of Vengeance* (1921–22), and the long-running drama featuring a water-drenched hooker, *Rain* (running for 648 performances in 1922), among scores of other prostitute dramas. By 1924 Belasco was at it again with his staging of the transparently titled *Ladies of the Evening*. In 1926 he joined Edward Sheldon and Charles MacArthur to stage *Lulu Bell*, the tale of an African-American courtesan. We might well conclude that given such disparate theatrical fates, if censorship did exist, it was quite erratic.

But the key question to ask here is: *how* did censorship function? John Houchin argues that censoring behavior in twentieth-century theatre was "indicative of a conservative society, one whose energy is used to maintain its political, moral, and social infrastructure."[65] This is true, but it is only half of the story. For a careful look at turn-of-the-century theatre reveals that in the midst of intense censorship on the New York stage a vast array of plays about prostitution were not only allowed to be produced, but in some instances became hits. Given this inconsistency, any useful account of censorship must focus not only on that which was censored, but also on that which was staged. The task is not only to reintroduce forgotten texts to the cultural consciousness, but also to explicate the cultural work of those texts, some of which were shut down, and others of which flew under the regulatory radar. In so doing, it is vital to examine historical artifacts as well as the performative elements of cultural discourse that constructed bodies of sexual knowledge – in and out of the brothel, on and off the stage. It is also crucial to move beyond a purely juridical reading of censorship, one that locates power exclusively with figures like Comstock, or New York Police Commissioner McAdoo. While they had their role in shaping sex discourse, they were not the only, or even primary, forces at work. The task, to borrow Michel Foucault's words, is to "at the same time conceive of sex without the law, and power without the king" – in other words, to eschew a model that views power exclusively as the domain of government officials and instead see it as a regulatory matrix of institutions and laws.[66] The underworld illuminates, perhaps not unexpectedly, how the stage was both producer *and* censor of gender and sexuality within a larger array of sex discourse.

Each play's performance history, with its wide array of elements (including the play text, revisions, actresses' performance choices, and cultural interventions), reveals the performativity, or the cultural work, of each dramatic text in affirming *and* resisting cultural and legal discourses. Sexual imperatives sometimes succeed, but they also misfire, engendering ruptures, subversions, and resistance – if only for a few moments on the stage or page. An integral part of the censorship story, is, in other words, the story of resistance. Yet, just as performance can subvert power, so too it can reinscribe hegemony. As Jon McKenzie reminds us, performance theory tends to over-emphasize the subversive potential of counter-performances (usually invoking Judith Butler's work on gender performance and subversion), overlooking how performance also reiterates normative structures.[67] Both the subversive and hegemonic modes are at work in the reception history of the brothel drama. What is astonishing about some of these brothel plays' censorship is their ultimate return to the stage. Those permanently squelched, too, sometimes provided extraordinary moments of resistance to that suppression. Even in performances that largely represented hegemonic notions of gender and sexuality, characters or

actresses sometimes defied the overarching logic of the play. In conventional white slave dramas, for instance, most plots are predictably
formulaic defenses of regressive gender politics. Yet, in the midst of this
conventionality, women occasionally take up make-shift weapons, defend
other women, and sometimes, fight their way out of the brothel. While
conservative characters often dominate such scripts, madams and prostitutes have short – and often radical – speeches that rub against the play's
conventional sex discourse. Accounting for the diverse and conflicting
threads of performance reception can thus enrich theatre history
scholarship.

A map of sin

This project begins by examining how "performing women" became conflated with the figure of the prostitute at the turn of the twentieth century.
Part I, "The female performer as prostitute," reconstructs the history of
three plays that feature performing women (music hall performer, artist
model, and actress) who are repeatedly conflated with prostitutes. In
chapter 1 of this section, Mrs. Leslie Carter's performance of the titillating
music-hall performer in David Belasco's *Zaza* (1899) escaped theatrical
censorship because Zaza redeemed herself from her sexual fall, ultimately
affirming conservative sexual mores. Carter's "cult of celebrity," as well as
her social standing in society and the fact she was a mother, worked to
neutralize Carter's provocative undressing on stage, allowing her to escape
charges of obscenity. Just one year after *Zaza*, however, Olga Nethersole's
infamous staging of Clyde Fitch's *Sapho* became the first American play of
the century to be closed by the police on charges of obscenity. Chapter 2
shows how Nethersole's production caused an uproar because she displayed
a radical female sexuality imbued with signs of New Womanhood. The
production was also doomed by Nethersole's reputation as female producer
and feminist activist. Chapter 3 considers the actress, a figure who, like the
music hall performer and artist model, was both desired and reviled.
Although most theatre histories remember *The Easiest Way* for David
Belasco's painstaking realism and sympathetic depiction of Laura Murdock,
an actress-turned-prostitute, this chapter argues that much of the success of
the play rested upon the actress-as-whore myth as well as anxieties about
women who exceed their roles as commodities exchanged between men.
Functioning as a morality tale in social control, the title ultimately says it

all: performing women, unregulated, are apt to take the easiest way in that
slippery slope to whoredom.

The second part of the book, "Working girls," probes a tempting figure
in Progressive popular culture. Working women had to negotiate the
unsteady terrain between selling commodities and commodifying themselves. In referencing both kinds of work, this chapter seeks to capture the
tension inherent in the plight of Progressive Era working women, unsettling the seemingly clear opposition between honest worker and prostitute.
As demonstrated in chapter 4, the popularity of musicals such as *The Shop
Girl* (1895), *Only A Shop Girl* (1903), *The Earl and Girl* (1905), and *The Girl
Behind the Counter* (1907) shows how fantasies about shop girls tapped into
obsessions with conspicuous consumption, male scopophilia, and the conflation of worker and hooker in increasingly fluid public spaces. These
infatuations were also at work in Bernard Shaw's *Mrs Warren's Profession*
(1905), the American premiere of which spawned an infamous obscenity
trial as seen in chapter 5. In rejecting both the morality that condemned
sexually active women and the double standard on sexuality that sustained
that perspective, Bernard Shaw dispensed with previous prostitution
mythologies, portraying instead the drudgery of women who belonged to
what we would now call the working poor. While several theatre historians
have reconstructed this remarkable event, their readings rarely consider the
larger context of antiprostitution discourse and ignore responses from
female audiences and lead actress Mary Shaw. By inserting those voices,
this chapter demonstrates that the objections to obscenity were largely
driven by male anxiety over women gaining control over sexual discourse.

Part III shows how the white slave panic of the 1910s – the fear that
white, upper-class women were being kidnapped and forced into prostitution – was intimately connected to deeper anxieties about immigration,
class mobility, and miscegenation. Chapter 6, "White slave plays in progressive era theatre," documents the construction of the white slave figure
as a paradoxical fantasy of the *virginal* and "racially pure" prostitute. Of the
scores of plays about prostitution in the Progressive Era, the white slave
play was by far the most popular and ubiquitous, resulting in scores of
productions in three discernable white slave subgenres: country-girl white
slave plays, urban white slave plays, and opium-den or harem plays.
Chapter 7 is a study of the hits of the 1913–1914 white slave season.
Revisiting the censorship cases of *The Lure*, *The Fight*, *Ourselves*, and *The
House of Bondage*, this chapter maps out the seemingly illogical politics
governing the regulation of white slave dramas on Broadway. While

The Lure and *The Fight* were successfully remounted after "voluntary" censorship of the brothel scenes, *The House of Bondage* ended in utter failure and the brutal arrest of its female producer and lead actress, Cecil Spooner. Meanwhile the best of all the white slave plays, Rachel Crothers's *Ourselves*, was denied endorsement by the Drama League and had a tepid run. The 1913–14 season reveals many moments of social control, theatrical censorship, and the theatre's participation in the regulation of sexuality. But we also see moments of resistance and rupture in this regulatory machinery, such as suffragettes giving curtain speeches during *The Fight*, audiences picketing the police station after the closing of *The House of Bondage*, or Crothers's prescient use of community-based theatre with female delinquents.

Part IV offers three end-case studies. Chapter 8, "*Damaged Goods*: Sex hysteria and the *prostitute fatale*," disputes the idea that the 1913 American premiere of Eugène Brieux's *Damaged Goods*, the first play dealing explicitly with venereal disease, broke a conspiracy of silence regarding sexual discourse. Showing that technologies of sex were indeed long operative in the theatre, this chapter examines the cultural work they performed not only in the American premiere of *Damaged Goods*, but also in antiprostitution reform and the social hygiene movement. None of the success of *Damaged Goods* (including its production as a command performance for the White House) could have been possible without a national panic about racial purity, which was perceived to be threatened by venereal disease. Moreover, while *Damaged Goods* represented itself as promoting a liberal social hygiene agenda, closer analysis reveals that the text undermines itself repeatedly, expressing regressive reform ideologies, particularly in terms of gender and sexuality. These conflicting tensions reconcile in one instance: the text's negative posture towards prostitutes and the creation of what might be called the *prostitute fatale*. Both the stage and film versions of *Damaged Goods* constructed the national subject in opposition to the "damaged" prostitute. Utilized in the pedagogical machinery of social hygiene reform, and adopted by the US military in its efforts against venereal disease, *Damaged Goods* was a major participant in the production of sexual knowledge in early twentieth-century America. The final chapter, "The repentant courtesan in '*Anna Christie*', and the lesbian prostitute in *The God of Vengeance*," begins by focusing on Eugene O'Neill's classic prostitution tale, the first brothel drama to garner a Pulitzer Prize. In revisiting the debate regarding "*Anna Christie*"'s much-contested happy ending, it becomes clear that this closure comes at a conventional price: the only way that Anna can experience forgiveness is by renouncing her female rage and assuming a traditional relationship with the men in her life. The contrived happy-ending marriage and reconciliation with her father is a device to facilitate the male bonding of her lover and her father. In addition to textual analysis, this chapter looks at performance choices by actress Pauline Lord and the curious response to Lord's unconventional (or, as some put it, "homely") looks. Because Lord positioned herself as naïve and respectable, Anna's character was ghosted by a certain innocence that rendered her non-threatening. Such dramaturgical respectability made sense, given that prostitutes were just swept off the streets by reformist movements. In sum, it may have appeared that O'Neill gave the prostitute-figure a dramaturgical face-life, but in many respects Anna is the same repentant courtesan-figure audiences had seen so many times before.

Finally, this chapter concludes with an investigation of the lesbian prostitute in Sholom Asch's *The God of Vengeance*. Although several brothel dramas had been charged with obscenity throughout the early twentieth century, *The God of Vengeance* was the first instance where the actors and manager were found guilty. Originally performed in Yiddish, the play ran successfully in New York for seventeen years in obscure downtown theatres. After it was translated into English and moved to an uptown venue, however, *The God of Vengeance* sparked enormous controversy. Offered as a final coda to the discussion of the brothel drama, *The God of Vengeance*'s English-speaking debut demonstrates the limits of portraying a nonrepentant prostitute, unconventional brothel interiors, and nonnormative sexual desire.

Part I

The female performer as prostitute

As America entered the twentieth century a visible shift occurred in the public perception of prostitution. The 1899 Broadway season was dominated by David Belasco's staging of *Zaza*, a portrait of a music-hall performer whom drama critic William Winter called "an obtruding harlot" of the stage.[1] Though found too risqué by some theatre-goers, *Zaza* was a smashing success, titillating New York audiences with the sexual rehabilitation of a brassy stage star. Yet, just a few months later, New York City rang in the new century by closing down Olga Nethersole's "sin-stained" *Sapho* and arresting Nethersole on charges of obscenity. That same year the vice commission New York Committee of Fifteen was formed and numerous antiprostitution groups – a disparate collection of preventative societies, vigilantes, feminists, and Progressives – were born. But just as *Zaza* was not censored from the stage, so not all harlots were removed from the street, in spite of new laws regulating both theatrical representations of prostitutes (and fallen women) and their real counterparts on the street. Though efforts to control dramatic images of prostitute figures paralleled Progressive antiprostitution reform efforts, both endeavors were highly erratic.

My intention in revisiting the performance histories of David Belasco's *Zaza* (1899), Clyde Fitch's *Sapho* (1900), and Eugene Walter's *The Easiest Way* (1909) is to examine how the "performing woman" (that is, the music-hall performer, model and actress) became conflated with the figure of the prostitute at the turn of the millennium. The respective leading characters in these plays – Zaza, Fanny, and Laura – were repeatedly labeled "harlots," "courtesans," and "tainted women," yet they are not prostitutes at all. Rather, these characters were *perceived* to be prostitutes because they were sexually active, unmarried – that is, "fallen" – women. This labeling of non-marital female sexuality as aberrant, while long circulating in dominant culture, gained particular momentum throughout the Progressive Era framing of antiprostitution discourse. More important to the conflation of the stage with the underworld, however, was that the lead characters of *Zaza*, *Sapho*, and *The Easiest Way* are all "performing women" – women who, as music-hall performer, model, and actress, respectively – support themselves in work that relies upon a display economy. Their presence in visual trades is precisely what marked their liminal performances as prostitution.

Early twentieth-century American popular culture was smitten with the figure of the actress. Countless novels, short stories, articles, and plays about actresses at the turn of the century reveal a cultural fascination with a purportedly champagne-drinking, lobster-eating, and sexually naughty Broadway girl. The actress was so exposed to the public eye that most facets of her life – from the mundane to the sensational, from her clothing to her politics – were of interest to readers.[2] Articles such as "The Actress in Her Automobile" (1904), "The Actress and Her Clothes" (1910), "Actresses and Woman Suffrage" (1909), and "The Actress as a Human Being" (1912), reveal an intense curiosity with every detail of actresses' lives.[3] By 1909, as Linda Mizejewski has shown, New York was referred to as "a chorus girl factory."[4]

Many dramas on the New York stage at the turn of the twentieth century featured a Broadway girl as the main character, especially the ubiquitous "girl" musicals. Particularly popular were *The Dancing Girl* (1891), *A Gaiety Girl* (1894), *The Ballet Girl* (1897), *The Singing Girl* (1899), *The Knickerbocker Girl* (1900), *The Casino Girl* (1900), *The Show Girl* (1902), *The Belle of Broadway* (1902), *The Hurdy-Gurdy Girl* (1907), *The Century Girl* (1916) and *The Girl in the Spotlight* (1920).[5] Championed by burlesque producer George Edwardes, these productions featured the erotic spectacle of dancing, scantily-clad women known as the "girl chorus." Representations of the Broadway girl were obsessed with objectifying her sexuality. "Every possible excuse," John Degen writes, "was found to place them in revealing tights."[6] Such mythical portrayals of the sexy Broadway girl rested upon a rigid bifurcated schema: either she was a naive girl who was lured to the stage and seduced by a "Broadway Bloke," or she was an irresistible seducer of men, often with powers endowed to her through her position in the theatre.

There is little question that such depictions influenced the production of more serious literature. Novels about the slippery slope between working women and fallen women – such as Stephen Crane's *Maggie: A Girl of the*

THE FEMALE PERFORMER AS PROSTITUTE

Streets (A Story of New York) (1893), Theodore Dreiser's *Sister Carrie* (1900), and Edith Wharton's *The House of Mirth* (1905) – linked fallen women's sexuality and prostitution to the stage by featuring a seemingly obligatory scene in which the heroine attends or acts in the theatre shortly before her fall.

Popular discourse increasingly portrayed actresses traversing the New York underworld. In his celebrated (though unscientific) 1869 study, *The Women of New York, or The Under-World of the Great City*, George Ellington captured the cultural ambivalence regarding actresses:

> The New York actress is, indeed, a very fair specimen of the morality, industry and sobriety of the sex … On the other hand, there are a number of young actresses in the city whose fair proportions and fascinating manners have not only ruined a great number of young men, but have all but ruined the women themselves.[7]

In Ellington's account the actress was both a liminal figure of the steamy underworld and a specimen of morality. Such ambivalence toward the actress – who was both "fair specimen," but also a "ruiner" of men – would come to typify the characterization of prostitution in modernist discourse.

With all the temptations of commodities in a rising retail industry, which itself increasingly relied upon aesthetic displays, plays about the chorus girl were often morality tales about the lure of capitalism and male patronage. James Forbes's popular play *The Chorus Lady* (1909) offers a typical representation of the Broadway girl's predicaments. While chorus girls were frequently represented as luxury-loving ladies who indulged their male sugar daddies, in *The Chorus Lady* sisters Patricia and Nora are chorus girls who resolve to resist this life of opulence. The play's smarmy Dick Crawford complicates matters when he threatens to ruin the younger sister after loaning her money she cannot repay. In the end it is "a firm grip on home" that keeps Nora in line. Both Patricia and Nora leave the theatre and return to their country farm, thus solidifying the popular myth of the city as an urban jungle that ruined innocent country girls. The message of *The Chorus Lady*, like so many brothel dramas, is clear: avoid the stage, and leave the city.

The theme of the performing woman poised on the precipice of sexual immorality was recycled in numerous plays throughout the first two decades of the twentieth century, in creations such as *The Climax* (1909), *Lulu's Husbands* (1910), *Two Women* (1910), *That Sort* (1914), *The Show Shop* (1914), *The Brat* (1917), *The Claim* (1917), *The Case of Lady Camber* (1917), *Parlour, Bedroom & Bath* (1917), and *The Gold Diggers* (1919). Indeed, by 1917 plays featuring chorus girls were so numerous that James Metcalfe of *Life Magazine* wrote that it was "open season for chorus girls," with so many appearing on stage it was impossible to keep track of them.[8] Metcalfe sardonically suggested eliminating names from the program altogether and numbering the girls like horses at the track. Faceless and ubiquitous, the Broadway girl appeared in numerous popular culture texts, hopelessly trapped in the impossible space of polarized representation.

Conflating actresses with prostitutes

At the same time that popular culture was circulating the idea of the "actress-as-whore," researchers were studying the profile of the prostitute. William W. Sanger's classic *History of Prostitution: Its Extent, Causes, and Effects Throughout the World* (1858) was the first widely read American study that focused on prostitution in New York.[9] As chief resident physician at Blackwell's Island, a prison hospital, Sanger conducted interviews with two thousand prostitutes about why they turned to prostitution. Significantly, *none* of the respondents said they had been actresses before they became prostitutes. Another influential study of prostitution, George J. Kneeland's *Commercialized Prostitution in New York* (1913), supported Sanger's conclusions. Conducted at the State Reformatory for Women at Bedford Hills, New York in 1912, as well as at other institutions, Kneeland's research revealed that relatively low numbers of actresses turned to commercialized sex. Of the Bedford prostitutes only 2.8 percent had previously done theatrical work and only 2.2 percent said they had combined prostitution with a theatrical trade.[10] At institutions other than Bedford only 3 percent of the women surveyed cited theatrical work as their trade before entering prostitution and less than 1 percent worked in the theatre after turning to prostitution.[11] Of streetwalkers surveyed, 6.5 percent said they were in theatrical work before turning to prostitution and 7.9 percent claimed they were involved in the theatre after entering prostitution.[12]

Theatre historian Tracy Davis has illustrated the same conflation of actress and whore in England. "Logistic evidence shows that identifications of the lower theatrical ranks as prostitutes were erroneous," Davis writes. "Open prostitution for any type of female performer was out of the question ..."[13] In comparison with other professions, then, the theatre fed relatively *few* women into prostitution. Beginning with Sanger, over sixty years of research reveals a stunning cultural fiction; yet the popular notion that actresses were prostitutes, or would become prostitutes, was simply inaccurate.

But if statistics show that actresses were *not* inclined to become prostitutes – one of the *least* inclined professions, in fact – how are we to understand portrayals to the contrary on stage, in literature, and in popular culture? If not based on facts, what is the basis of this popular cultural myth?

Sanger's study suggests one reason. According to the Blackwell's Island interviews, first-class prostitutes would take "an afternoon promenade on the fashionable side of Broadway," just as upper-class women did.[14] Broadway was a hybrid site in other words, where the paths of society women, actresses, and prostitutes intersected. As Maureen Montgomery has shown, New York's nouveau riches depended upon a gendered display culture: "By appearing in public and displaying luxury, particularly in places of nighttime entertainment where conspicuous dress was allowed, the society woman took on the role of the courtesan in exhibiting herself as the possession of one man and evoking the envy of others."[15] The rise of the new leisure class in New York necessitated new negotiations of space, as the paths of the monde and demimonde "were becoming increasingly coextensive," to use Montgomery's words.[16] Nowhere was this commingling more clear than in the theatre district. Broadway was a fluid space that was marked, according to Peter G. Buckley, by "a coalescence of the classes, sexes, and races in an ever-increasing frequency of cultural exchange."[17]

Central to the promenade and other public displays of the Broadway girl was the necessity of exhibiting herself for an elite male gaze. New actresses, for instance, often "exhibit[ed] themselves on the street," noted Ellington:

> Indeed, this was a favorite method of advertising during the season of last winter; and half a score of pretty women could be pointed out any fine day on Broadway, flaunting in costly raiment among the wealthiest of our dowagers and the proudest of our belles ... [N]one of them value their profession so much as their good looks.[18]

Baudelaire likewise understood how actresses relied upon securing male endorsement. He noted: "What can be said of the courtesan can also be said, with reservations, of the actress; for the latter, too, is a manufactured confection and a thing of public pleasure."[19] If such suppositions are correct, then both actresses and prostitutes found it professionally savvy to exhibit themselves on the very same section of Broadway where the upper class would take their afternoon promenades. With both professions relying upon eliciting visual pleasure it is no wonder that they might be confused for one another.

The gender and class dynamics of this Broadway conflation were undoubtedly enhanced by what Walter Benjamin called the "modern spectatorial consumer." As Lauren Rabinovitz has shown in her study of women and cinema in turn-of-the-century Chicago, the nineteenth-century European *flâneur* is emblematic of the new urban subjectivity of the period. Rabinovitz uses Benjamin's theory to define the *flâneur* as one who engages in "the elite practice of aimless strolls, of joyfully mingling with the crowd as a way of knowing the city." Until the rise of the female urban workforce, this stroller was exclusively male and elite. "For a woman to assume *flânerie* in the nineteenth century," Rabinovitz writes, "was to risk being viewed as a prostitute."[20] Indeed, the freedom to walk the streets paralleled the male proclivity to consume goods and cast his gaze. Thus, in linking the pleasures of consumerism and scopophilia with the gendered subjectivity of the *flâneur*, we can better understand why the gaze would engender a spectatorship of consumption (whether it is directed at store goods or women). This model also explains why the actress, as one who "assume[s] *flânerie*" when parading on Broadway, would disrupt the kinetic space and scopophilia typically reserved for a male *flâneur*. An actress's assumption of *flânerie* – her invasion of previously male spaces, and the visual field – marked her, as it marked her sister in sin, the prostitute, as transgressive.

Yet another reason why actresses were conflated with prostitutes had to do with the increasing fictional depictions of actresses in pornography and erotica. Readers could pursue their sexual fantasies through the ersatz-figure of the actress. As Davis has observed:

> [P]rostitutes were not considered a suitable or desirable subject of conversation for middle-class ladies but actresses (individually and collectively) were a conversationally acceptable substitute in almost every social group. The lessons that could be extracted (or the thrills that could be generated) were equatable. The press was obliged to reinforce stereotypes while gratifying voracious interest in sexuality and to satiate prurient tastes with news of a substitute bohemian group.[21]

Many pulp novels featuring actresses, with steamy titles like *The Position of Peggy* (1911), *The Price She Paid* (1912), and *Out of The Wreck I Rise* (1913), bordered on pornography. Thus, the line between acting and whoredom became even more blurred. "Victorian erotica," writes Davis, "verified in a fictive (but for readers, a real) sense that the actress was inseparable from the whore and synonymous with sex."[22] With these popular novels drawing on pornography and functioning as a kind of erotica, Progressive Era readers could experience similar arousal yet rest assured that social conventions would be reinforced at the narrative's end – usually with the death of the sexually errant heroine.

One of the most compelling reasons that actresses were viewed as morally suspicious was due to their ability to earn a substantial living. As one article in *Theatre Magazine* from the period noted, "Twenty-five dollars a week is a more sensible wage than $15.00 or $10.00 or $8.00 – yes, or even $6.00, isn't it? That's why there are so many stage struck girls ... because it pays in every way."[23] These are salaries that only prostitution could rival. Yet early twentieth-century Western societies were still sorting out their discomfort with women earning money and entering the public realm. During the 1880s and 1890s, as Rabinovitz points out, the female labor force in American cities increased by more than twice the rise in the female population. These new urban female workers, or "women adrift," as Rabinovitz calls them, "suddenly appeared alone on city streets in such large numbers that their public wanderings became a new mobile visible signifier of an independent female sexuality."[24] Such wage earners caused a rift in the semiotics of early twentieth-century logic and *flâneur* spectatorship, a rift that the actress epitomized. Instead of woman as object to be consumed, the actress became a subject who was both consumed and *consumer*. Indeed, the idea of actress-as-whore emerged, in part, in response to the collapse of this familiar binary. As we shall see, the figure of the actress navigated the uncharted territory between sexual freedom and respectability as few women could.

I

Zaza: *That "obtruding harlot" of the stage*

The torrential rainfall during the American premiere of *Zaza* may well have been an omen. "The rain was coming down in torrents," the *New York Telegram* reported, "but there was a great rush of women at the Lafayette Square Theatre in Washington and the proceedings became so riotous that it was necessary to call in the police."[1] The police were there not to stop the show, but rather to facilitate its opening. And while the Belasco staging of *Zaza* was born in the midst of a storm it played in theatres and cinemas for over forty years – in German, French, and Russian – in countless stage revivals, opera performances, and three movie versions.[2]

Originally scripted by French authors Pierre Berton and Charles Simon, *Zaza* was made popular by the great actress Réjane on May 12, 1898 at the Théâtre du Vaudeville in Paris.[3] In the house that night was David Belasco, the so-called Bishop of Broadway, who would adapt the play eight months later for American audiences. *Zaza* premiered in the US at Lafayette Square Opera House in Washington, DC on December 26, 1898. It then moved to New York's Garrick Theatre on January 9, 1899, where it played for 184 performances. Belasco not only altered the French version with changes in character, dialogue, and mise-en-scène. He also sought to redeem Zaza from the iconic traps of whoredom. Belasco's adaptation of the French script outraged the original authors, who allegedly stormed out of a performance. Five years after the premiere, when Réjane restaged the play in New York, the French authors and Belasco were still at odds.[4] Launching a public relations campaign, Berton and Simon sent the American press copies of their original *Zaza* script, asking for "a public verdict on the question" because, according to one article, they "felt injured by the billing of Mr. Belasco as the author of the piece."[5] In spite of their

objections, Belasco's adaptation would prevail, playing in American theatres for over forty years.

Belasco's intentions in changing the script were seemingly benign: he
sought to offer a more sympathetic view of Zaza. According to William
Winter, he merely wanted "to find some excuse for Zaza's past and to have
less pity for the wife [of the man with whom Zaza has an affair]."[6] Hillary
Bell from the *New York Herald* observed that Belasco's changes were
successful in adding a new humanity to Zaza: "In the original version she
begins in vice and ends in it, having a holiday of sentiment meanwhile. In
the new version Belasco has humanized the heroine and after her virtuous
vacation, as it may be termed in contrast to her previous life, Zaza maintains
herself in decorum."[7] But at what price did Zaza's taming come? In order to
establish Zaza's decorum by making the French whore respectable, Belasco
eradicated much of her independence (especially her sexual autonomy). In
so doing, he resorted to traditional notions of female virtue and proper
gender performance, reforming Zaza much in the same way women's
sexuality was regulated throughout the period of antiprostitution reform.
Belasco's adaptation of the script therefore was an analogue for the reform
of fallen women during the Progressive Era.

Belasco's rehabilitation of Zaza can be seen in several dramaturgical
choices. First, he toned down the coarseness of Zaza's background and
character by eliminating her mother's alcoholism. In the original script,
Zaza survives a bitter childhood with a drunkard mother, becoming "utterly
unlovely, a girl of the tenements, thrust on the streets in her early childhood," as one *New York Times* critic put it.[8] Social determinist theories of
the time asserted that alcoholism was inherited and thus inescapable. Had
Belasco kept the mother character, then Zaza would have been perceived as
permanently tarnished by her mother's disease. Instead, Belasco replaced
Zaza's mother with an alcoholic aunt who adopts her, a change that
distanced Zaza from the faulty familial genes. Thus Zaza's decline is no
longer inevitable and Belasco could retell the longstanding American myth
of self-making and social transcendence. With resolve, natural talent, and
assistance from a stage friend, Zaza struggles to make something of herself
on the stage. Years later, as a music-hall success, her dressing room is filled
with tokens from admirers – men with whom she toys for sport.

Zaza, as originally conceived, came from a long tradition of theatrical
French sirens – a tradition that runs from Camille to Sapho – and her story
also referenced the sexual underworld, including the popular French-run
bordellos in New York City's sex district, Soubrette Row. Belasco worked

vigorously to clean up these sexual subtexts. As drama critic Alan Dale remarked in 1899, Belasco "steered away from all repugnance. He must have gone at the play with an exterminator and dashed away the vermin of its suggestiveness from its surface."[9] Most noticeably, Belasco sought to sanitize the sexual undercurrent of the music hall in which Zaza works. If actresses were perceived as sexually suspicious in American culture, then music-hall singers were even more so. As Kathy Peiss points out in *Cheap Amusements*, her study of working women and entertainment in turn-of-the-century New York, music halls were "closely tied to the male subculture of public amusements" where "crude jokes, bawdy comedy sketches, and scantily clad singers entertained the drinkers."[10] Moreover, music halls were notorious as sites for heterosexual assignations between female performers, waitresses, and male spectators. Simply by virtue of their presence in these liminal leisure sites, women who worked in, or attended, such spaces were often branded whores. "The phenomenon of independent, working-class women engaging in commerce in a working-class theatrical space," notes Robert C. Allen, "was perceived by those in a position to make laws as tantamount to criminal sexuality."[11] As we shall see, performing women, as well as women in performance spaces, were often those branded as sexual outlaws.

Because of the licentious character of urban music halls, Belasco's version tidied up moral ambiguities by altering the performance spaces in which Zaza works. According to one source, instead of setting the first act in "a resort that might almost have been called a dive" as the French script calls for, Belasco set it in "a scene of a provincial theatre and added enormously to the interest of the act by introducing a variety of amusing details of the life there."[12] This move from an urban to a country setting distanced Zaza from the commercialized vice world and its symbiotic relationship with lowbrow entertainments.

Given that music halls were often incriminating spaces for women, it is interesting that Belasco fashioned Zaza's positive transformation within this framework. Indeed, in the last act the music hall becomes a legitimating space. When Zaza returns to Paris as the music-hall star of an upscale theatre on the Champs Elysées, she experiences status and respect for the first time in her life. She is now, as her theatrical friend Cascart puts it, "a great artist," commanding upper-class audiences that could be mistaken for the opera crowd.[13] Belasco's overhaul of the music-hall profession in his adaptation was in sync with the efforts of variety halls (like Proctor's) to clean up their acts and market themselves as respectable, primarily by trying to attract female audiences.[14] Now that Zaza is a music-hall star, and thus financially stable, she achieves a kind of moral wealth as well, for unlike a courtesan she doesn't need any man's money. As Nathalie, Zaza's maid, puts it, "Madame is rich – very rich." (5.6). When she is seen on The Great White Way, "wearing gowns and jewels that a duchess might envy," the public knows she is not "drinking champagne on [a] beer income," but rather that she has earned these luxuries herself.[15]

Belasco also changed the setting of the second act, substituting Zaza's lodging house in the industrial town of St. Etienne with "a little house in the woods" (2.1). Prior to this act, Zaza had won a bet with her entourage that she could seduce Bernard Dufrene, an earnest and handsome Parisian. In spite of herself, however, Zaza falls in love with Dufrene. Six months later, in act two, the couple live together for one month in this bucolic setting. Belasco himself called *Zaza* "a new *Camille*," and this act clearly borrows from Dumas's play, as the lovers live beyond the temptations and scrutiny of urban life.[16] For Zaza to resemble Camille she must leave the city – particularly the incriminating space of the music hall – to find true love. Belasco's dilution of the play's urban mise-en-scène paralleled the Progressive impulse to idealize the countryside and demonize the city (a strategy to combat the drain of country folk to the city, especially women seeking work). The lovers' Arcadian escape from the urban underworld allows Zaza to navigate her moral turnaround more effectively.

Transformed by love, Zaza becomes monogamous, utterly devoted to Dufrene. As she tells Cascart, her manager and friend, "The happiest existence for a woman is to live with the man she loves" (2.27). Like her dramaturgical predecessor, Camille, Zaza is rehabilitated by love. But unlike Camille's lover, Armand, Dufrene does not change. He makes repeated, secretive trips to Paris where, as Cascart tells Zaza, he has been seen at the theatre with another woman, "a lady, about twenty-five, refined, pretty, very pretty. They didn't shrink from being seen together; they sat [in an] opening in a box . . . If I had seen him with a – a woman of a certain kind, I would have told you nothing. You may believe me – this is serious" (2.31). In this unconventional morality, it is not "a woman of a certain kind" (i.e. a prostitute), but rather a refined lady – possibly Dufrene's wife – whom Cascart and Zaza find troubling. So upset by the news that it "throws her into a courtesan's rage," according to *Harper's Weekly*, Zaza travels to Paris to confront Dufrene.[17] At his home she confirms that Dufrene has been leading a double life and determines to reveal all to his wife in act 3.

Belasco changed the Berton and Simon script in another important way, softening Zaza's character by highlighting her maternalness. Belasco did so not only in the script, but also in the selection of Mrs. Leslie Carter for the role – a choice to which I will return. Act 3 initially promises to be a lowbrow catfight between Zaza and Dufrene's wife. As Zaza puts it, "Just wait till I meet this woman! I'll give her the finishing sweep!" (3.38). But in Belasco's adaptation this act was "materially softened and refined."[18] While waiting to meet Dufrene's wife, Zaza encounters his angelic daughter, Toto. In this scene Zaza is clearly out of place, her brassy costume (with its loud swirls and bold patterns) in clear juxtaposition to Toto's pure white dress and the tasteful bourgeois drawing room. These signifiers of class and sexuality are not lost on Toto, who "showed that she recognized the innate vulgarity of the cocotte," according to one critic.[19] However, after meeting the child, Zaza undergoes a melodramatic transformation:

> As soon as I saw the little one, I understood that I was done for . . . Ah! Some women are born to be happy! They are petted and caressed when they are little; everyone loves them and when they grow to womanhood, they are able to live honestly with the man they love (*looks at Toto*) and be the mother of his children! Yet such women don't count their blessings every hour! They don't know what it is to be poor creatures of chance like we are, who knew hunger and misery when we were babies and who can only escape from it through some man; and if we take it into our heads to love him in a good way, we soon find out we have asked too much – such happiness is not for us – What shall I become? Oh, God, what will become of me now! (3.22; original ellipsis)

In this tearful scene, Zaza is transformed from a sexual predator to a woman hungry for husband and child. She does the dignified thing and leaves Dufrene's home intact. Unlike Camille, who sacrifices herself for the social standing of her lover, Zaza sacrifices her happiness for her lover's *family*.

While this scene is similar in both versions of the play, what differs in the Belasco–Carter interpretation is how Carter emphasized the importance of motherhood in the press. "To me," she recounted to a reporter, "the great act of the play is the third. Most people consider the fourth the climax, but I live more in the third. For in that act, Zaza's womanliness is awakened. Awakened in the most subtle way by a little innocent child. A woman, you know, who cannot be moved by a child is indeed hopeless."[20] Zaza's individual pleasure is eclipsed in this scene by the trope of respectability, where female sexual desire is sacrificed to "womanliness" (which Carter aligns with motherhood). Thus, by the end of the third act, Belasco's steamy music-hall singer begins to look less like a whore and more like a nanny.

In the fourth act Zaza confronts Dufrene with his treachery, which he does not deny. When Dufrene discovers that Zaza has been to his home and spoken with his wife and Toto too ("Toto too?"!), he becomes furious. Zaza has ventured from her prescribed domain, threatening to spoil respectable society by her very presence. Angered at Dufrene's response, Zaza lies to him by saying that she has told his wife all about their affair. Believing Zaza's supposed betrayal, Dufrene expresses contempt, calling her "common – tawdry, betinselled Zaza!" He ends the affair, saying, "I have only one regret – the shame of ever having wasted one hour (*contemptuously, going to Zaza*) on a creature of your kind!" (4.40). Consumed by anger, Dufrene just stops short of striking Zaza. In this moment Zaza realizes that Dufrene can never fully love her. Ending their affair once and for all, she tells Dufrene that she did not, in fact, reveal their secret to his wife after all. In turn, Dufrene tries to re-ignite their affair, but Zaza refuses. In both scripts Zaza sends him away. Only in Belasco's version, however, does Zaza recover her dignity in such a pronounced way, replying, "I won't be the low thing you've just called me any longer" (4.41). Act 4 concludes with Zaza sacrificing her desires; respectability is restored.

But it is Belasco's fifth act – tellingly called "Love Redeems the World" – in which much of Zaza's redemption occurs. In this final act, Dufrene returns to Zaza two years after their tumultuous breakup, hoping to reconcile. Zaza's moral turnaround is not complete until she rejects Dufrene a dramatic second time. In the French script, Zaza sends Dufrene away, but suggests that she will continue to take lovers:

ZAZA.   I know what you are going to say – what I refuse you today, I'll give tomorrow to others, whom I don't love the way I love you.

DUFRENE. And who won't love you as much as I love you.

ZAZA.   Lovers for a month; I have enough that I could resell them.[21]

By contrast, Belasco makes no reference to Zaza's sexual past or future. Instead of making the above speech, Belasco's Zaza takes a vow of celibacy, promising Dufrene, "My heart will never beat again for any man. Yours was the last kiss – yours the last embrace. They will be the last. That much – my love for you – has done for me" (5.12). This scene suggests not only a virtuous sacrifice reminiscent of nineteenth-century drama, but also a desperate kind of love for a man who has been verbally and emotionally abusive to Zaza. Belasco's efforts to purify Zaza were not lost on critic John Corbin, who noted in 1904 that "the French version forebore [sic] to whitewash Zaza in the last act – as the American version did, giving her a candid robe of innocence."[22]

In addition to Zaza renouncing her sexual freedom, Belasco's script also adds an extra reference to Dufrene's daughter, Toto. Zaza says: "Let me send Toto back to her father." Dufrene bows his head and replies: "You make me ashamed!" (5.13). Zaza thus further redeems herself, and rises from wanton to moral woman. She not only castigates her former lover, but also supports the institution of marriage she once rebuked. Zaza accordingly assumes her new chaste role as a culturally intelligible subject in the heterosexual symbolic order. In the last few lines of the play Zaza makes her final break with Dufrene before climbing into her carriage. Zaza effaces her own desire for Dufrene and transfers it to Dufrene's daughter, telling him: "Kiss Toto for me – two big kisses – one on each cheek. She needn't know they come from me; promise you will" (5.13). Awakened by her apparently instinctive maternalness, Zaza's sexual promiscuity is overridden by her endorsement of monogamous marriage, heterosexual reproduction, and maternal concern for the child (a surrogate for the children she will never have).

Critical reception of Belasco's doctoring of Berton and Simon's script varied. In comparing the two versions Corbin criticized Belasco's softening of Zaza's character in the last act: "This sentimentalization of the courtesan is the mistake Dumas made in his *Dame aux Camelias* – and owned up to afterward."[23] In contrast to Belasco's Zaza, Corbin continued, the French Zaza "packed Bernard [Dufrene] about his business not because she had become a saint, but because she had become a woman."[24] In *Famous Actresses of the Day in America*, Lewis Strang also condemned Belasco's fifth act: "Mr. Belasco's artistic touch was sure until the last act, when he erred for the sake of a happy ending."[25]

But these critical voices would stand out against the bulk of other reviews, which applauded Zaza's virtue. As Bell put it, "Hitherto Zaza had been wholly depraved, now virtue suddenly seized hold of her."[26] Another reviewer agreed: "Her love for Dufrene remains, but it has made her surrender him to his family and has made of her a respectable woman."[27] According to Carter herself: "In the French[,] the play is unpresentable. Zaza remains bad to the end. But in Belasco's translation, Zaza is transformed by her love and by the appeal that the child makes to her latent goodness. She reforms."[28] Strang credited Carter for humanizing Zaza: "Mrs. Carter . . . made Zaza – the coarse, the low-bred – understandable,

and by making her understandable as a human being, she saved Zaza from
lasting condemnation . . ."[29] Strang clarified how Zaza differed from other
fallen women, most noticeably Pinero's Paula Tanqueray: "Right here was
the irreconcilable difference between *Zaza* and the *Second Mrs. Tanqueray.*
In Zaza, one pitied the woman and condemned her fault – in Pinero's play,
one also pitied the woman . . . but at the same time he found her sin most
abhorrent and hateful."[30] Why, we might ask, were critics like Strang and
actors like Carter so invested in celebrating Zaza's reform, given that Zaza's
story is a very old plot indeed?

Performing intertextual identity

One explanation for the astonishing investment in Zaza's moral recupera-
tion – by Belasco, Carter, and critics alike – is that Carter's own personal
circumstances mirrored some of Zaza's misfortune. Carter was unhappily
married to a Chicago industrialist, a wealthy, shrewd man who committed
her to a private sanitarium after one bitter marital battle. After her release,
Carter struck back by suing for divorce, citing unusual cruelty. Not to be
outdone, her husband charged her with adultery and countersued, winning
not only the lawsuit, but also custody of their son, Dudley. Financially and
socially ruined by this much-publicized trial, Mrs. Carter turned to Belasco
for help with a career on the stage. As the story is told in many accounts,
Carter pleaded with Belasco's butler for permission to see the director and
Belasco, overhearing "the dramatic power behind the tearful plea, flung
open the door" and began his mentoring of Carter.[31] Belasco was aware that
Carter's personal tragedy ghosted her performance of Zaza, a detail he
emphasized in his opening night speech (which he gave after the fourth
act): "Nine years ago a poor woman threw herself at my feet and asked me to
help her. Now she is the happiest woman in the world, for she can telegraph
to her son that you like her in *Zaza* and that the boy may be proud of his
mother."[32] Bell not only praised Belasco's rhetorical savvy, but also
acknowledged the speech's effect on Carter: her "maternal love and her
joy in hearing that she had earned the right to her son's love in return."[33]
One newspaper reported that her son, Dudley, had watched the play and
declared: "Zaza is alright [sic] and my mama is alright [sic]."[34] As this
second drama played out in the press, Carter's legitimacy was measured
by her own son, just as Zaza's was by Toto. Belasco's manipulation of the
intertextuality of these two women's lives was not lost on critic Norman
Hapgood:

Bravo, Mr. Belasco. Did not every woman's heart in that vast throng thrill with yours and Mrs. Carter's when it remembered that, through plot and counterplot, through the divorce court and the awful verdict of the judge on the mother's relation to her child, her maternal heart beat fondly on her offspring in this crowning hour of triumph?[35]

Indeed, Carter had much at stake in constructing an identity of respect-ability, both on and off stage, for it reflected her suitability to be a mother. Carter struggled with the stigma of being a divorcee and kept the name of her millionaire ex-husband "to keep her celebrity credentials"[36] as an "ex-Society woman."[37] The identities of Zaza and Mrs. Leslie Carter were interchangeable in the public mind, as Alan Dale made clear in the New York American: "This was Zaza, and Mrs. Carter was every bit of it. The role fitted her without a wrinkle ... Carter personified Zaza."[38] Thus, Carter's own personal triumph in her fall from and rise in society cast an uplifting moral light on Zaza's journey, and vice versa.

In addition to the social parallels between character and actress, Carter's financial worries ghosted her performance of Zaza. Her monetary difficulties culminated in bankruptcy on November 4, 1898 – just one month before the opening of Zaza in Washington.[39] After her triumph in Zaza however, Carter's career as a star was confirmed, and her success story strongly resembled the character she portrayed. Just as economic independence pro-vided moral relief for Zaza, so performing Zaza provided economic independ-ence for Mrs. Leslie Carter. This is just one of many ways in which Carter's personal history and the fictional life of Zaza became uncannily intertwined.

If Belasco fashioned Zaza's virtue on stage, Carter took it to the press. In many interviews Carter defended Zaza's character: "But I do not want my poor Zaza to be damned as immoral. I think she teaches a great moral lesson."[40] In fact, Carter also wrote an article for Broadway Magazine, called "Mrs. Leslie Carter Discusses Zaza and Morality," in which she professed the need for virtue to prevail over bodily pleasures.[41] Carter not only defended her portrayal of Zaza, but also, with an eye always to her public image, her career of portraying fallen women:

[I]n my portrayal of these so-called "bad women" of the stage I have seen the fullest justification of my career. For if it has been given me to portray them truly, then the labor, the study, the money I have expended has not been all in vain. For always these plays have shown more powerfully and strikingly than any dry-as-dust sermon could – that true happiness in life is to be measured always by goodness.[42]

While many great turn-of-the-century actresses portrayed fallen women, Carter was perhaps the most vocal in defending supposedly morally way-ward characters. Even as late as 1913 Carter was defending her reputation as a virtuous actress, according to critic Archie Bell: "Mrs. Carter's name, like that of Nethersole, is associated with the so-called 'bad woman of the stage.' ... Yet she, like Nethersole, protests that she has been preaching a lesson of virtue and that 'the wages of sin is death' ever since she started her career."[43] Thus, just as Carter remade herself out of the ruins of divorce, so Zaza was refashioned to promote sexual respectability and proper (maternal) location.

The press also played a role in the construction of Zaza's respectability. Some critics desexualized Mrs. Leslie Carter's body, repeatedly calling it "maternal" and "robust." Although Mrs. Carter spent a good deal of time dressing and undressing on stage, "exhibiting [her] stockings, arm, neck and back," reviewers interpreted this exposure as decidedly nonsexual, because Carter was seen as "the passionately maternal actress," to use Hapgood's words.[44] Even the *New York Times* commented positively about the weight that Mrs. Carter had put on during summer vacation: "Mrs. Carter came back fuller as to face, a trifle more robust, perhaps, and evidently thoroughly rested by her summer outing, for there was nothing of the jaded woman in her appearance ..."[45] An actress with a "robust, maternal" body seemed to work effectively against cultural expectations of licentiousness that a role like Zaza might imply. It seems, then, that Carter's maternalness – however that term was understood – not only constituted her respectability, but also neutralized her fallen sexuality.

Such descriptions of Carter are particularly intriguing because Carter had been known for her vibrant red hair, something which was often thought to mark the actress as feisty, temperamental, and sensual. The *New York Herald* wrote about "her fiery locks and temperament," while others described "Zaza of the red hair," "the auburn-haired singing girl," and "this artist's glorious shock of auburn hair."[46] The *Philadelphia Record* described Carter as "the beautiful actress with the Rossetti hair and the Burne-Jones figure" (see figure 1).[47] But during the run of *Zaza*, in a press release called "The Real Mrs. Carter," Carter's press secretary fought against certain assumptions about red hair: "It has come to be believed that Titian tresses and a peppery temper are synonymous. The theory sounds plausible enough, only it is not true – that is, so far as Mrs. Carter is concerned."[48] Another press release devoted entirely to Mrs. Carter's red hair, called "Mrs. Leslie Carter and Her Temperament," argued that

Figure 1. Postcard of actress Mrs. Leslie Carter. Author's personal collection.

"auburn tresses have always been popular and ever a badge and indicator of emotional genius," among great actresses, including "the Divine Sarah and Réjane," who "have hair as red as a bottle of ruling ink."[49] Carter and her publicist thus sought to construct an identity of propriety by neutralizing a reading of auburn hair as temperamental and sensual, and relocating it within the traditions of classical painting (Titian) and great acting (Bernhardt, Réjane).

With the hair eliminated as a fetish, it is perhaps clearer why the press fixated upon other parts of Mrs. Carter's body, especially those that signified as nude or semi-nude by the use of tights. As we recall from Hapgood, in portraying a musical-hall actress, Carter changed frequently on stage, "exhibiting [her] stockings, arm, neck and back."[50] As Tracy Davis has pointed out, tights were one of the primary signifiers in nineteenth-century pornography, pornography which, incidentally, often featured actresses. The sexual currency of tights permeated not only pornography, but also the theatre itself. According to Davis, "At theatres up and down the country, tights were the sign of the actress, legs were the locus of male enjoyment, and simulated nudity was the privileged interpretation of the voyeur."[51] Yet, what is quite unusual about Carter's performance of Zaza is that her use of tights and exposure of her body were perceived as nonerotic at a time when other plays were being censored for precisely the same sort of exposure. Though audience members saw plenty of simulated nudity, no one was shocked or incensed by Carter's body being exposed, or at the exposure of any of the other actresses portraying music-hall dancers, whose legs were regularly displayed in act one of Zaza. Indeed, Mrs. Carter's disrobing appears to have been received rather uneventfully. For example, in act 1, Carter changes out of her costume into a negligee, asking Dufrene coyly, "You don't mind, do you?" (1.58). In response to this and other scenes the New York Times reported dispassionately, "Zaza does a great deal of dressing and undressing before the public eye. She exhibits much of her person."[52] In a similarly detached manner, Alan Dale observed, "She removes her bodice in order to make way for her candor of these proceedings," noting, "it is only in Boston that they put trousers on statues."[53]

That critics received Carter's semi-nudity on stage with such indifference signals the extent to which Carter's respectable persona ghosted her performance. The performing, public body of the actress was inseparable from what Michael Quinn has called the cult of celebrity: her sexual politics, acting style, and off-stage performances of gender and sexuality.[54]

Indeed, as I have already noted, Carter's career was launched by Belasco, under whom she served as a model protégé. This professional union was broken only in 1906 when Carter married William Lewis Payne without Belasco's permission (itself a bizarre condition), which infuriated Belasco and ignited a twenty-five year dispute.[55] Their much-publicized feud, which both sides upheld until just before Belasco's death, was not unlike a second divorce. Interestingly, after that split, Carter strove to construct a new identity separate from Belasco. For example, one press release argued that Mrs. Carter was not taught to act – especially not by Belasco and his rigorous training schedule – but rather that she was "a great actress" who possessed "a natural gift of God, a self-known instinct."[56] In spite of these efforts, when Carter attempted to produce her own work, she failed. "Following a disastrous attempt to act in a capacity of manager, producer and star," wrote the *Evening Telegram*, "Mrs. Carter fled to England."[57] In fact, Carter never achieved the same star status she had under Belasco's wing and in 1908 was forced once again to declare bankruptcy.[58]

Returning to the premiere of *Zaza*, we can see that Carter was a product and beneficiary of a male theatre production system. If *Zaza* ruffled any feathers it was not because Carter ventured into hostile entrepreneurial waters. Indeed, *Zaza* was safe from the censor's wrath in part because of Belasco's air-brushed adaptation.

Class voyeurism

For all of Belasco's whitewashing of Zaza's character, there was one aspect of her life that he chose not to sugarcoat. Just as Zaza is a performer not of the legitimate stage, but rather of the music hall, so she is equally characterized as illegitimate in terms of her class. Given that vaudeville and music halls were the choice entertainment of working-class men and women during the late 1800s and early 1900s, the very space in which Zaza performs is already marked as inferior to her audience's bourgeois domain. Although Belasco toned down some elements of the original Zaza's tenement lifestyle, as discussed earlier in this chapter, he nonetheless retained Zaza's lower-class mannerisms. As Bell reported in the *New York Herald*, "She sings the coarse songs that please the dull and the insignificant . . . There are no good people of the social standard in her life, there are only those who do not know the rules of behavior set down in the codes of civilized society."[59] *Harper's* also praised Carter's display of coarseness, specifically in terms of class vulgarity:

She is so tawdry and betinselled that the eyes get sore in watching her;
she is so low and vulgar in the commoner workings of her nature that one
may quite reasonably, if he chooses, refuse to spend an evening in the
same theatre . . . It is a marvel to see how many kinds of tawdriness and
vulgarity, distinctly and finely discriminated, one woman can show.[60]

Why would Belasco eradicate Zaza's sexual promiscuity only to retain other
elements of her lower-class affect?

In many ways *Zaza* engendered a kind of class voyeurism, in so far as the
leisured and business class greatly outnumbered the working class in audiences in standard theaters.[61] *Zaza* prefigured social-problem plays in
American drama, which, with just a few exceptions, had yet to find their
way to the stage. Both Belasco and Carter approached the play with journalistic exactitude characteristic of realism, making some scenes of *Zaza* resemble an ethnographic study of lower-class women. According to one
newspaper account, while Belasco worked on the script, Mrs. Carter "studied
first hand the little French girls whose lives inspired the play . . . [S]he visited
dance halls and cabarets of the French capital and penetrated the homes of
hundreds of 'Zazas.' "[62] While actors might have conducted some such
research, the kind of extensive interviewing and sociological study that
Carter performed was unusual, especially for a single actress of her day.

The most visible markers of Zaza's class were not her bodily acts (indeed,
I have argued that Carter's body performed against the sexual expectations
of the role), but rather her lower-class speech acts.[63] Her East Side slang
captivated the fashionable bourgeois and upper-class audience at the
Garrick Theatre, "a very select audience – that is, an audience of men
who pay their taxes punctually, who have money, lands, stocks, libraries
of beautiful and scarce books. The women were of the most exclusive,
fashionable society."[64] Utterances like "Zut!," "Tch! Tch!," "Hump!,"
"Skedaddle!," and "Come in boys. We're going to crack a bottle of fiz,"
(1.26, 1.34, 1.39, 1.52, 1.41) were, as Bell noted, "slang that fashionable people
do not hear often. It amused distinguished women at the Garrick last night,
and they laughed at it impulsively."[65] Slumming, it appears, had great
appeal for bourgeois audiences, who were both repulsed and attracted to
the less fortunate. The class voyeurism in the theatre replicated the slumming by men in various demi-monde entertainment establishments such
as concert saloons. As M. Alison Kibler points out in her excellent study
of vaudeville, *Rank Ladies: Gender and Cultural Hierarchy in American
Vaudeville*, "Many concert saloons attracted middle-class men, 'slumming

voyeurs' who were eager to sample the city's mysterious underside and to mingle with poor or immigrant women."[66] In 1899 Bell noted that a similar kind of voyeurism motivated audiences to see *Zaza*: "She is as ill-mannered as a girl can ever be. Her attitude, her gestures, her way of walking, of talking, of doing anything ... are abominable. Zaza could not appear in a drawing room that respected itself and remain there an instant."[67] This is precisely the point: Zaza could not appear in any fashionable drawing room. However, she could appear on stage where "men of learning and men mighty in affairs; women of society and of the stage" could view her from afar.[68] The hypocrisy of such a stance is conceded in the same review:

> Surely, no one in the audience at the Garrick last night would wish to be cited as an authority on the realism of *Zaza*. No one would wish it to be printed of him that his remark was, at the end of the play, "I know a woman like Zaza. There is absolute fidelity to the type in Mrs. Leslie Carter's representation." Zaza's audience makes her acquaintance intimately. Zaza's audience knows her almost as well as ... other acquaintances of the play know her.[69]

The intimacy that Bell suggests that audiences have with Zaza is perhaps only partly true, particularly when this encounter occurs in the realm of representation. Indeed, culture can work as an ambivalent force with conflicting urges, especially, as Lawrence Levine has noted, in sites where highbrow meets lowbrow.[70] Yet the dual fascination and repulsion that audiences felt towards characters like Zaza is framed safely, given the respectability of the Garrick, Zaza's moral rehabilitation, and Carter's persona as an ex-society woman. What the bourgeoisie was slumming, in other words, was a construction of their own making – a reformed Broadway girl with family values. A virtuous version of the old rags-to-riches tale, *Zaza* had won over the theatre-goers, according to Bell: "The entire audience wept with Zaza, laughed with Zaza, was sarcastic, savage, repentant with Zaza."[71]

In the larger landscape of antiprostitution reform, which was just gaining steam in American Progressive culture, the domesticated version of *Zaza* would shape ensuing debates regarding obscenity, sexuality, prostitution, women's work, and, of course, American drama. Seemingly a play about a modern, sexually liberated woman, *Zaza* actually recycled dominant sexual ideology and fallen woman dramaturgy. Seen in such a light, it becomes clear why *Zaza* escaped the clutches of Anthony Comstock and other censors of the New York stage: the play advocated marital fidelity on the one hand, and allowed bourgeois audiences to slum in the underworld within the respectable frame of legitimate theatre on the other. One thing is certain: *Zaza*, "the patchouly-scented heroine of this tainted trash," to recall Winter's phrase, would leave an indelible mark on American theatre history, and, like Camille, pave the way for her future sisters in sin.[72]

2

That "sin-stained" Sapho

One of the first plays of the century – and one of the most scandalous productions in twentieth-century American history – was produced by a woman. Marginalized by most theatre historians, Olga Nethersole became a cause célèbre with her titillating production of Clyde Fitch's *Sapho* in New York on February 5, 1900.[1] Nethersole had made a career of playing fallen women, but none were as objectionable as the smoldering Sapho, named after the ancient lesbian poetess, Sappho. Several years before *Sapho*, in her performance of *Carmen*, Nethersole had become famous for what became known as "the Nethersole Kiss" – a kiss on the lips that lasted so long that stagehands were rumored to lay bets on its duration each evening. In *Sapho*, Nethersole scandalized her audiences not only with a kiss, but also with her whole body. While the model Fanny, known in the art world as Sapho, is not a prostitute in the official sense, she was perceived, in Abe Laufe's words, as "a courtesan who lured and then discarded men."[2] *Sapho* therefore provides insight into how fallen women, especially those who were also performing women, became conflated with prostitutes. As District Attorney Gardiner stated, "If I were called upon to characterize it, I would call it *Sapho*: the Career of the Princess of Parisian Prostitutes; or, Vice Made Attractive."[3] While it is true that Fanny had many lovers who supported her, a common practice at the time, the story of *Sapho* is about Fanny finding true love – and reckoning with her sexual past.

In the wake of *Zaza*'s success the censorship case surrounding *Sapho* can be seen as a watershed moment in Progressive America, for this production intersected with the very beginning of antiprostitution efforts, as censors and reformers alike were struggling over how to regulate female sexuality. Within the context of antiprostitution reform, *Zaza* and *Sapho*'s divergent production histories demonstrate contradictory impulses that both controlled and tolerated the sexual female body on stage. These contradictions were mirrored in early antiprostitution debates between regulatory groups, who argued for government-monitored prostitution, and purity groups, who fought for complete elimination of the social evil. Insofar as *Zaza* told a certain story about redeeming a fallen woman's sexuality, it served to stage dominant, even "official," sexual truths. *Sapho*, on the other hand, demonstrates another regulatory function: the sexually aberrant woman who must be censored, contained, and disciplined through juridical structures. *Sapho* may be, moreover, the first expression of such Progressive influences in American theatre. While censorship had long occurred in the theatre, it was not until the turn of the twentieth century that it became so forcefully directed at a single target: a woman who took pleasure or profit from her sexuality.

Representations of Sappho, the ancient poetess, permeated Victorian culture. Spurred on by Henry Thornton Wharton's influential text in 1885, *Sappho: Memoir, Text, Selected Renderings and a Literal Translation*, late Victorian writers on both sides of the Atlantic (from Ezra Pound to Olive Shreiner) drew on Sappho for artistic inspiration. As Yopi Prins has shown in *Victorian Sappho*, "Sappho represents different ideas of Victorian womanhood, and like the Queen she becomes a 'representative' woman who embodies the very possibility of such representations, allowing them to multiply in often contradictory forms."[4] Well before the Fitch–Nethersole production, therefore, Victorian invocations of Sappho engendered varied, and often contradictory, notions of gender and sexuality. Recovered and rewritten by scholars and poets alike, Sappho signified differently in various contexts. Paradoxically, the lesbian reading of Sappho was often eclipsed by the late nineteenth century's unease with the woman question. As Margaret Reynolds has shown in *The Sappho Companion*, "As so often in Sappho's story, she was co-opted into New Womanhood because she offered a model of female achievement in the past."[5] Robert Appleton's *Violet: The American Sappho . . . A Realistic Novel of Bohemia* from 1894 is particularly noteworthy for our discussion of the Fitch–Nethersole *Sapho* because it likewise portrayed "an actress with a 'past,'" who is "beautiful, confident and predatory."[6] In the slippery terrain of representation then, the Sapphic figure oscillated between signifying Victorian respectability and, as Prins has shown, "the suffering of 'woman' as an overdetermined heterosexual identification: doomed to die for love."[7] While all historic deployments of the Sapphic figure are important to the performance history of the Fitch-Nethersole adaptation, what is of interest for this study is the intersection of the suffering woman, an actress with a past, and the New Woman. Nethersole drew upon all of these contradictory signifiers in her production.

The source text for the Fitch–Nethersole production was Alphonse Daudet's 1884 novel, *Sapho*, which "was written as a warning to [Daudet's] sons against becoming entangled with a woman of inferior station," according to C. Hayward's *Dictionary of Courtesans*.[8] Clyde Fitch adapted Daudet's novel to the stage after receiving suggestions from Nethersole to be more sympathetic to the character Fanny (alias Sapho). Although Fitch penned the adaptation, according to Nethersole the project was hers: "I have been working on it for four years, and Mr. Fitch undertook the dramatization at my request."[9] While adapting the text, according to Fitch's correspondence, he received "daily letters from Louis Nethersole with requests for details for his sister."[10] Nethersole's name might not have been on the script, but she was instrumental in shaping the project.

The Fitch–Nethersole dramatization of *Sapho* portrays the love affair of the alluring Fanny Legrand and Jean Gaussin, an innocent country boy with a promising future as a foreign consul. Inexperienced in love, Jean becomes enraptured with Fanny, whom he meets at a masked ball in Paris. Before the evening is over, Jean becomes intrigued with Fanny, unable to ignore her allure. Meanwhile, Fanny's former lover, Flamant, arrives at the party, confessing that he committed forgery in order to support Fanny and their illegitimate baby. During the ball Flamant is arrested and taken away, leaving Fanny to be escorted home by Jean. They start an affair.

As the play unfolds in act 2, Fanny and Jean are living together in a country cottage while Jean studies for his examinations. Jean becomes disillusioned when he learns Fanny's former identity: the model known as Sapho, the sensual muse who posed as "that naked Sappho that every eye in Paris can inspect" (2.16). Although Fanny has convinced Jean to adopt her child, Joseph, without telling Jean his true identity, Jean soon discovers who the youngster really is. With pressures from his family to provide for them and save himself from ruin, Jean feels trapped. When he flees following a terrible argument, Fanny tries unsuccessfully to poison herself. Shortly thereafter Flamant returns from jail, professing his love for Fanny, and asks to assume his duties as father. Recognizing the sacrifice she must make for her child, Fanny accepts Flamant's proposal and thus selflessly gives up her own happiness. The play ends with a tear-filled scene, in which Fanny leaves her true love, Jean.

The story of a sexually experienced woman having affairs with men outside of marriage was not new to the New York stage, but the astonishing controversy over *Sapho* was. In Belasco's *Zaza*, staged just a year earlier, a similar plot-line had been advanced: a music-hall performer lives with a married man in the country for six months. Yet, while *Zaza* was often compared to *Sapho*, it encountered none of the controversy that *Sapho* did. What, then, was so vexing about Nethersole's *Sapho*? "Why all this shouting against Sapho" as one editorial asked, when "there are numerous performances running in this city that are much worse than *Sapho* ever dared to be. Why are they not stopped?"[11] As drama editor and theatrical agent T. Allston Brown noted in 1903, "The season of 1899–1900 saw many immoral plays in New York"; yet, none of them were censored.[12] *Camille* had, after all, offered a similar plot decades before, playing hundreds of times without incident. Nethersole herself had played Camille and Carmen dozens of times before 1900; they were popular stock pieces in her American repertory tours after 1895. As the *New York Sun* noted, "Olga Nethersole's choices of heroines to enact have shown a preference for viciously immoral creatures."[13] The basic subject matter of *Sapho*, as one editorial articulated, "has been presented on our stage many times before by Mme. Bernhardt and Duse, Mrs. Kendal and Miss Nethersole in *Camille*, *The Second Mrs. Tanqueray*, and other plays. Yet no one has ever seriously proposed to stop those plays."[14]

Another way to read the controversy is to recognize the act of censorship as regulating sexuality. Cultural conservatives represented the *Sapho* conflict as unduly sullying American sexual mores – utilizing, in short, the "repressive hypothesis," to use Michel Foucault's term, to cast themselves as protectors of morality.[15] Marking *Sapho* as obscene and censoring it from the public was, of course, another kind of sexual performance. Yet, as some critics observed in 1900, such regulatory efforts were themselves another kind of sex discourse – and hypocritical at that. As Bruce MacDonal reported in the *New York Telegraph*, "there is nothing in [*Sapho*] to surprise New York. The affectation of ignorance of certain existing conditions and relations between men and women is stupid and provincial."[16] In spite of the fact that "there are Camilles, Zazas and Fanny Legrands in New York by the thousand," the controversy surrounding the production of *Sapho* would reveal the limits of staging sexuality, especially when staged by a woman.[17]

Seen in this light, what follows is not a complete reconstruction of the performance, for though the scholarship on *Sapho* is scarce, Anne Callis, John Houchin, Randy Kapelle, and Joyce Reilly have documented many details of the controversy. What I wish to focus on is how sexuality is deployed through discursive and performative mechanisms of the stage, press, and jurisprudence. By including the character Fanny Legrand, as well as actress Olga Nethersole, in the framework of performing women, this chapter seeks to link their work as model, actress, and muse to the logic of display culture and its conflation of such work with prostitution. In tracing the arrest of Nethersole and company, the closing of the play, and the eventual trial, it becomes clear that much was at stake in protecting the familiar Victorian readings of Sappho as the woman who must die for her sexual sins. What *Sapho*'s censorship proves, then, is that only specific representations of fallen women's sexuality were allowed in the public domain. Sex, Foucault reminds us, "was a thing one administered; . . . it had to be taken charge of by analytical discourses."[18] The theatre, it turns out, was a crucial mechanism in policing – and producing – sexuality. However, as Nethersole's eventual triumph also shows, there was space for critical interventions within this discursive matrix.

Sympathetic *Sapho*

Some critics, like theatre historian John Houchin, have viewed Fanny Legrand from *Sapho* as a "notorious *femme fatale*" . . . who "challenged the belief that prostitutes were victims of male aggression . . ."[19] My reading seeks to dispute these two familiar archetypes invoked by Houchin and others (*femme fatale* and prostitute), showing that Fanny was neither; instead, Nethersole made Fanny a casualty of her circumstances, a selfless woman whose crime is but that she loves. Unlike Daudet's novel, which portrayed "man as the victim of woman," according to critic Murray Sachs, Fitch's version gave a sympathetic treatment of Fanny – at Nethersole's insistence.[20] Rather than devour the weak-willed country boy, as in Daudet's story, the sexually experienced Fanny in the Fitch–Nethersole version recognizes Jean's virginal status and warns him to stay away from her. She cautions him:

FANNY. You are so young yet. Love wisely. Leave Paris, go back to the country. Choose some pure young girl. In scenes like this, no happiness is found. It is love for a day. Fickle, casual, drinking parties in the country, mask balls like this[,] horse play in the studies, engagements, conquests. (*sadly*) I know it all. (*despairing gesture*) Heaven help me, I know it all. (1.15)

The sexually domineering woman is therefore softened in the Fitch–Nethersole version, offering more insight and sympathy into Fanny's plight. Although Daudet began his novel with the masked ball, the Daudet-Belot script omits this initial scene altogether, beginning their play after the affair has begun. Fitch and Nethersole restored the ball scene not only to underscore the sensuality of Fanny and Jean's relationship – for, as Timothy J. Gilfoyle has noted, masked (or French) balls were notorious for "testing the boundaries of urban sexual behavior" – but also to portray Fanny as a more complex character who is critical of the very ribaldry with which she is associated.[21] In denouncing the ball and "love for a day," as she puts it, Fanny comes across as a woman who is searching for love in all the wrong places. This was precisely the problem, according to the *World*, the newspaper that ran a smear campaign against *Sapho*. While Daudet's novel showed "how easy it is for a young man's life to be completely wrecked by association with a depraved woman," in the Fitch–Nethersole version, according to reporter Sidney Sharp, "hardly a vestige of this meaning is apparent. Sapho is made the center of interest throughout, and numerous attempts of a clap-trap nature are made to gain our sympathy for her."[22]

The Nethersole–Fitch portrayal also offered a more sympathetic view of Fanny by increasing the visibility of Fanny's boy, "the boy without whom I cannot exist," as Fanny puts it in act 4 (4.14–15). Such scenes often received the most applause. Described in the stage directions as "mother hungry," Fanny can rise out of her sexual disgrace only through the transcendent role of mother (3.24). No longer able to depend upon Jean, a "respectable" man who will ultimately dump her, she chooses nevertheless to marry Flamant, an ex-convict whom she doesn't love, in order to gain respectability for her bastard child. While *Sapho*'s ending provides insight into how women were limited by sexual morality, the plot also recycles the Victorian valorization of maternity. As Justice Fursman, the presiding judge over the obscenity trial in the Criminal Branch of the Supreme Court, put it, "The play depicts the life of a common woman, and yet it is not without its moral. It shows that a man and a woman may be bound together in the honest bonds of matrimony by the love of an innocent child."[23] Yet, this is not the whole story, for the "moral of a bad woman turned good for the love of her child," as the *New York Times* noted, was not unique to this play.[24] A similar ending is used in *Zaza*; something else, then, must account for *Sapho*'s sensationalism other than plot. In order to understand what was at stake in *Sapho*'s performance history, we must look at Nethersole's performance choices, particularly how she signified – as both actress and public figure.

Performative subversions

At the heart of the *Sapho* controversy was a cultural breach, to use Victor
Turner's formation, created by Nethersole's performance, not by playwright
Fitch's words.[25] For as Kim Marra has shown, Clyde Fitch was "driven to
stage the American Girl," who "signified not only WASP racial purity but
also gender and sexual purity," in part to mask his own homosexuality.[26]
Nethersole's Fanny could hardly be mistaken for the pure American Girl.
Accordingly, she and others in the company were charged with causing a
public nuisance. During the trial in February 1900, it was Nethersole who
was attacked most routinely for her performance choices. As Joyce Reilly
observes, Nethersole's "own innovations were the most hotly debated
moments in the *Sapho fracases*."[27] Nethersole was perceived as a public
nuisance because of her feminist politics and performative subversions of
expected sexual codes. Unlike other actresses portraying fallen women,
Nethersole simultaneously unsettled and reclaimed certain erotic tropes.
Nethersole's self-conscious exploitation and subversion of erotic codes
reveals an astute awareness of identity performance. Yet it was precisely
this performativity, particularly its citation of feminism and sexual libera-
tion, which provoked anxiety. Indeed, the obscenity charges brought
against Nethersole reflected this discomfort with a sensual and independent
woman who toyed with erotic images on stage.

One of the most objectionable moments of the play was the infamous
staircase scene at the end of the French ball in act 1. Because Fanny is too
tired to climb the stairs herself – or so she says – Jean carries her up in his
arms to his bedroom. To show the passage of time while the couple was
upstairs, as well as to suggest the sexual act ensuing, the curtain rose and
fell, according to some accounts, as many as five times.[28] The staircase
scene was Nethersole's own invention and was played in front of the main
curtain. Owen Davis, one the most prolific American playwrights of the
twentieth century, recalled the scene this way: "Olga Nethersole ... was
being carried, mark you, upstairs in an actor's arms. Walking upstairs in
those days was always significant of the very worst intentions on the part
of the walker, and to be carried was indicative of nothing that nice people
could mention. It was dreadfully gay and bawdy."[29] In the trial, this scene
was actually staged in court and became a central piece of evidence against
Nethersole.

What made the staircase scene most inflammatory, however, was
Nethersole's delivery of her lines. Witnesses at the trial reported that

although Nethersole said "no" to Jean, she said it in such a way as to mean "yes."[30] One witness went so far as to imitate Nethersole's sexy four-syllable "no" during his testimony as follows: "The witness leaned back in his chair, threw out his arms appealingly toward Justice Fursman, and opened his mouth to its widest extent. 'No-o-o-o,' he roared. The witness's voice is a strong baritone, and he threw a note of yearning into his imitation that made every one in the courtroom jump. Justice Fursman reproved the witness."[31] Given the ephemeral quality of performance, scrutinizing Nethersole was more difficult than it appeared. Precisely because the script did not – nor could not – convey Nethersole's performance choices, the court had to rely upon witnesses mimicking, often badly, how Nethersole performed certain scenes.

Although Nethersole was criticized for sexual innuendos in act 1, her acting style as a whole was also critiqued for defying notions of traditional femininity. The *New York Times* gave an unusually acerbic review of *Sapho*, focusing on Nethersole's disregard for acting and etiquette standards: "It is too late in the day to dwell upon the deficiencies of Miss Nethersole's acting," the review noted. "She is not fascinating or graceful, and her violence, uncertainty, artificiality, and awkwardness were never more unpleasantly in evidence than in this performance."[32] The review faults Nethersole for not being graceful or pleasant – in short, for being improperly feminine and lacking bourgeois etiquette. Another reviewer called Nethersole a "rough, spasmodic, inartistic actress, fit only for violent melodrama."[33] William Winter added his usual acerbic critique: "Miss Nethersole was duly spasmodic, in her usual vein, but being of an unsympathetic temperament, and as an actress always artificial, she prevailed, in as far as she prevailed at all, by physical force, not by either well simulated feeling or fine art."[34] Perceived as a transgressor of fine art, Nethersole's acting also subverted expectations of genteel womanhood.

In addition to resisting the performative gestures of bourgeois female identity, Nethersole was also charged with performing "divers lewd, indecent, obscene, filthy, scandalous, lascivious, and disgusting motions."[35] The *New York Dramatic Mirror* invoked the classic myth of dangerous female sexuality, reporting: "Her Sapho is a languorous, insinuating siren."[36] Put another way, Nethersole's Sapho was "[e]ndowed with rare powers of fascination and witchery," as the *Sketch* put it.[37] When not drawing on classical myths of perilous female sexuality, other reviewers labeled Nethersole's sexuality as animalistic. The *Sun* reported, for instance, "It would be impolite, and perhaps not wholly true, to say that her mimicry of love is necessarily animal."[38] Perplexed by the contradictory signs afloat, the article continued, "She is handsome in a gross way," denoting "a tigress of a woman, who purred when stroked, but bit when struck ..." The *World* advanced another animal metaphor: "Olga Nethersole acted with a great deal of feline grace."[39] While Nethersole manipulated erotic codes to her benefit, she also took offense to charges that she was recklessly vulgar. In May 1900, she filed suit against a pastor of a Presbyterian church in Washington for a sermon in which he called her a "lewd woman."[40] Some years later Nethersole responded to how critics viewed her work and the changing attitudes:

> I was [called] "vulgar" in all of these things a few years ago. Nobody would criticize an actress to-day for turning her back to the audience. Nobody would find cause for complaint if an emotional actress blew her nose during a scene of weeping. Bare feet have lost their "sting" for an audience; and as for vital matters of health, purity and right living, these are now openly discussed in the plays of the day, in magazines and newspapers that cater to family circulation, and nobody winces at the mention of the body, as if it were something unholy and unmentionable.[41]

If Nethersole eschewed the so-called finer arts of acting in 1900, she also emphasized Fanny's strength, drawing from the iconography of New Womanhood. During the performance Nethersole used smoking to signify Fanny's independence and sensuality. Smoking women were perceived by dominant culture as either sexually effusive or as feminist. In this role, as in real life, Nethersole was both. A few years before *Sapho*'s premiere, Nethersole had modeled provocatively for Ogden's Cigarettes wearing her costume from *Carmen* (see figure 2). Nethersole also appeared on the front of a tobacco card from Sweet Caporal-Kinney Brothers Cigarettes. Her performance of *Sapho* was thus ghosted not only by her sexy rendering of *Carmen* – "a controversial, innovatively unromantic portrait of a calculating, streetwise trollop" and "dirty cigarette girl," as Reilly notes – but also by advertising tobacco for women, most of whom were subverting decorum by smoking.[42]

In the final act of *Sapho*, when Fanny leaves Jean, Nethersole lit a cigarette before walking out the door – yet another Nethersole addition to the Fitch script.[43] While the original Daudet–Belot script emphasizes Fanny's selfless self-sacrifice for her child, Nethersole's performance of this scene doesn't wallow in self-pity. Quoting Ibsen's Nora, Nethersole added another liberatory gesture before leaving her man – she deliberately lit a cigarette, inhaled deeply, and walked offstage with cigarette in hand.

Figure 2. Olga Nethersole as Carmen, posing for Ogden Cigarettes. Author's personal collection.

At a time when a woman smoking in public was deemed risqué, the smoking Sapho instantly became an iconic image for the production. *Sapho*'s publicity posters show a cartoon of Nethersole smirking, eyes sensually half-closed, smoking a cigarette, and provocatively returning the gaze (see figure 3).[44] In 1900 such gestures signified the New Woman and, like bloomers and the bicycle, were unmistakably feminist. When *Theatre Magazine* contemplated the censorship case twenty-five years later it still described Nethersole as "very daringly [lighting] a cigarette."[45] Her defiant, sexy, and assertive portrayal demonstrates the destabilizing force of a woman's cigarette, a performative gesture that reads against the grain of the more conservative elements of the script. Thus, Nethersole combined sexiness with independence, subverting the idea that the New Woman was asexual or masculine – popular representations at the time – or that a sensual woman was out of control, sexually excessive, and hopelessly degenerate.

Of all the objections to Nethersole's performance, however, the most important had to do with her provocative costuming. Known for her exquisite costumes, Nethersole had drawn public interest when, portraying *Camille* in 1894 and 1899, she resurrected the "exact reproductions of the styles in vogue at the time of Marie Duplessis," the prostitute on whom *Camille* was modeled.[46] On and off stage Nethersole knew very well how to manipulate herself as visual spectacle in the display economy of the theatre. Because Nethersole routinely donned sensational costumes, there was much anticipation about how she would approach *Sapho*. Even before *Sapho* opened Nethersole was asked several times about her clothing. Everyone was wondering just how provocative Nethersole would be, as one reporter's question revealed: "Will you wear, that, – er, remarkable costume in the first act?"[47]

And indeed, Nethersole did not disappoint, appearing in a spectacular costume for in the first act's masked ball. Dressed as Sappho, the ancient poetess, Nethersole wore an off the shoulder, gauze-like white toga. The gown was slit up the side, but secured with large buttons at mid thigh (see figure 4). Even by today's standards this costume is somewhat revealing, but in 1900 the costume clearly connoted nudity, as this headline made clear: "Partial Disrobing of the Heroine the Most Startling Thing in the Daudet-Fitch Piece."[48] Much of the press, like the following review, became obsessed with how Nethersole achieved the nude effect: "Olga Nethersole has arrived in *Sapho* at the secret of wearing clothes that reveal, rather than conceal, the figure. Even the dimples in her form were artfully suggested, and, although ostensibly covered with drapery, she presented an appearance of nudity."[49] *World* reporter W. O. Inglis testified: "She wears a Grecian costume, which reveals her figure. She appears to be naked down to the apex of the heart; the shoulder is bare right down to the shoulder blade.

Figure 3. Olga Nethersole in publicity poster for *Sapho*, smoking. Author's personal collection.

Figure 4. Olga Nethersole in the controversial see-through gown from *Sapho*. Photo by Byron, courtesy the Museum of the City of New York.

The rest of the costume is almost transparent and you can see the entire outline of the body."[50] The *New York Dramatic Mirror* also focused on Nethersole's tight-fitting dresses: "The actress wore some gowns of amazing clingingness, her first act dress quite out-clinging anything yet seen here in its line."[51] During the trial, drama critic Hilary Bell testified that Nethersole's costumes were "diaphanous" and revealing: "Fanny wore tights . . . and when she stood with her back to the light you could pretty well see through her costume."[52]

That Bell focused on the tights may well provide a clue to the scandalous nature of Nethersole's attire. As Tracy Davis has pointed out, tights were one of the primary signifiers in Victorian era pornography – which often featured actresses – drawing attention and the male gaze to fetishized parts of the female body.[53] Similarly, at the turn of the twentieth century, sexual encodings, on stage or in pornography, were usually created by men for their erotically fluent male consumers. Nethersole upset this gendered visual economy, however, by capitalizing on what Davis has called the "erotic lexicography of male culture" and then subverting it.[54] Therefore, the imitation of a nude female body was not the real transgression here, for simulated nudity had occurred on the American stage long before; rather, it was Nethersole's assumption and subversion of erotic tropes that provoked anxiety.

Another problematic aspect about Nethersole's perceived nudity was the fact that she was portraying a model at work. In the first act Fanny assumes her role as artistic muse and appears on a pedestal in a Grecian costume. As Inglis recounted: "Then a very strong light is thrown upon the stage and it reveals Miss Nethersole standing on a pedestal, a very beautiful woman, with a very beautiful figure."[55] This is a masked ball, after all, but Fanny means to unmask herself here. Nethersole foregrounded, in other words, her position as a performing woman. More than this, she was portraying a character who was herself performing a role. Nethersole heightened this performative citationality by making explicit her various roles: as muse, as Grecian Goddess, and as erotic spectacle. Nethersole denaturalized the representational apparatus that objectified her at the very same time she utilized it toward her own ends.

Just as Nethersole's costuming was the center of the controversy, so her clothing became one of the primary matters of concern during the trial. Nethersole's attire was described daily in the newspapers. So blurred were the lines between the character Nethersole played and her real person that the public expected Nethersole to wear shocking clothing in the courtroom just as she had on stage. The *New York Times* reported that whenever Nethersole entered the courtroom there was "a buzz of excitement and a general rising among the numerous women in the crowd who wanted to get a good look at the actress' clothes."[56] Before reporting a single fact from the trial, the *New York Herald* stated that Nethersole "was radiantly dressed in a pale blue gown, with rich furs."[57] Observing how the courtroom was itself a performance space, the *New York Times* used theatrical metaphors to note that "all three defendants made a complete change of costume" since their last day in court. Nethersole's outfits interested the *Times* so much that they were described with almost obsessive detail: "Miss Nethersole wore a long, loose cloak of brocaded lavender silk, which trailed flashes of brilliant white whenever its lining was exposed. A sable collarette fell gracefully around her shoulders, while a lavender velvet hat with ostrich plumes and fur trimming cast a deep shadow over her eyes."[58] A sketch of Nethersole in the *New York Herald* shows her in this outfit. With a confident look on her face, she literally dwarfs her attorney, Abraham H. Hummel, who is almost half her size in the background. While the *Times* and other papers noted briefly what leading man Hamilton Revelle was wearing, Nethersole was undoubtedly the focus, for she "made a brilliant spot of color in the otherwise somber-looking courtroom."[59] Such repeated preoccupations with Nethersole's attire not only linked the actress to her character's flamboyant costumes, but also sutured her into the position of object of the gaze.

If Nethersole was perceived in part as a visual fetish, she was also described as a Medusa-like figure who turned men to stone with her mesmerizing gaze. One witness at the trial, Henry Brevoort Kane, "was apparently very much disturbed by the intense searching gaze which Miss Nethersole fixed upon him," according to the *New York Times*.[60] In assuming the gaze Nethersole refused to signify simply as a figure that passively invites it. Occupying both roles – as visual spectacle in her flamboyant ostrich-plume outfit and as the monstrous Medusa – Nethersole not only returned the look, but also assumed a position of power as female spectator and producer of meaning. Nethersole negotiated back and forth between multiple identities, refusing to be sutured into a single subject position. This instability provoked anxiety in Kane, who, as his testimony unfolded, became enraptured by Nethersole: "The witness," the *Times* continued, "who had been gazing at Miss Nethersole as if she were some strange enigma, started violently," when the Assistant District Attorney asked him his next question.[61] Rendered impotent, or, as Freud would have it, castrated, by this reversal of the gaze, Kane "had been apparently been brought almost to a state of collapse by Miss Nethersole's earnest scrutiny, [and] jumped lightly from the stand and hurried out of the courtroom with the greatest precipitation."[62]

In addition to utilizing a powerful gaze during the trial, Nethersole also staged "courtroom maneuvers," which Reilly has called "among the best-staged pieces of acting in her career."[63] Some reporters noted, for instance, that Nethersole looked "bored" or "annoyed" during the trial.[64] When Inglis gave "his testimony in half pantomime and half recitation," regarding Sapho's posing as a model on the pedestal, "Miss Nethersole placed her gloved hand over her mouth and yawned audibly. This disconcerted Inglis so much that he turned away and glued his eyes upon Magistrate Mott, who seemed especially pleased with the efforts to reproduce some of the acting on the stage."[65] At other times during the trial the prosecuting District Attorney was required to ask Nethersole for her help in reciting the lines since he couldn't remember them. Nethersole was cooperative, but "perfectly cool and self-possessed," as she "prompted Mr. Hummel with his lines."[66] By manipulating such moments, Nethersole both assisted and subverted the legal proceedings.

Both fetish and monster, Nethersole seemed to entrance her accusers before summarily disarming them. In both inviting and returning the gaze, Nethersole unsettled the rigid binaries that fueled scopophilic desire.

Nethersole: A "strenuous" producer

In comparing Carter's *Zaza* to Nethersole's *Sapho* it is clear that the nude, or simulated-nude, female body itself was not at issue in 1899, for such exposures were acceptable in a variety of contexts, including pulp fiction, *tableaux vivants*, and painting. What was at issue, rather, was how the female body challenged dominant sexual ideology. As producer of *Sapho*, and its sexual images, Nethersole rejected prevailing conceptions of female identity, performing instead nontraditional female sexuality and displaying signs of New Womanhood. Nethersole's assumption and subversion of erotic tropes – as actress and producer – transgressed hegemonic expectations of gender, class, and sexuality.

Additionally, Nethersole was singled out partly because she was one of the few female producers of her day. Such work was stressful, and highly unusual for women at that time. In an article entitled, "My Struggles to Succeed," which appeared in *Cosmopolitan* a year before the *Sapho* scandal,

Nethersole wrote about the "heart-wearing and spirit-breaking" work in the theatre. "I have worked and struggled incessantly," she continued, "and often it has seemed that I was rolling a stone up a hill only to have it fall back threatening to crush the spirit out of me."[67] Though she was grateful for her success, she strongly advised other women against seeking a career in the theatre, writing that it "is too great a price to pay."[68] Nonetheless, Nethersole persevered in the Sisyphean task of producing her own work. She believed so much in *Sapho* that "she bought it and backed its production with her own money, and played it with such realism that she divided the whole land for and against her," as Lavinia Hart pointed out in her 1901 article about Nethersole.[69] In a letter to acquaintances in 1899, Nethersole wrote, " 'Sapho' I am thankful to say is a great success so far, in Chicago, and Milwaukee. Enormous business, ah if it only continues and I can save some money. The production has cost us 4000 pounds."[70] As producer she exercised unusual control over the production, insisting on artistic control and taking financial risks.

Equally unsettling was Nethersole's challenge to the male power-lock on theatre production. The *Sun* accused Nethersole of deliberately staging the controversy for her own profit: "Discussion of that question [of the play's depravity] will not settle it," the newspaper reported, "but will put money into the pocket of the actress by increasing the publicity of her exploit."[71] Similarly, the *New York Tribune* denounced "the paltry motive of its producers ..."[72] Attuned to such accusations, Nethersole defended the play and her motives:

> [I]f I felt that Sapho [were morally bad] do you suppose for one moment that I would have given the time and thought and spent the money I have upon this production? Perhaps the public may not be aware that it is all my own money that has gone into Sapho. If you will allow the expression, I am my own "angel" in this case.[73]

But Nethersole was soon to be reminded that the angel's role was in the house, not the theatre.

Perhaps because she was a female producer, Nethersole had a reputation for being difficult. James Metcalfe's review in *Life Magazine* notes, "Miss Nethersole's requirements are strenuous. To meet some of her abilities would tax the genius of a more experienced writer of erotic literature than Mr. Fitch."[74] A British reviewer cautioned that Nethersole should tone down her assertiveness, writing, "she must not envelope her public (in this country) like a sirocco as she does in *Sapho*."[75] It is difficult not to compare the discourse about Nethersole with the criticisms that surround contemporary pop stars such as Madonna: a star who is likewise too assertive, too sexy, too contradictory – in short, too independent. Certainly in 1900 the stakes for being all of these things were much higher than today. And hence, Sapho, as producer and New Woman – as difficult woman – had to be censored.

For all of Nethersole's interventions, the outcome of the trial had very real material consequences. By arresting Nethersole, her leading man, Hamilton Revelle, her manager, Marcus Mayer, and Theodore Moss, the proprietor of Wallack's (Fitch was curiously not arrested), and by shutting down the production, Chief of Police Devery threatened Nethersole's livelihood. In fact the arrests came as a surprise, because, according to Nethersole's attorney, "a promise had been given that the performance would not be interfered with," which the District Attorney denied.[76] Moreover, the order on March 5 to cease production did not arrive at the theatre until nearly 7:00 pm, thus not giving Nethersole's team time to rearrange another performance for that night. With capital invested in the show, but drawing no box office receipts, Nethersole was in a very precarious position.

In order to cover her costs during the month between the show's closing and the trial, the resourceful Nethersole staged a repertoire of fallen women plays, beginning with *The Second Mrs. Tanqueray*. Performing in a play that was "admittedly naughtier than *Sapho*," according to the *New York Herald*, Nethersole seemed to be sending a signal about the hypocrisy surrounding her censorship case.[77] The support for Nethersole was significant: "In spite of the fact that there was little time for the sale of tickets and the exchange of seats already bought for *Sapho*, Wallack's Theatre was crowded last night to see Miss Nethersole in *The Second Mrs. Tanqueray*."[78] The crowd "applauded her liberally at the close of every scene," and she was repeatedly called in front of the curtain after each act "until she was scarcely able to make her acknowledgements" due to fatigue.[79] Ten days later Nethersole switched tactics from portraying "two types of the 'lost woman,'" as the *New York Times* put it, to performing "the preternaturally virtuous British matron" from Pinero's *The Profligate*.[80] In a brilliant and ironic reversal, Nethersole portrayed a young and tender woman who is wronged by a deceitful, adulterous husband. Her transformation from an innocent to "injured and protesting woman" in this role mirrored Nethersole's own sense of injury by the New York censors.[81] And one has to wonder how this role ghosted, and perhaps aided, Nethersole's projection of herself as unduly persecuted by the District Attorney and press.

The verdict

Sapho had been closed by order of the police since March 5. On April 5, after just two days of trial testimony, Nethersole and company were acquitted of all charges. The jury in the Criminal Branch of the Supreme Court deliberated for only fifteen minutes. After the verdict had been given, "a sort of cheer went up" despite orders to the contrary given by Justice Fursman.[82] In his summing up the judge pointed out the hypocrisy regarding public perception of Nethersole's costumes: "On every ballet stage in New York there will be found costumes exposing more that this costume of *Sapho* did."[83] Revealing the stress she had endured, Nethersole sobbed during much of the reading of the verdict.

Nethersole's victory was especially appreciated by women, who swarmed to the courtroom to hear it. "For ten minutes after the jurors had left," the *New York Times* reported, "Miss Nethersole was kissed and hugged by all the women in the courtroom."[84] According to Nethersole, the support that she received from women was the strongest: "All the abuse that I have had since I started to produce *Sapho* has come from men ... Again, I thank the women who attended today. Where the women go, the men will follow."[85] Nethersole's triumph over censorship proved that she had successfully resisted social norms that sought to define and regulate her. Nethersole left the courthouse in "a triumphal procession," comprised of "an excited crowd [which] followed her with joyful shouts."[86]

The very next day, Nethersole returned to performing *Sapho* to standing ovations and sold-out houses for fifty-five performances. The *New York Times* reported: "From an audience that packed every available inch of room in the auditorium of Wallack's Theatre, Miss Olga Nethersole last night received one of the most remarkable ovations that has ever been accorded to an actress in this city."[87] Audiences often rewarded Nethersole for the very moments for which she was attacked in the trial. When she appeared "wearing the much-discussed Greek gown ... the audience rose and applauded for fully ten minutes."[88] The staircase scene was another triumph for Nethersole: "There was another great burst of applause for her ... [As] the curtain went down on the famous staircase scene, where Jean carries Fanny up stairs, the house rose again and shouted its delight and approval."[89] There was a clear delight in seeing Nethersole perform "that naughty Sapho scene," as one publicity poster called it.[90] Much was at stake, as several productions of *Sapho* throughout the country depended upon this verdict.[91] Nethersole played *Sapho* to large houses until May 29, when she set sail again for England. The sold-out closing night crowd supported Nethersole enthusiastically, according to the *New York Times*: "After the third act, an ovation was accorded Miss Nethersole that equaled the one given her the first night of her reappearance after the recent trial."[92] The contrast between the enthusiasm of her audiences and the moralizing of her critics demonstrates how divided society was about the representation of sexual excess on stage. Yet Nethersole's victory, in court and at the box office, signals an important cultural moment that would set a precedent for matters of representation in the twentieth century.

Regardless of its popularity and controversy, Nethersole's transgressive performance – one of the first images of women's sexuality produced by a woman, and the first obscenity trial of the century – would stand out as an exception, and then fade into oblivion. Yet Nethersole's *Sapho* helps elucidate how the Progressive Era's perceptions of "fallen women," "harlots," "courtesans," and "prostitutes" drew upon a general conception of pathologized female sexuality. It is particularly useful to see how, within this discourse, the performing woman's body simultaneously utilized and disrupted erotic signs. Nethersole's smoldering *Sapho* rang in the New Year by challenging New York's representations of fallen women on stage just as The Committee of Fifteen, New York's first vice commission, was mounting what would be a long and failed attempt to control prostitution. Nethersole's triumph, though brief, subverted the very signs that would later be used to characterize, regulate, and reform her sisters in sin – both on the stage and in the streets.

3

The Easiest Way *and the actress-as-whore myth*

New York, and every other big city for that matter, is full of Laura Murdocks. They are to be found – thousands of them – wherever the pleasure call is strong, in the gay restaurants and lobster places of the Great White Way, drinking champagne on beer incomes, riding in their own automobiles, wearing gowns and jewels that a duchess might envy. Many of these girls started their careers as manicures, cloak models, chorus girls, actresses.[1]

Theatre Magazine, March 1909

If we believe the above description, the Great White Way was over-crowded with lavishly decorated Broadway girls like Laura Murdock – the infamous character in *The Easiest Way*, Eugene Walter's popular 1909 play about an actress who falls into prostitution – looking for men to buy them luxuries. Because their excessive displays could seemingly never be obtained on beer incomes – the wages paid to chorus girls and minor actresses – they must, like the ill-fated Laura, be mistresses kept on champagne incomes by wealthy men.

Such extravagance was found disturbing not only because of the garish display of sexual indiscretion, but also because women were leaving traditional cultural roles in order to challenge men as wage earners. Although women had long been consumers in the private sphere, their entrance into public spaces as wage earners and consumers (rather than as objects of consumption) was relatively new and disorienting. In interpreting the scene above the author never considers that the Broadway girl could be a serious wage earner herself and too easily discounts her ability to earn a handsome income. Her extravagance seems only possible to him through prostitution. Whether perceived as a working woman in the age-old sense of prostitution or a wage earner in the more modern understanding of the term, the Broadway girl was imagined as an excessive figure, one who breached not only decorum, but also whose excessive appetite challenged prevailing gender and sexual ideology. The theatre, in short, was seen as a space in which women exceeded their bounds.

David Belasco's staging of Eugene Walter's *The Easiest Way* capitalized on this fascination with the Broadway girl. Walter's portrayal of a down-on-her-luck actress who falls into prostitution was dubbed the smash hit of the season and ran for an impressive two years in New York City. Owen Davis remembered *The Easiest Way*'s premiere as one of the "most thrilling first nights" ever and later claimed that Walter's drama was the best American play in the first half of the twentieth century.[2] Early twentieth-century critics viewed *The Easiest Way* as "one of the few instances of American triumph in modern tragedy," and "the first American work of real dramatic art."[3] The *New York Times* called it a "remarkable drama, quite the most remarkable of its type, that any American author has yet produced ..."[4] Indeed, *The Easiest Way* earned the distinction of being selected as the best play of 1909 retrospectively by John Gassner.[5]

Yet, in spite of its success, *The Easiest Way* provoked critics to wonder about the state of American drama. As James Metcalfe of *Life Magazine* wrote in 1909:

> When Mr. Eugene Walter, who has jumped to a place among our leading dramatists and Mr. David Belasco, recognized as first among American producing managers, put on the stage of the Stuyvesant, one of New York's highest-class theatres, a play like "The Easiest Way," what are we to say about the condition of the American drama? And when "The Easiest Way" receives the patronage of the representative theatre-going public – not the Tenderloin and out-of-town crowd ... but audiences drawn largely from our refined and cultured circles – what are we to say about the condition of the American theatre-going public?[6]

Metcalfe had a point: a representational threshold seemed to have been crossed. What *was* the Tenderloin doing on the New York's refined stages?

As has been shown throughout this book, the Tenderloin was not novel to New York's stages, in spite of repeated claims to the contrary. What was new about *The Easiest Way* is that it was the first American play about performing women and prostitution that was successfully embraced by the mainstream. Walter and Belasco recycled operative assumptions about the actress and prostitute, demonstrating a clear trajectory from working the stage to walking the streets. In so doing the play not only invoked the excessive, luxury-loving actress figure, but also anxieties about women who exceeded their roles as commodities exchanged between men. Functioning as a morality tale in social control, the title ultimately says it all: performing women, unregulated, are apt to take the easiest way in that slippery slope to whoredom.

Given the history of censorship on the New York stage, what was perhaps most stunning about *The Easiest Way* was its escape from the clutches of the New York Society for the Suppression of Vice. *The Easiest Way*'s long run on Broadway coincided with the passing of Penal Law 1140a in 1909. This anti-obscenity law was designed to prevent what the antiprostitution Committee of Fourteen called "plays of an uncommonly low grade presented in New York City the past two years."[7] The legislation did not, however, go into effect until September 1, 1909 – well into the lengthy run of *The Easiest Way*, which had opened on January 19 of the same year. While the authors of the law could have characterized *The Easiest Way* as an "obscene, indecent, immoral or impure drama," which might corrupt "the morals of youth or others," this did not happen.[8] While there were other "plays under fire," as Channing Pollock characterized them,[9] the Committee of Fourteen's vice report noted that there was "the production of a somewhat different class of plays for the season of 1909–10."[10] Why was *The Easiest Way*, just four years after the notorious censorship of *Mrs Warren's Profession*, deemed different from previous plays about performing women and prostitution? And what did its enormous success suggest about the state of American drama and the staging of sexuality?

Staging morality, exchanging women

One way of understanding *The Easiest Way*'s appeal to mainstream audiences and censors is to envision the play as representing not a sympathetic prostitute, but rather an immoral performing woman. *The Easiest Way* was less invested in staging "environmental determinism," as Brenda Murphy has written, than in portraying a morality tale that documented the decline of Laura Murdock, a capable, but not overly talented, actress.[11] Consequently, the play fails to interrogate the conditions that ensnared working women in the theatre, resorting, perhaps even unconsciously, to platitudes about pleasure-loving Broadway girls and fueling the actress-as-whore myth.

It is Laura Murdock who takes "the easiest way" by becoming the mistress of Willard Brockton, a rich, older man who not only keeps her in a life of luxury, but also provides her with acting parts in New York theatre. While on tour in Colorado Laura falls in love with John Madison, a newspaper reporter with a modest income. Aware of her previous life, Madison asks her to break off her ties with Brockton and support herself while Madison makes his fortune in Colorado. "If I ask you to be my wife," Madison says, "you'll have to give it up; you'll have to go back to New York and struggle on your own hook until I get enough to come for you ... Do you love me enough to stick out for the right thing?" (1.626). In asking Laura to support herself, Madison assumes her decision to work is merely a moral one, that if Laura wishes to do "the right thing," as he puts it, she can. It is no coincidence that Madison makes his fortune out West, far from the demands of the urban jungle, in a rugged terrain where men could profit by conquering nature. Caught up in his own self-making, he even uses the phrase "struggle on your own hook" without realizing that hooking may be, ultimately, Laura's only option. One drama critic observed in 1913 that Madison's excursion out West "is an almost unpardonable expedient for leaving the girl alone to fight her losing battle."[12] Not surprisingly, all the male characters in *The Easiest Way* are able to support themselves, while the women cannot (or, as the play would have us believe, will not).

To complete their pact, Madison asks Laura to end her affair with Brockton in front of him because, as he explains, "I ought to be in on any important transaction like that" (1.627). Madison's use of the word "transaction" makes clear that Laura is an item of exchange between two men, traded as mistress for the more esteemed position of wife-to-be.[13] As the *New York Dramatic Mirror* put it, Laura holds "the same position as the piano – something that has been bought and paid for."[14] When Brockton and Madison clinch their business deal, Laura, the traded commodity, leaves both men alone so that they can craft a gentleman's agreement about Laura's future. On one level, this meeting merely establishes that the rivals will fight for Laura's affection. Yet the stormy relationship between Brockton and Madison also suggests a particularly intense male bonding. Brockton assures Madison that in the unlikely event that Laura should ever go back to him, he will have Laura notify his rival. Laura's future is thus decided without her participation and sealed with a gentleman's handshake.

William Winter took note of the puzzling magnetism between Brockton and Madison: "[E]ach feels a sort of brotherly attraction for the other – a phenomenal feeling, under the circumstances, since each has the best of all reasons, as humanity is constituted, not only for dislike but hatred."[15] Another critic described Brockton and Madison's pact as "rather puny and pitiful in their little mutual egotistical triumph."[16] Alan Dale found this scene "the real weak spot" of the play.[17] Perhaps the most critical viewpoint came from overseas. When *The Easiest Way* opened in London in 1912, a reviewer commented, "the men in the play exhibit towards her much silliness and brutality," noting that the play "throws lurid light upon American manhood and the methods of the American impresario."[18] And Ronald Wainscott has recently described the gentlemen's agreement of this scene as underwritten by "sexism and paternalis[m]."[19]

As strange as this agreement might seem, *The Easiest Way*'s love triangle makes great sense in the geometry of homosociality. As Eve Kosofsky Sedgwick has shown, "in any erotic rivalry, the bond that links the two rivals is as intense and potent as the bond that links either of the rivals to the beloved."[20] This triangle, it is important to note, is asymmetrical: the woman is "a conduit of a relationship" between men.[21] As an anonymous article in the *Craftsman* put it, Laura was "just a matter of barter" between the two male characters.[22] This relationship was captured in a publicity poster showing Laura desperately dwarfed by the two men (see figure 5). Eclipsed by their larger bodies, Laura looks frantically into the distance, while Brockton and Madison gaze intensely into each other's eyes. The first act ends with the two men alone on stage, smoking. The slow sunset throughout the act is now complete, according to the stage directions: "By this time the stage is black and all that can be seen is the glow of the two cigars" (1.630). Their phallic cigars glowing in the dark, the men conclude this act not unlike two lovers having a postcoital smoke, the tobacco sealing the transaction.

If the first act concludes with male homosocial bonding, the remaining three acts dwell on Laura's deceit and subsequent fall from actress to whore. Act 2 shows Laura six months later, in what has become Belasco's famous portrayal of a cheap boarding house in the theatre district of New York. She has not had an acting job for a long time because Brockton had blacklisted her for withholding sexual favors from him. Laura struggles, but cannot hold out any longer. Desperate for money, she returns to Brockton at the urging of Elfie St. Clair, a former chorus girl and the current mistress of another sugar daddy. Accordingly, Brockton honors his pledge with Madison and forces Laura to notify him that she is Brockton's mistress once again. Laura never mails the letter, however, following Elfie's advice: "The thing to do is to lie to all men – they all lie to you. Protect yourself" (3.660). The scene therefore establishes these two women – both of whom are actresses – as deceitful and predatory, suggesting that performing women are not to be trusted.

Figure 5. Publicity poster for *The Easiest Way* depicting the love triangle of Madison, Laura, and Brockton. Image courtesy of the Museum of the City of New York.

Laura's dishonesty is underscored by Brockton's peculiar insistence on truth, which only strengthens his alliance with Madison. Upon discovering that Laura had deceived them both, Brockton becomes indignant that Laura has lied. He tells her, "I'm going to tell him the truth. It isn't you I care for – he's got to know" (3.666). The homosocial subtext of that statement rings all too clear: it *is* Madison whom Brockton cares for, and he means to honor their pact. But Brockton is deluded about what counts as honesty. He does not intend to tell Madison, for example, that he has arranged for Laura to be out of work, all but guaranteeing her decline.

The concluding act of the play escalates Laura's tragic decline toward deceit and whoredom. Unaware of Laura's situation, Madison returns to New York, having made his fortune, and asks her to marry him. Just as Laura and Madison are ready to leave together, Brockton enters her apartment with his own latchkey. The sound cue of the key in the door is a climatic moment that theatre historians have compared to Nora's slamming of the door in *A Doll's House*. One critic described this scene as follows: "But, in a momentary lull, there is the sound of a key in the lock, a sharp, metallic rattle. This key is in the broker's hand, and it needs no explanation. For Laura Murdock it means a calamity swift and irrevocable. Again the action is silent. From exaltation to black despair – by the turning of a key!"[23] After a moment of stunned silence Madison understands he has been duped and Laura tries desperately to defend herself:

> LAURA. I couldn't help it. I was so poor, and I had to live, and he wouldn't let me work, and he's only let me live one way, and I was hungry. Do you know what that means? I was hungry and didn't have clothes to keep me warm, and I tried, oh, Madison, I tried so hard to do the other thing – the right thing, – but I couldn't. (4.673)

While this is perhaps Walter's attempt at a kind of Shavian sympathy for his fallen woman, the plot soon turns against Laura. As Alan Dale put it in his 1909 review, "A slight effort is made to enlist sympathy for Laura. It does not succeed . . ."[24] Madison won't hear her excuses. More than anything, from his perspective, her lying unravels the relationship. As Madison clarifies: "perhaps I could have forgiven you if you hadn't lied to me" (4.673).

Rather than showing the appalling conditions by which women are forced to turn to prostitution and rallying sympathy for its heroine – as

Mrs Warren's Profession does, for instance – the play retreats to a moral condemnation of Laura, a point repeatedly underscored by the press. *Town and Country* remarked that Laura was "incapable even of that elemental honesty."[25] Dale caustically called Laura "a weak little drab of a vacuous, aimless woman, too puerile to be moral, and almost too cowardly to be brazenly immoral, pitted against two lovers."[26] Walter himself supported this view in a 1911 article in *Current Literature*: "Laura Murdock is a type not uncommon in the theatrical life of New York ... She had never made an honest effort to be an honest woman."[27]

While most of the press lambasted Laura, the Matinee Girl, a regular columnist for the *New York Dramatic Mirror*, pointed out that some women interpreted this issue differently from men:

> Of course she lied and lied and lied. Every woman in the audience understood, if no man did. The little liar was a relic of the brute age when man ruled woman with a heavy hand and the corporeal punishment of wives and mistresses had not been abolished. And every woman sympathized, inwardly at least, with the spinner of the web of untruth.[28]

Yet the Matinee Girl stood out against other reviewers who seized upon the moralistic vision of the title and reproached Laura for making such an "easy" choice.

Dwelling on lying and sexual betrayal, *The Easiest Way* thus makes Laura's deceit her tragic flaw. The male characters, on the other hand, have an easier journey in telling the truth than the female characters do. When, for example, Madison reproaches Brockton for not honoring their agreement, Brockton defends his honor – and their accord: "I'm not going to let you think that I didn't do the right thing with you. She came to me voluntarily ... If there's been a lie she told it. I didn't" (4.673). Brockton glosses over Laura's "voluntary" return to him, and while he leaves without his mistress, he claims the moral high ground by insisting that he told the truth. When Brockton exits, the triangle is broken and the lover's relationship is also doomed. Madison now turns on Laura and, echoing the title of the play, delivers his judgment: "With you it is the easy way, and it will always be. You'll go on and on until you're finally left a wreck, just the type of the common woman. And you'll sink until you're down to the very bedrock of depravity. I pity you" (4.674). After Laura threatens to kill herself to get him to stay, Madison suggests that suicide is precisely the decent thing to do. He then leaves her.

Ultimately this modern play, as several reviewers called it, resorts to very old dramaturgy in resurrecting the heroine's tragic fall. As Wainscott has written, "the action of Walter's play traverses disastrous territory for the fallen woman who wishes to go straight," harkening back to the tragedies befalling characters like Camille and Olympe.[29] What is new here, however, is that Walter has Laura commit social suicide by seeking *not* death, but rather the underworld. This is a penitent whore who does not die, but in fact sinks more deeply into whoredom. Finding herself rejected by both Brockton and Madison, and penniless, Laura desperately turns to her only alternative: finding other men to support her. Laura's final words, spoken to her maid, are also memorable: "Annie . . . get me my prettiest dress. Hurry up. Get my new hat, dress up my body and paint up my face. It's all they've left of me . . . I'm going to Rector's to make a hit, and to hell with the rest" (4.676). Rector's, the famous restaurant and hotel, was the hotbed of sporting life in New York. Frequented by fashionable businessmen and actors, it had the reputation of offering opportunities for sexual liaisons.[30] Like the main character in *The Girl From Rector's*, which was running at the same time as *The Easiest Way*, Laura prepares for "the illicit joys of little old New York" by cruising its most infamous public spot.[31] The final sound cue of *The Easiest Way* definitively signals Laura's decline into the underworld. The stage directions indicate that a hurdy-gurdy ragtime is heard from the street, "peculiarly suggestive of the low life, the criminality and prostitution that constitute the night excitement of that section of New York City known as the Tenderloin" (4.767). The ending leaves little doubt about Laura's intention to prostitute herself in the shadows of the Great White Way.

The "luxury loving" actress

While in many ways *The Easiest Way* painted a "familiar picture of the theatre-woman, struggling for her virtue amid the alleged temptations of Broadway," as critic Alan Dale put it, the play recycled myths about actresses' vanity, greed, and sexual corruption.[32] Critics repeatedly called Laura "weak," and "luxury-loving."[33] Dale found Laura, and indeed actresses like her, so distasteful that he wondered "why two men were so unduly interested in such a woman. One wonders all the time why the genial Broadway bloke was so cursedly addicted to *such a whining, flabby little imbecile*" (my emphasis).[34] William Winter particularly vilified Laura's character, calling the play "a long-drawn portrayal expositive of the immoral character, unchaste conduct, and necessarily wretched retributive experience, of a courtesan."[35] Belasco himself said in no uncertain terms that Laura was "one of those unfortunate women who wish to live in luxury on nothing a week – a pitifully weak, unmoral, constitutionally mendacious creature who drifts to perdition along the path of least resistance."[36] Of course, this charge of being "unmoral" and "constitutionally mendacious" is both gendered and classed – Brockton's lavish tastes are not scrutinized in the play, and upper-class women of the time had no need to provide for themselves. As Thorstein Veblen put it in his *Theory of the Leisure Class*, "It grates painfully on our nerves to contemplate the necessity of any well-bred woman earning a livelihood by useful work."[37] Working women, on the other hand, especially *single* working women within the theatre, transgressed the conceptual framework of the patriarchal leisure class in not only working, but also in consuming commodities.

Such descriptions of Laura the actress are strikingly akin to George Kneeland's description of prostitutes in his 1913 study *Commercialized Prostitution in New York*: "With few exceptions, the girls are characterized as weak, vain and ignorant, fond of pleasure, – not, of course, at the beginning, necessarily vicious pleasure, – easily led, – now by natural emotion, again by cunning design."[38] This is precisely the charge leveled against Laura: she simply can't give up her luxuries, as Brockton warned Madison. Unlike *Zaza*, where the actress can redeem herself through the theatre, *The Easiest Way* portrays the theatre as an incriminating space that can only spawn self-indulgent, immoral, unchaste women, to use Winter's words. Insofar as the play advances such a view it promulgates regressive ideologies regarding working women, sexuality, and women in the public sphere.

It is unclear why the phrase "the easiest way" became shorthand for prostitution. To be sure *some* prostitutes viewed their work as "easy" in the early twentieth century.[39] However, most prostitutes viewed their work as one of the few lucrative options available to women. In her research on American prostitutes in the early twentieth century, social historian Ruth Rosen compared several studies conducted from 1911–1916 in which prostitutes were interviewed. Of the reasons why prostitutes turned to prostitution only 9.5 percent of the respondents gave the answers "own choice, 'easy money,' tired of work," whereas 15.5 percent of the women cited "economic need" and 17.2 percent cited "bad home conditions" as the reason. Significantly, 11.3 percent of respondents said they were "betrayed, deceived, seduced."[40] Far from choosing the easiest way, most women made the best choices they could in dire circumstances, not unlike Laura.

In spite of Walter's plot suggesting that women sought "the easiest way," some critics took issue with the phrase. This writer in the *Craftsman*, for instance, questioned the dramaturgical logic:

One wonders just how much satire the playwright had in mind when he called "the easiest way" a pathway where a woman's soul is a negligible quantity, her heart the inspiration for sterling masculine wit, her tenderness, which may have sprung from the hidden fires of maternity, just a matter of barter ... There is not always work to be found, even at the lowest salaries, at shops or factories. Girls have been known to walk until they fainted in New York City to get a position where they could work ten hours a day for three dollars a week ... "[T]he easiest way" at times has a way of seeming to be the only way ...[41]

Emma Goldman also understood that for many women this was the only way. In her review, she wrote: "The easiest way is the path mapped out for her from time immemorial. She could follow no other."[42] But these voices were outnumbered by the mainstream press's denunciation of Laura as morally depraved. As the *Bookman* put it, describing a 1921 revival, *The Easiest Way* was still considered "the best title a play ever had."[43]

Aptly titled or not, *The Easiest Way* worked as a confessional morality tale and testimonies of its influence on young women began appearing in the papers. One story, which was printed in the *Evening Sun* in 1911, related how a chorus girl had changed her life after seeing the play. Prior to her transformation she had gone "to and from the theatre in her private motor and ha[d] jewels galore and of such great intrinsic value that they make the stars of the company's few pearls look like rhinestones in comparison." Yet, after seeing *The Easiest Way*, she promptly quit her job to return home. According to the article "there are at least fifty men and women connected with the theatre where she was playing who will vouch for the truth of this story."[44] This confessional, like the plot of *The Easiest Way*, functioned as a discursive regulator of female sexuality. "If there is a lesson" to the play, as Metcalfe explained, "it is as a deterrent to women."[45] Yet, as *Munsey's Magazine* noted with irony, the play's reach was limited: "As to the women themselves, if we are to believe Mr. Walter, they will be acting in other theaters, and will not have the opportunity to see for themselves whither the apparently easy route they are following leads. So much for the ethics of the piece."[46] As an ethically precarious text and performance, *The Easiest Way* not only disciplined the women it constructed as whores, it also warned against the dangers of women attempting to earn a wage in the city.

Best if all these women, like the repentant chorus girl, packed it in and returned home.

A new actress type

This chapter has argued thus far that the plot of Eugene Walter's *The Easiest Way* prolonged the actress-as-whore myth, but to what extent was Belasco culpable of this? At first glance it appears that Belasco steered away from such signification. Casting against type, Belasco used innocent-looking Frances Starr – called "the Cinderella of the Stage" by *Theatre Magazine* – in the role of Laura.[47] Belasco's casting of Starr was surprising to some because, according to the *New York Dramatic Mirror*, Walter wrote *The Easiest Way* for his wife, Charlotte Walter.[48] For the detail-obsessed Belasco, Starr offered something new. As Allen Churchill noted in his memoir of Broadway, Starr's innocence jarred the recognizable iconography of fallen women established by actresses like Nethersole and Bernhardt. "Here was no Sapho or Camille," he wrote. "One could pass Laura Murdock in the street without realizing that she was a soiled Broadway butterfly ... and this, perhaps, was the most shocking feature about *The Easiest Way*."[49] And indeed, Laura did not signify within recognizable prostitute iconography.

Starr's interpretation of Laura differed from previous actresses' portrayals of courtesan figures. Her body type and acting style conveyed "a new type of livery lady," as Channing Pollock put it in 1909. Laura was "a courtesan with all modern improvements ... Our Camilles, our Sapphos and our Zazas have been large women."[50] Starr's frail body type, the *Evening Journal* reported, worked in her favor: "You will weep with this girl Laura ... because of her utter humanness and fragility."[51] Laura's weakness, unlike Zaza's strength, typified her humanity, as Louis V. Defoe wrote in the *World*: "the miserable heroine proved too weak to live and too weak to die, weak enough only to drift to perdition along the treacherous path of least resistance."[52] Some critics, like William Winter, identified Starr's quality as childlike: "Childishness was often denoted by the expedient of drawing up the feet beneath the body, when in a seated attitude."[53] Belasco himself was attracted to her "expressive face and pretty, girlish figure" when he was first scouting her in other roles.[54] Indeed, Starr was childlike offstage as well; the Matinee Girl reported that in Starr's dressing room "hung a golden-curled doll the company had presented to her" in a previous play.[55] She still had it with her. The *New York Dramatic Mirror* explained that a frail actress was necessary for this part because "a woman physically larger, less dainty in her appearance, would never gain one atom of sympathy."[56] Belasco's own comment is perhaps the most telling: "I have found in Miss Starr a new type. We used to think it required a big, torrential woman to play such emotional scenes as these. Such a woman would have coarsened this play. She would have killed it. A little woman can play tragic scenes. I have proven it to-night."[57] Frances Starr also acknowledged that her persona as "the Cinderella ingénue," shaped the play: "But the wise Belasco knew that a frail young ingénue was what the play needed for Laura, and how right he was!"[58] This new interest in a "new type," as Belasco put it, demonstrated a shift away from the suffragist/ actress (Nethersole, Shaw), and toward a more diminutive Cinderella. Gone were both the sexually potent character and the powerful actress who produced her own work. The feminist politics of the big women had been overshadowed, paradoxically, by the little women of Broadway.

Mediated realism

More than being remembered for inaugurating a new actress type, *The Easiest Way* is known for Belasco's meticulous staging of a boardinghouse with the realistic exactitude that became his trademark. Some critics credited *The Easiest Way* "as the first naturalistic play of the American theatre."[59] Indeed, Belasco's staging was described as "photographically real, and tremendously vigorous."[60] *The New York Herald* remarked that the play demonstrated "all the convincing evidence of photography with the realism of life added."[61] *Munsey's Magazine* praised the production's attention to detail: "every accessory was absolutely faithful in its realism" in showing "the dregs of Tenderloin life."[62] Alan Dale reported (perhaps somewhat revealingly), "I have seen garrets and boarding house rooms, and the squalid resorts of the shabby genteel a thousand times, but never have I seen anything so unmistakable as Laura's furnished room . . . all indescribably real."[63] A subsequent article in *Munsey's* described *The Easiest Way* as "the *pièce de résistance* in scenic accuracy."[64] And modern theatre critics, like Lise-Lone Marker, still laud Belasco for "the startlingly authentic quality of the final stage set" and the "unflinching verisimilitude of the stage picture."[65]

Belasco, whom Ethan Mordden has called the "father of realism in American theatre," produced his stagecraft through the relentless pursuit of the real.[66] Because he and his stage designer, Ernest Gros, had difficulty constructing an authentic-looking theatre boardinghouse in their scene shops, Belasco took to the streets of the Tenderloin in search of inspiration.

As recorded in his memoir, *The Theatre Through Its Stage Door*, he located the shabbiest boardinghouse he could find and "bought the entire interior of one of its most dilapidated rooms – patched furniture, threadbare carpet, tarnished and broken gas fixtures, tumbledown cupboards, dingy doors and window casings, and even the faded paper on the walls," offering to replace the furnishings with new ones.[67] Belasco literally brought a slice of life onto the stage. " 'Never fake,' Belasco once said. 'The public will always catch you and never forgive you.' "[68]

While it is true that Belasco was a great pioneer in creating American realism on stage, *The Easiest Way* offered a kind of mediated realism of the lower-class underworld. The scene that captured most attention was, tellingly, one that depicted Laura's living quarters, a voyeuristic glimpse into an impoverished female space. What dominates the notorious second act is an old bed, "the Belasco trademark," as Marker observes, a symbol of "the pervading decay of the entire interior."[69] As the curtain rises, it reveals the intimate details of her life: her bed, clothes, washbasin, letters, silk stockings, and food. This elaborate inventory of Laura's room is remarkable not only for its precise details (consisting of two pages of stage directions), but also, as Marker notes, because "every single item, in business too tedious to catalogue, was *used* during the act" (original emphasis).[70] This was precisely the point: to show the private details of the working poor. Such fine points had an almost fetishistic appeal, according to *Munsey's Magazine*: "Never before, probably, has there been seen on the stage such a striking example of that prodigal disarray of personal belongings that means poverty rather than wealth."[71] And as Frances Starr recalled, "People still tell me about the things I did as Laura – brushing the snow off the milk bottle, sewing a glove, sitting on the trunk at the close of the play," the last of which became an iconic moment, often used in posters for the play.[72] There were distinct pleasures in viewing the lower class, especially its female members, in the new realism on stage. "Theatrical realism fed a hunger for objects," writes Elin Diamond, "that supplied evidence, characters who supplied testimony, plots that cried out for interpretive acuity and, pleasurably, judgment."[73] Such scopophilic pleasures were ample in *The Easiest Way*. In explicating the ideological underpinnings of this urban American drama, we see that such plots were heavily invested in the depiction of female and lower-class bodies – bodies to be invaded, investigated, and consumed.

The success of *The Easiest Way* reveals much about the state of the American drama in 1909. The mythological portrayal of the actress was anchored to the notion of excess that performing women seemingly invoked: excessive clothing, verbal utterances, appetites (for food and sex), and unregulated movement through the public sphere. No longer just an object to be consumed, but now a consumer herself, the actress provoked enormous uncertainty. Accordingly, *The Easiest Way* needed to offer dramaturgical closure by moralizing the sexual fall of the actress. Laura's eventual slide into prostitution is therefore hardly coincidental: it epitomizes her assumption of her "proper" role not as a consumer, but as something to be consumed. The very Progressive reformers who would decide how the other half lived were the same people caught up in the pleasures of voyeuristic spectatorship. Unlike *Mrs Warren's Profession*, *The Easiest Way* doesn't make the case on behalf of a woman who turns to prostitution out of economic necessity. Walter's flaw, as Ludwig Lewisohn of the *Nation* put it in 1921, was that "he made no effort to see through things. He dispensed with a raisonneur, with any choric character, not because he had, like the great naturalists, the power of infinite critical implication, but because he had literally no comment to make. He accepted the world seen by his creatures."[74] Disapointingly, *The Easiest Way* recycles familiar myths about luxury-loving Broadway girls. The moral of the play, as Francis Hackett from the *New Republic* put it in 1921, was clear: "Once a prostitute, always a defective."[75]

As we have seen throughout this section, the performing woman, like the prostitute, was seen as defective. The music-hall performer, artist model, and actress all became conflated with the figure of the prostitute, in part due to their professions, but also because of their independence, sexual politics, and manipulation of identity performance. Performing women's personae also ghosted the characters they were performing (who were themselves performers). The fascination with the Broadway girl continued throughout the Progressive Era, even as antiprostitution efforts gained momentum. Sexual myths would continue to underwrite the common portrayal of the champagne-drinking, lobster-loving Broadway girl who takes the easiest way, only to fall from grace. In the wake of *Zaza*, *Sapho*, and *The Easiest Way*, scores of dramas about sisters in sin would emerge with diverse fates. Some would be censored, while others would go on to become the toast of the season. This seemingly illogical reception demonstrates, over and over again, that debates about obscenity focused upon the sexually errant female body: a thing to be contained, regulated, and redeemed. Yet, as all three of these dramas make clear, performing women indexed a wide array of unsettling discourses, demonstrating that performance can never be fully regulated or contained.

Part II

Working girls

"The working-girl," as Willa Cather noted in 1913, "seems to be a tempting bait to playwrights just now."[1] As women began entering the workforce, fiction, reportage, music, and plays documented the bitter details of the working girl's life. There are ample tales of wage-earning women in the American literature of this time: Dreiser's *Sister Carrie*, Crane's *Maggie: A Girl of the Street*, and James's *The Lawton Girl*, to name just a few. While some attention has been given to American "Tales of the Working Girl," as Laura Hapke calls them, very little attention has been given to working women in the American drama of this period.[2] Particularly of interest for this study is the cultural fascination with the working girl's seemingly inevitable fall into prostitution. The working girl was understood to occupy liminal spaces with a foot on either side of the threshold separating respectability and the underworld. The term "working girl" is not only a pun on turning trades and tricks; it also connotes the slippery terrain that many working women negotiated between selling commodities (the shop girl) and commodifying themselves (the girl shop). In playfully referencing both kinds of working (and, indeed, both kinds of shopping), this section of the book seeks to capture the tension inherent in the plight of Progressive Era working women, unsettling the seemingly clear binary between honest worker and prostitute.

This section begins by charting a trajectory from the rise of department stores and the associated fantasies about the new breed of shop girls who worked in them, to Bernard Shaw's sobering materialist account of prostitution.[3] What inevitably drives working-girl dramas is the tension between working behind the counter and working beyond it: that is, the so-called slide into prostitution. It is not coincidental that the rise and fall of the working-girl figure corresponds with the arc of late Progressive Era anti-prostitution discourse. The body of plays from this period suggests that prostitution was a last resort for working-class women's economic survival, not merely a social evil, as Progressives repeatedly theorized it. Myths about the shop girl tapped into rising cultural obsessions with conspicuous consumption, male scopophilia, and the conflation of worker and hooker in increasingly fluid public spaces. The theatre, we shall see, was a formative discourse that portrayed these conflicting tensions.

4

The shop girl: Working-girl dramas

According to the 1890 census, almost 20 percent of American women were employed.[1] Of the jobs open to them, department store work was seen as the most desirable. As women entered the urban workforce in record numbers, working women began appearing on stage, primarily as the archetypical shop girl. While plays about working women were not unusual, shop-girl plays were innovative because they dramatized the economic pressures that forced working women to contemplate (and sometimes turn to) a life of prostitution.[2] Although there were some important precursors to the shop-girl character in American theatre in the latter part of the nineteenth century, most plays of this ilk tended to be about women involved in manual labor (such as *The Seamstress of New York*, *The New York Factory Girls*, *Hidden Help or A Working-girl's Luck*, *The Workgirl*, *The Match Girl of New York*, *The East Side of New York*, and *Bertha, the Sewing Machine Girl, or Death at the Wheel*).[3] What was new about the early Progressive Era shop-girl plays was first, their intense interest in department store workers as visual spectacles, and second, their musical comedy form. The backdrop to all of these productions about shop girls was the specter of the "girl shop": prostitution.

   Musicals about women working in shops and department stores became popular in New York beginning with the 1895 musical farce *The Shop Girl* by British author George Edwardes, adapted for the American stage by H. J. W. Dam and Ivan Caryll.[4] Heralded as one of the first modern musicals and based on Edwardes's research in large department stores, *The Shop Girl* sought to quench the public's thirst for "the local and the real . . . the life of today," as Edwardes put it in an interview.[5] Numerous "Girl" musicals increasingly portrayed women's work in detail. "Dramatists," Peter Bailey writes, "drew their typical heroines from young working women in the burgeoning new service sector of the economy, those who held court from behind a counter in telegraph offices, bars, teashops and, most prominently, department stores."[6] *The Shop Girl* gestured toward new scientific working theories, celebrating the "noble institution of financial evolution," as one musical number put it, in the rise of the big department store.[7]

Another central focus of *The Shop Girl*, like the manipulative obsession of Edwardes himself, was on stage beauties, characters that appeared as eye candy for male spectators. As the second verse of "The Song of the Shop" reveals:

> And they all make eyes at the Shop Girl,
> Sweet little neat little Shop Girl!
> That's what they do, Married men, too –
> Really they never will stop.[8]

The virtuous shop girl was juxtaposed with the ubiquitous gaiety girl, whom Edwardes was famous for promoting. Not just one gaiety girl, but a chorus of stage beauties found their way into this musical as show girls performing for a charity bazaar in the department store. The "Chorus of Stage Beauties," as the number was called, literally invites the male gaze:

> In us of course you see
> A charming coterie,
> Whose fascinations all confess
> Please to gaze upon the grace
> Of each pretty little face
> And admire our very dainty dress.[9]

Sumptuously lit, with scantily clad showgirls, *The Shop Girl*'s success hinged upon visual spectacle that catered to heterosexual male desire, an optic economy that was likewise utilized to commodify goods in department stores.

1895 was the year, it seems, that Manhattan was singing about "The Shop Girls of New York," as the popular song by Charles E. Pratt and George Cooper made clear. These "maidens grand," the lyrics tell us, are "full of fun, yes, ev'ry one, The Shop Girls of New York!"[10] The 1903 debut of the musical *Only a Shop Girl* at the West End Theatre demonstrated the symbiotic relationship between the theatre and shopping, premiering, as it did, only months after the opening of Macy's new Herald Square branch, the largest department store in the world at that time. *Only a Shop Girl* portrayed a young woman who loses her position at the department store, as well as her lodgings, after men in the store give her unwanted attention.[11] The musical's songs romanticized the position of the shop girl; suggesting that her visibility in the store might allow her to be swept away by a wealthy man if she were beautiful enough. Although "She's only a shop girl at Macy's," the refrain tells us, "she is able to marry a baron, if she got a chance."[12] The notion of rich men whisking shop girls away was repeated in other smash musical hits like *The Earl and Girl*, which premiered in the US in 1905, and *The Rich Mr. Hoggenheimer*, which premiered in 1906. Though the upbeat music of such productions told audiences that "Heaven will Protect the Working Girl," as Marie Dresser cooed in the 1909 burlesque ballad, the fact remained that few barons married shop girls at Macy's.[13]

One of the most difficult dilemmas for a shop girl was negotiating between male scopophilia on the one hand, and the necessity of making herself presentable on the other. The shop girl was, in other words, not only selling merchandise but also an image of herself to more wealthy customers. This dual role created a variety of new challenges, not only for women, but also for the merchants who employed those women. As Mary Rankin Cranston explained in her article "The Girl Behind the Counter" in 1906: "A pretty, attractive girl is prominently placed and thus becomes the target for the attentions of male admirers, employees and customers."[14] Shop-girl musicals, as Joel H. Kaplan and Sheila Stowell have written, engendered a kind of escapism that readily objectified its heroines, linking desire for commodities on stage with those in the store. One critic from that time noted, "Occasionally one is tempted to forget 'she' is anything more than a lay-figure, intended for the exhibition of magnificent costumes."[15] Diana Hirschler summed up the role of the shop girl when she proclaimed in 1912: "cultivate an agreeable speaking voice and don't invite criticism and distract your customer's attention from the goods you are selling with elaborate coiffures, pungent perfumes, untidiness and jewelry."[16] The end goal, Hirschler reminded her readers, was always "your goods," a cruel misnomer for commodities that most clerks could often not afford. As Susan Porter Benson has shown, saleswomen in department stores "played both sides of the counter, selling in their roles as workers, consuming in their roles as women, and merging the two roles in ways which showed in high relief the tensions in a society of mass consumption."[17] The shop girl was, as Willa Cather astutely put it, a kind of bait. The paradox of the shop girl, therefore, was that while she was put on display as bait, she assisted leisure-class

men and women in their conspicuous display of wealth, while not posses-
sing the capital to purchase the items herself.

Another way for women to negotiate this tension was to barter with
what Bailey has called "sex on the installment plan, with no guarantee on
either side of final payment."[18] In *The Girl From Kay's*, a popular musical
which ran for 205 performances in New York in 1903, this sort of transaction
is made clear in a song called "The Bonnet Shop." According to the lyrics, a
"girl of common sense" need only "snare a millionaire" before she can set up
her own bonnet shop.[19] Romance is, in other words, a business transaction,
and all a level-headed girl has to do is properly mortgage her attentions
until she has bankrolled her independence.

One of the longer running performances of the New York 1907–08
season was the British musical comedy *The Girl Behind the Counter* adapted
for American audiences by Edgar Smith. Though labeled "an irresponsible
and disconnected musical" by *Life Magazine*'s James Metcalfe in 1907, *The
Girl Behind the Counter* was "right in the line of what seems to be New
York's present favorite kind of entertainment" with its ability to "catch the
fancy of the clubbite and Waldorfer as well as that of the Tenderloiner."[20]
Contrasting the story of Winnie, the "good" shop girl, with Ninette, a
flirtatious "coquette," the musical portrays women's sexuality in the familiar
Madonna/whore paradigm, suggesting women should stand firmly on one
side of the counter. As seen in the 1909 song "The Girl Behind the Counter
is the Girl I Love," the myth of upper-class men romancing the shop girl
pervaded popular culture, masking the gender and class inequities which
were central to capitalism.[21]

When not the object of romance songs the working girl was also studied
by Progressive reformers. In *How the Other Half Lives* (1890) Jacob Riis
devoted a chapter to working women in New York. He cited a report from
the Working Women's Society, which maintained that "it is simply impossible for any woman to live without assistance on the low salary a sales-
woman earns . . . It is inevitable that they must in many instances resort to
evil."[22] While Riis documented the unbearable working conditions for
women, he also applauded their pluck and paid tribute to them: "To the
everlasting credit of New York's working-girl let it be said that, rough
though her road be, all but hopeless her battle with life, only in the rarest
instances does she go astray. As a class she is brave, virtuous, and true."[23]

The shop-girl figure also appeared in mainstream periodicals like the
Ladies' Home Journal and *McClure's Magazine*. As Linda Hess points out,
approximately fifty articles on shop girls appeared between 1890 and 1920.[24]

Unlike musicals, which represented the mythical figure of the working girl, these literary pieces gave extensive realistic details about the dismal working conditions facing working women, primarily in New York City. One series of articles, which appeared in *McClure's* in the fall of 1910, is paradigmatic of the Progressive journalism that strove to educate readers about working conditions for women (and that was often written by women).[25] Based on investigations conducted by the National Consumers' League, one article from this series cited compelling case studies of working women who lived from hand-to-mouth – standing up to ten hours a day, eating very little, only to return to their flats at night and launder their own clothing. This "starvation in pleasure," the authors noted, was compounded by "low wages and overwork" as well as the "conditions of temptation" created by men who offered clothing, food, or money in exchange for companionship (and, of course, for sex).[26]

While such reporting was an important corrective to the phantasmal characterizations otherwise, these narratives also dwelt upon shop girls prostituting themselves. As Benson has shown, often these charges of prostitution were not true: "perhaps the most damaging, and certainly the most sensational, charge was that department-store saleswomen were in special peril of prostitution, whether professional or occasional."[27] A year-long study of working conditions in New York department stores, which was published in 1913, came to the same conclusion (though for different ideological purposes): a "gross injustice has been done department-store girls, and working girls in general, through comments linking the wage-scale with the so-called 'white-slave' problem."[28] Why, then, did Progressive culture worry about "starvation in pleasure" or on which side of the counter the girl worked?

Illusory romances like *The Girl Behind the Counter* functioned as narrative antidotes to soothe cultural sores about women entering the workforce and the supposed "girl problem," or female criminal behavior. As Ruth Alexander shows, working-class female adolescents were labeled as problems precisely when they rejected "Victorian standards of girlhood virtue to lay claim to sexual desire, erotic expression, and social autonomy."[29] Female delinquency was perceived to be on the rise – a factor more of classification than actual fact. Just as working-class girls were constructed as problems for Progressive Era culture to regulate and reform, so shop girls were imagined as just a counter-top away from sin. As we shall see, the "girl problem" infused not only the dominant culture's handling of female delinquency, but also the management of sexuality itself.

Maggie of the shops: working-girl dramas

As the popularity of shop-girl musicals waned, more serious dramas about working women began appearing on the New York stage in the early 1900s. It is worth noting that while these dramas often negatively represented women's work, they nonetheless featured women in central, and very active, roles. Unlike their bourgeois or upper-class female counterparts, working girls were more heavily involved in the action. Precisely because they fell out of respectability, working-girl characters could maneuver more successfully; they earned money, beat back the villains, overcame sexual harassment, and plotted their revenge. Nonetheless, working-girl dramas steered toward a specific construct, preferring the mythical over the realistic, as the short-lived run of Cicely Hamilton's ultra realistic portrayal of working women, *Diana of Dobson's*, demonstrated in New York in 1908.[30]

One of the proto-working girls was the title character of *Maggie Pepper* by Charles Klein (published in 1909 and performed 147 times in 1911).[31] A drama about a levelheaded, female worker with a strong business sense, the play explores the challenges facing working women, especially the lure of prostitution, as the title character's name suggests (Maggie was the main character of Stephen Crane's *Maggie, a Girl of the Streets* [1900], one of the first American novels about a young woman's fall into prostitution).[32] Unlike Stephen Crane's working girl-turned prostitute, Maggie Pepper never contemplates working the streets, and indeed her character is, if anything, too industrious and heroic. Nonetheless, she is an important figure in the dramatic landscape of the representation of women's work, although compared to Bernard Shaw's intricate analysis of the oppression encountered by working women, *Maggie Pepper* offers little more than the seasoning that the name implies. According to Channing Pollock's 1911 review, it was "crude and elemental and filled with glaring improbabilities and incongruities."[33] Still, the play hints at the injustices suffered by women who were exploited as "one of the human products of the bargain emporium system," and, according to James Metcalfe, the play can be seen as "a telling indictment against the tyrannies of our department store princes of trade."[34]

While *Maggie Pepper* demonstrated that a woman could make a career by working in a department store, subsequent plays about women's work on Broadway grew increasingly grim, repeatedly tracing a trajectory from department store to brothel. A 1913 performance of *By-Products* by Joseph Medill Patterson, for instance, showed a mother and her two daughters,

Mary and Rosie, living in a tenement in abject poverty. Although the mother holds down two low-paying jobs, Mary is the only household member to make a decent wage as a department-store clerk (Rosie is ill with consumption). When the credit collector arrives and threatens to rip out the family's stove and jeopardize Rosie's precarious health, Mary runs out to meet with one of her store customers and returns with a wad of bills. She pays the collector and has enough to send her sister and mother to Colorado where they can both tend to their health. The play ends with the chilling point that while Mary has saved her sister and mother, she has lost herself, as she puts it, to "that long journey the fortune teller told me about."[35]

The journey from the department store into prostitution became a common dramaturgical path, shown in John Reed's little-known one-act play *Moondown*, which appeared in *The Masses* in September 1913 and was performed in a season of one-act plays by the Washington Square Players in 1915.[36] The short sketch portrays two women, "one a cynical, disillusioned victim of circumstances, the other clinging to the romance of youth."[37] A seasoned prostitute, Mame, shares a room in a New York boardinghouse with Sylvia, a young girl in search of work who believes "that a girl can keep straight and get work if she wants to."[38] However, Sylvia has to quit her job after her boss sexually harasses her and unable to find other work, and down to her last dime and subway ticket, she has put her faith in a man who promised to marry her and take her away. But as the moon goes down – on their agreed-upon meeting time – it is clear he is not going to show. Accordingly, she accepts her fate as a prostitute.

Although the bulk of the working-girl dramas were performed in the early to mid 1910s, the shop-girl story was revived in Dodson Mitchell's *Cornered*, which ran for 143 performances in 1920. *Cornered* portrayed the frustrations of a former prostitute who tries to make it on a shop girl's salary. Sexually harassed by her boss and frustrated by her meager income, she "is lured back to the old life on the promise of her pals that they 'will turn one more trick and quit.'"[39] The sizable run demonstrates that while the shop-girl story had been told repeatedly, New York audiences had not lost interest in it at the end of the Progressive Era.

In the early part of the twentieth century, therefore, numerous dramas, comedies, and musicals explored the lives of working women and the supposedly inevitable slide towards prostitution. In the mid to late 1910s, dramas about prostitution showed a waning interest in representing the conflict between "honest" work and prostitution and a growing curiosity in

the life of hooking itself. This shift in representation signaled a rejection of
conceiving prostitution as a fixed and pathological identity. Increasingly,
prostitution was viewed as a *transitory* occupation. As Barbara Meil Hobson
has concluded, the Victorian figures of the fallen or outcast woman "totally
misrepresented the social reality of prostitution: that it was short-term; that
women moved between prostitution and other employments; and that a
vast majority of women practiced the trade occasionally seasonally, or off
hours from regular jobs."[40] Such a perspective, however, was at odds with
theories of female sexual deviancy and the concomitant reform efforts. The
ensuing sex debates, legislation, and reform efforts in Progressive America
were a manifestation of these conflicting ideological views. In the midst of
this discursive production America still had yet to receive a full-length
drama that explored in detail the life of a working girl/prostitute – that is
until 1905.

5

The girl shop: Mrs Warren's Profession

Drag in a brothel, and they will never have seen so great a play as yours.

Max Beerbohm, 1898[1]

Just as playwrights were decorating the stage with shop girls so the theatre began dragging in brothels, though not initially with success, as theatre critic Max Beerbohm sardonically indicated. In fact, the New York premiere of Bernard Shaw's *Mrs Warren's Profession* on October 30, 1905 created the kind of riotous controversy of which few openings in American theatre history can boast. On opening night, a "struggling mass of people, who were shrieking and howling and bidding for seats and behaving generally like maniacs," waited impatiently outside the Garrick Theatre. They were packed in so tightly that traffic was brought to a standstill; the only way the actors could pierce the impenetrable mob was with a police escort.[2] After just one night, however, this memorable production was shut down on obscenity charges and banned for two years in America.[3] What had drawn this huge crowd to the Garrick Theatre that night? More importantly: why was this production perceived as "'the limit' of stage indecency," as the *New York Herald* put it, when prostitutes had appeared on stage long before Kitty Warren?[4]

Mrs Warren's Profession was the first full-length play to appear on Broadway that not only created a sympathetic portrait of a former-prostitute-turned-madam (Kitty Warren), but that also provided an extensive account of the socio-economic conditions that forced women to turn to prostitution. Rivaling previous dramaturgy, *Mrs Warren's Profession* presented a new type of working girl – what James Huneker called in 1905 "the Unpleasant Girl" – that shattered all previous models for staging the prostitute.[5] In rejecting the moral world that condemned sexually active

91

women, and the double standard on sexuality that sustained that perspective, Bernard Shaw dispensed with previous shop-girl mythologies,
portraying instead the drudgery of women who belonged to what we
would now call the working poor.

Bernard Shaw also rejected the romanticized hooker-with-a-heart-of-
gold so popular on the American stage, creating the "anti-type ... of the
Courtesan Play," to use Martin Meisel's words.[6] While Olga Nethersole's
staging of *Sapho* in 1900 challenged some of the romanticized notions about
fallen women's sexuality – a kind of sexuality that became *confused* with
prostitution, primarily through performative strategies instead of textual
ones – *Mrs Warren's Profession* was one of the first prostitute plays that did
not dramaturgically punish its heroine, require her to make some kind of
sacrifice, or rally the audience's sympathies entirely against her. In his
defense of *Mrs Warren's Profession*, Bernard Shaw pointed out the hypocrisy
behind the previous, popular *Camille*-inspired plots that had saturated
the stage:

> [C]onsider the unending line of plays which maintain an association in
> the imagination of the spectators between prostitution and fashionable
> beauty, luxury, and refinement! Sometimes a formal sop is offered to
> morality by making the lady commit suicide or die of consumption at
> the end; but as suicide is the one illegality that your thoroughgoing
> voluptuary never commits, and as honest women die of consumption as
> often as prostitutes, this artificial "moral" is not convincing.[7]

Arnold Daly, the actor/manager who produced the American premiere
of *Mrs Warren's Profession*, made a similar distinction: "The difference
between *Camille* and *Mrs Warren's Profession* is this: If a girl sees Camille
she says of the courtesan: 'How grand, how noble, I want to be like
Camille.' If she sees *Mrs Warren's Profession*, she finds Mrs. Warren
and the type which Mrs. Warren represents repellant."[8] In fact, audiences wanted to see their Camilles more than Bernard Shaw or Daly
anticipated.

In creating this new prostitute figure, rather than blaming the working
girl or pathologizing her "fall" into prostitution, Bernard Shaw criticized
the economic structures that caused prostitution. In short, instead of
reproducing the shop girl, he gave us the girl shop. In the preface to *Mrs
Warren's Profession*, Bernard Shaw wrote: "[P]rostitution is caused, not by
female depravity and male licentiousness, but simply by underpaying,
undervaluing, and overworking women so shamefully that the poorest of

them are forced to resort to prostitution to keep body and soul together."[9] Bernard Shaw's resuscitation of the prostitute figure, a figure previously demonized in this field of representation, was praised by feminist Emma Goldman in her 1914 collection of theatre criticism:

> Time was when the Mrs. Warrens were looked upon as possessed by the devil . . . And while we continue to drive them from pillar to post, while we still punish them as criminals and deny them the simplest humanities one gives even to the dumb beast, the light turned on this subject by men like George Bernard Shaw has helped to expose the lie of inherent evil tendencies and natural depravity.[10]

In *Mrs Warren's Profession*, both the working girl and the concept of "working" are demystified by specifying concrete economic details about women's work and the difficulty of securing what we would now call a living wage. In one monologue, for example, Mrs. Warren explains the drudgery of factory work to her daughter Vivie, who, having been educated away from home in the finest of boarding schools, is isolated from the working class. Mrs. Warren describes the fate of her working-class half-sisters – a fate that would have been hers had she not resorted to hooking:

> MRS. WARREN. One of them worked in a whitelead factory twelve hours a day for nine shillings a week until she died of lead poisoning. She only expected to get her hands a little paralyzed; but she died. The other was always held up to us as a model because she married a Government laborer in the Deptford victualling yard, and kept his room and the three children neat and tidy on eighteen shillings a week – until he took to drink. That was worth being respectable for, wasn't it?
>
> (2.247)

The material reality of women's work thus served as a backdrop for challenging supposed upper-class respectability and what Bernard Shaw believed were hypocritical sexual mores. By critiquing the class politics of prostitution, Bernard Shaw emphasized that prostitution was a societal problem, produced by the rise of modern capitalism. In drawing our attention to the girl shop, and by subverting the shop-girl myth, Bernard Shaw revealed the grave realities of women's work in a capitalistic system that readily offered women for sale.

Rivaling working (girl) ethics

Mrs Warren's Profession portrays the conflicting work ethics embodied by two working girls: Mrs. Warren and her daughter Vivie. Bernard Shaw cleverly juxtaposes the New Woman with the fallen woman, showing not only how the two possess differing worldviews, but also how they are undeniably connected.[11] Having placed highly in her studies at Cambridge, Vivie wishes to enter the male world of business. As she puts it, "I shall set up chambers in the city and work at actuarial calculations and conveyancing. Under the cover of that I shall do some law, with one eye on the Stock Exchange all the time" (1.217). Audiences were intrigued not only by Bernard Shaw's characterization of the New Woman, according to drama critic Fannie Fair, but also how Vivie's role would be performed: "[E]very one is wondering whether the girl who plays the part will smoke a cigar on the stage and put her feet up on the desk or if she will compromise on cigarettes, as Vivie is obliged to do in the last act because the women in her office object to the cigar smoke."[12] Here the interest was as much in how working is performed as it was in the signs of first-wave feminism. As demonstrated in Olga Nethersole's production of *Sapho* (see chapter 2), a woman smoking on stage signaled New Womanhood, much like bloomers and the bicycle. And thus the issue of women working, Bernard Shaw reminds us, was ineluctably tied to the feminist agenda of achieving equal rights.

The second working-girl ethic is embodied by Mrs. Warren, who believes that prostitution is a viable way for women to make money. For Mrs. Warren, business as a madam has been so profitable that she has remained in the profession for years, running brothels throughout Europe. Instead of repenting for making a living as a sex worker and entrepreneur, Mrs. Warren is proud of her business acumen. As she explains to Vivie, "No: I never was a bit shamed really. I consider I had a right to be proud of how we managed everything so respectably . . ." (2.251). Mrs. Warren's use of the word respectable to describe the running of a brothel is a Shavian dig at cultural respectability. Indeed, critics faulted Bernard Shaw for placing a heady businesswoman in a brothel, as did Constance A. Barnicoat in 1906: "When Mr. Shaw does endow a woman with business ability and managing facilities, what does she do with them? Engages in the White Slave Traffic, and waxes fat thereon!"[13] Barnicoat, like many others at that time, expressed a nostalgic desire for more traditional characters like Maggie Pepper and the working girls before her.

In the underworld culture itself, however, turning one's business acumen to madaming was an achievement of sorts. According to social historian

Ruth Rosen, turn-of-the-century madams viewed their work with pride, experiencing success in business as few other women could. One madam viewed her work as a kind of calling: "Madaming is the sort of thing that happens to you, like getting a battlefield commission or becoming the Dean of Women at Stanford University . . . Many are called, I always say, but few are chosen; and for me it has been a steppingstone to bigger and more profitable things."[14] As different as a madam and the Dean of Women at Stanford are, both roles helped young women prosper economically and socially (each, clearly, within class constraints). As Rosen notes, madams usually took 50 percent of each prostitute's daily earnings and could earn as much as fifty-thousand dollars in a year, though there were few who ever earned that much.

The two competing ethics of labor in *Mrs Warren's Profession* clash when Vivie discovers that her mother still manages a brothel. Even though Mrs. Warren has overcome economic hardship, Vivie is outraged that she continues with her work. Vivie has little moral ground to stand on, however, as Mrs. Warren's business partner, Crofts, points out, "you've always lived on it. It paid for your education and the dress you have on your back. Don't turn up your nose at business, Miss Vivie; where would your Newnhams and Girtons be without it?" (3.263). Indeed, while both characters are drawn to their work, each is a different kind of working girl:

> MRS. WARREN. I must have work and excitement or I should go mel-
> ancholy mad . . . The life suits me: I'm fit for it and not
> for anything else . . .
>
> VIVIE. No: I am my mother's daughter. I am like you: I must
> have work, and must make more money than I spend.
> But my work is not your work, and my way not your
> way. We must part. (4.283–84)

If Bernard Shaw offers two working girl ethics for us to evaluate, he does not do so simplistically. Vivie admonishes her mother, but not for being radical, as we might think: "If I had been you, mother, I might have done as you did; but I should not have lived one life and believed in another. You are a conventional woman at heart. That is why I am bidding you good-bye now" (4.286). Vivie thus rejects her mother, not because of her unconventional sexual politics, but because she strives for upper-class respectability. To Vivie's New Woman mind-set, achieving a conventional life is not in the least admirable. Bernard Shaw critiques Vivie's hypocrisy by portraying her renunciation of her mother as callous and cold. The play ends with Vivie resuming "her work with a plunge," signaling that New Womanhood cannot neatly solve the new century's problems (4.286). *Mrs Warren's Profession* therefore portrays two complicated portraits of working, neither of which is a satisfying representation of the working girl. Nevertheless, Bernard Shaw provides enough socio-materialist context for audiences to know that the girl behind the counter is caught in the jaws of the capitalistic machine, never to be rescued by a baron at Macy's.

No haven at New Haven

Just three days before the New York premiere a performance of *Mrs Warren's Profession* was given in New Haven as a trial run. The New Haven performance, as many scholars have shown, was a raucous event, a prelude to the eventual censorship awaiting the play in New York.[15] In revisiting that sensational performance my intent is less to document incendiary reactions to the play than to draw attention to the controversial performativity of prostitution, specifically as it is foregrounded by class disparity and the problem of prostitutes passing in respectable society.

Before the New York opening of *Mrs Warren's Profession*, Anthony Comstock, founder of the Society for the Suppression of Vice in New York City, threatened to stop the production.[16] In a letter in the *New York Times*, Comstock warned actor/manager Arnold Daly not to produce one of "Bernard Shaw's filthy products."[17] Their exchange was a literary battle that took place in the press for several days. Given the threat of arrest, Daly tested the waters by opening in New Haven on October 27, three days before the New York engagement. Daly chose this satellite town because he "thought the students would in the first place be profound enough to grasp the lesson which the play teaches and flippant enough to guy anything in it which they thought salacious."[18] Daly misjudged his New Haven audience, however, just as he would miscalculate Broadway.

Nowhere could have class disparity been more clearly framed than within the privileged Yale audience. Indeed, theatre historians have under-estimated how Mrs. Warren's low-class accent, and other markers of class performance, provoked both censors and audience members. As the show entered the second act – the act which Bernard Shaw himself removed when he failed to have the play approved by the Lord Chamberlain in England – the Yale undergraduates in the balcony broke into pandemo-nium, countered by professors below, who demanded order. According to actress Mary Shaw, the outbreak occurred during the scene in which

Figure 6. Act 2 of the American premiere of *Mrs Warren's Profession* with Catherine Countess as Vivie and Many Shaw as Mrs. Warren. Photo courtesy of the Museum of the City of New York.

Mrs. Warren explains her profession. Discovering that her mother is a brothel madam, Vivie asks, "Who was my father?" Mrs. Warren replies, "You don't know what you're asking. I can't tell you" (2.244; see figure 6). The prevailing explanation for the resulting pandemonium is that it was a response to Mrs. Warren's admission of having had so many sexual partners that she couldn't be sure of her daughter's father. While this was clearly one reason for the mayhem, what happens a few lines later may have equally determined the reaction. According to the stage directions, when Mrs. Warren becomes exasperated by Vivie's questioning, she "suddenly breaks out vehemently in her natural tongue – the dialect of a woman of the people – with all her affectations of maternal authority and conventional

manners gone, and an overwhelming inspiration of true conviction and
scorn in her" (2.245–46). Mary Shaw recalled that while this battle between
the students and professors raged, the show stopped completely; the
actresses had to wait patiently on stage for order to resume. Shaw then
recounts the moment when, in her view, she rescued the play:

[A] sudden conviction came upon me that it was going to be impossible to
play Kitty Warren as Kitty Warren should be played, in the vulgar cockney
dialect to which she reverted in strong feeling. Knowing something of the
methods of controlling mob spirit in audiences, I strode to the head of the
table, took on the manner of Lady Macbeth, and played the entire scene in
loud, sonorous tones with menace in every one of them. An appalling
silence fell upon the theater. There was no more trouble of any kind from
the undergraduates, and when the curtain fell upon the second act they paid
the tribute that cowards always pay to the courageous, and gave us about
ten curtain calls . . . [A]t its close some distinguished men and women met
us on the stage and expressed their appreciation of the performance.[19]

Mary Shaw thus regained control, not only by effacing the vulgarity of
Mrs. Warren and converting her cockney accent into an aristocratic one,
but also by evoking a classical performance style and the respectability of
Shakespeare. She instinctively offset the excessive sexuality associated with
both prostitution and the lower class by evoking Lady Macbeth, a character
who is "unsexed." Order was restored when Mrs. Warren became less "a
certain class of female harp[y]," as the *Herald* put it, and more a desexualized lady.[20] Shaw's performance of class respectability is therefore what
stopped the students from acting like former "Bowery B'hoys" in the
gallery, reminding them of her and their own, bourgeois origins.

Class performance

Once the show transferred to New York, Shaw's relapse into cockney left an
indelible impression on the press. One unidentified clipping, for instance,
criticized Shaw for her "vernacular of the slums:"

Miss Mary Shaw . . . makes the mistake of playing the part from the
outset in too Cockney a key. This woman, as Shaw conceived her, has
rubbed off some of the external polish of the men she has associated with.
When in her anger at her daughter she should relapse into a vernacular of
the slums, no effective contrast is possible.[21]

The *New York Times* likewise objected: "In the acting of the chief role there
was exactly the overemphasis of its more repugnant features that might

have been expected."[22] While crediting Mary Shaw for being "an artist of broad experience and undoubted ability," the same review faulted her for being too explicit: "Miss Shaw lays on her colors too heavily."[23] In layering excessive vulgarity, like applying the heavy makeup of a prostitute, Mary Shaw transgressed not only good taste, but also expectations about class and social decorum. Decades later, prominent theatre critic Barnard Hewitt repeated this critique, stating that Mary Shaw's use of a lower-class accent during this scene, "somewhat spoiled the complete effectiveness of her work."[24] One contributing factor to Mrs. Warren's purported indecency was therefore her class transgression.

While there is ample evidence to suggest that certain class performances were the hitch in the critical reception, a less obvious, but equally vital, problem was performativity itself. Using the term performativity, I draw on Judith Butler's definition which, in turn, is indebted to J. L. Austin. Butler expands on Austin's observation that words "do" things: "Within speech act theory, a performative is that discursive practice that enacts or produces that which it names."[25] Performativity, in other words, enacts cultural work. The fear of how *Mrs Warren's Profession* would signify as performative was precisely what drove the need for social control. The *New York Times* made this clear: "The play itself is fit for publication only as a document for the sociologist and reformer ... Acted, it is incredibly worse. The full force of the utterance and gestures only add to its vulgarity and the necessity of acting up to the parts makes it equally repulsive."[26] What the press and the censors feared, in other words, was the "full force" of such texts, the ways in which all performatives rely upon citationality. "Performativity," Butler writes, "is thus not a singular 'act,' for it is always a reiteration of a norm or set of norms, and the extent that it acquires an act-like status in the present, it conceals or dissimulates the conventions of which it is a repetition."[27] Performativity was dangerous in this case, the *New York Herald* cautioned, because "the better it was acted the more impurity and degeneracy of the characters, the situations and the lines were made apparent."[28] The potential iteration of transgressive signs was perceived as limitless, and volatile.

The fear of lower-class and underworld performativity can be seen by examining Police Commissioner McAdoo's response to a public reading of *Mrs Warren's Profession* (by "a well-known woman reader," according to Mary Shaw) at the Berkeley Lyceum just days after the play had been censored at the Garrick.[29] Instead of shutting it down, however, McAdoo allowed the reading to continue. Mary Shaw's account of this exception – as full of wit as Bernard Shaw – offers an interesting insight:

Just for fun, I called up Commissioner McAdoo on the telephone, speaking as if I were some outraged citizen of New York. I informed him of the fact that this reading was to take place, and asked him whether he was going to permit the performance. He curtly informed me that he had nothing whatever to do with it: that they had a perfect right to read *Mrs Warren's Profession* if they wished, but he would permit no scenery to be used.[30]

How, we might wonder, only a few days after a scandal that shook New York, could the very same play be deemed harmless once stripped of its scenery, costumes, and blocking? This example demonstrates how the respectable status of the (unnamed) reader marked her performance. Here, a reputable woman, cloaked in the respectability of her class, wears her own bourgeois clothing (a costume in its own right), and speaks without employing a working-class dialect. More importantly, there is no scenery or blocking – simply her reading of the script. This reading conveys a certain kind of decorum, one that Mary Shaw, whose performance cited feminism and activism, could not marshal. The public reading of the text was allowed because it was contained. Such an example also demonstrates that performative framings – in this case, the "well-known reader's" respectability – contribute to semiotic intelligibility.

If all's well that ends well, then New Haven was no haven for *Mrs Warren's Profession*. Although Daly and Mary Shaw both remember the New Haven performance as having been well received, *Mrs Warren's Profession* was shut down by the aptly named Mayor Studley after just one performance. What would await the cast in New York, they hoped, was vindication. Respectability would be restored. Daly felt so strongly about this that he put his faith in the critics' hands, proclaiming, "The play will be positively presented to-night, and if it is condemned by the jury of critics it will be withdrawn."[31] Once again, Daly and others miscalculated the extent to which the performance of a prostitute drama would provoke the press and censors. In 1905, *Mrs Warren's Profession* could exist in New York's brothels, but not on the stage.

New York, respectable New York

If the supposedly enlightened New Haven crowd judged *Mrs Warren's Profession* as "the most shockingly immoral dialogue ever publicly repeated," then there was a great deal to worry about in New York.[32] Daly put his trust in the press, but hadn't reckoned that Comstock would turn his wrath onto him. With threats of arrest ringing in his ears and Bernard Shaw's quip from England that "a few months' rest and quiet [in prison] would do Daly a great deal of good" still fresh in his mind, Daly acted quickly.[33] When the production moved to New York three days after New Haven, anxiety drove Daly to edit from the script "every single line which is capable of double construction," as he put it.[34] At first, many were "purely changes of words," as Daly had been summoned to hand over the revised prompt book to New York Police Commissioner McAdoo before the curtain went up.[35] However, as opening night in New York drew near, Daly turned his attention to censoring the performance of prostitution as well. Stage directions describe Mrs. Warren as "showily dressed in a brilliant hat and a gay blouse fitting tightly over her bust and flanked by fashionable sleeves." Although described as "decidedly vulgar," Bernard Shaw takes pains that Kitty Warren should not be caricatured by the traditional signs of prostitution: "on the whole, a genial and fairly presentable old blackguard of a woman" (1.220). In the New Haven performance, however, Daly resorted to classic, if not clichéd, signs of prostitution. According to Mary Shaw, "My original make-up for the part of Kitty Warren was a blonde wig and striking [red] costume, the idea of the management being to emphasize her well-dressed vulgarity. In this get-up I had played the part in New Haven."[36] Worried the cast would be arrested in New York, however, Daly went a step further to dilute the signs of prostitution. As Shaw recounted, "But to-night, Mr. Daly, when he saw me, was seized with a sudden panic, and asked me to go downstairs, take off my wig, wear my own hair, and in every way tone down Mrs. Warren's appearance."[37] Daly described his self-censorship as follows: "[I]t has been decided to cut out all objectionable lines and to present Mrs. Warren in what I might term a high-neck and long-sleeve gown."[38] Evoking the metaphor of Victorian respectability, Daly's production strove to make Mrs. Warren more reputable through both performance and textual changes.

Daly's efforts to dilute the performative signs of prostitution in Mrs. Warren's character may have had, paradoxically, the opposite effect. Once the classic signs of prostitution – a blonde wig, red dress, lower-class accent – were eliminated, the character had the unsettling effect of being indistinguishable from ladies in society. The Daly production thus underscored one of Bernard Shaw's textual points: Kitty Warren *passed* in mainstream contexts, specifically in bourgeois society. As a successful brothel manager and former prostitute, Mrs. Warren infiltrated society and remained camouflaged as a businesswoman for many years. No one, not even her own daughter, suspected her real profession. Moreover, Kitty Warren further inverted existing models of prostitution by implying that a prostitute could be a good mother – one who can afford the very best boarding schools, no less. Violating the very essence of Edwardian womanhood, Mrs. Warren claims the cultural space reserved for respectable women. In passing as a lady, she is "a vigorous whore," as Charles A. Berst crudely observes, who has duped society.[39]

There were many such whores who passed as ladies. The demands of display culture, as Maureen E. Montgomery has shown, made it difficult to discern between them: "Certainly, in the 1890s and 1900s the boundaries between the monde and the demimonde were becoming much more fluid as women became more mobile and began to push against the constrains upon their activities in public space. In fact the spaces of the worlds were becoming increasingly coextensive."[40] It is no wonder, then, that viewers became confused as the borders between brothel and boudoir became blurred. This liminality paralleled the anxiety that Progressive Era culture had about prostitution invading and infecting parts of the city. As Police Commissioner McAdoo wrote in his memoir, *Guarding a Great City*, one consequence of shutting down red-light districts was that prostitutes could be found scattered throughout the city:

> There can be no question whatever but that the vicious woman is more to be feared in a tenement or apartment house than in a house notoriously used for immoral purposes. The mechanic's daughter across the hall, who works hard all day in a feather or tobacco factory, is apt to become curious about the woman who does no work and who wears fine clothes and jewels, to become dissatisfied with her lot and envious of the easy life of the other, and, finally, after an acquaintance, to join the vast army of unfortunate women who seem to increase rather than decrease with the march of civilization.[41]

Since "vicious women" could be found everywhere, this logic tells us, then the task of hunting out prostitutes became difficult indeed. The apprehension therefore at the Garrick Theatre, like that in New Haven, paralleled the angst (and pleasure) of encountering a prostitute, who passed in mainstream contexts.

Policing female spectators

The anxiety about the ambiguous way in which prostitution signified was echoed in the extreme nervousness exhibited by the press about female audience members. Opening night reviews made repeated observations about women in the theatre, scrutinizing their physical appearance, class, etiquette, and sexual politics. McAdoo was quoted in the *New York Times* as asking: "Remarkable isn't it, what a lot of young girls there were in the house tonight?"[42] Another review reported the "presence of beautiful women, many of whom watched every detail."[43] Women were studied not only inside the theatre, but also in the "dense crowds" outside the Garrick where "there were as many women as men in the throng."[44] When not portrayed as beautiful, young, or otherwise diminutive, female audience members were derided as inept. One review, for example, suggested that many women didn't quite understand the play: "Many [prospective buyers of tickets] were women, some who looked as though they had no idea of the kind of play [they were watching]."[45]

Why comment on the female audience members' beauty, attention span, or intelligence? This question was pondered by Professor Felix Adler in a public lecture that filled Carnegie Hall just six days after the premiere. Adler speculated, like McAdoo, that young women had "the most frivolous of motives" in their "itching desire to be in the fashion." But Alder's real irritation was with women, especially young women and girls, engaging in sex discourse: "It is deplored that in cultivated circles and in certain colleges for girls so much attention is given to the recent phenomenon in literature."[46] The *New York Times* perhaps best summarized the anxiety about women seeing the play: "It tells working girls that it is much better to live a carefully calculated life of vice rather than of honest work."[47] Such comments, like the censorship efforts by McAdoo and Comstock, revealed dominant culture's investment in managing and literally policing sex discourse. The inordinate attention on female spectators was not lost on Bernard Shaw, who wrote in the preface to the play, "Those who were 'surprised to see ladies present' were men" (200). The *New York Times* agreed: "It may be the fear of our wives and daughters being brought face to face with such a phase of life as that shown in the Mrs. Warren play . . . that is keeping the movement toward suppression alive."[48] The policing, therefore, mapped out a specifically gendered terrain, where women could not be spectators much less participants in sex discourse. An article in the *New Haven Register* made this political agenda clear: "Such a play as *Mrs Warren's Profession* cannot under any circumstances be given before a mixed [gender] audience."[49]

The idea of policing sexuality became literalized in the figure of McAdoo, who acted simultaneously as Police Commissioner, censor, self-appointed gatekeeper of morality, and even theatre critic. McAdoo believed he was "guarding a great city," as his own book characterized it. In an article in *Current Opinion*, McAdoo warned, "If New York should adopt his [Shaw's] moral code, I would resign my police commissionership in an hour."[50] McAdoo was in the habit of lecturing on the topic of "proper" sexuality in a variety of venues. Three weeks before the New York premiere, in a speech to the men of the YMCA, McAdoo gave his views on sexual virtue. "Be virtuous and you will be happy ... You must be morally and physically clean and strong."[51] In addition, McAdoo ventured into theatre criticism, critiquing not only Bernard Shaw's dramas, but also the genre of problem plays themselves, waxing nostalgically for "the old melodrama, where the hero was always a man, and a gentleman at that; the villain all that should be hissed, and everything came out right in the end. I want the old days, with the good plays, and there were many of them."[52] For McAdoo, the theatre had much force as a discursive power, but creative energies had been misplaced since the good old days of melodrama. As he put it, "The three great forces in New York to-day are the Church, the press, and the theatre."[53]

If the theatre was a great force in the production of sexual behavior, then much was at stake in policing spectatorship. Some reports that dwelled on female theatre-goers revealed anxiety that women in the audience were themselves prostitutes. For if Mrs. Warren could be indistinguishable from any society lady and freely circulate within society, so too could she be camouflaged in the audience. According to one review of the opening night: "Nearly all appeared refined, intelligent and well-dressed. There were some who were undoubtedly ... of the same professional calling [as Mrs. Warren]."[54] Whether these women *were* actually prostitutes is less interesting than their interpellation as such. Yet, this intense surveillance of women in the theatre reveals that neither the signs of respectability, nor those of the brothel, could always be readily decoded.

The concern over young women sitting in the audience during *Mrs Warren's Profession* echoes the unfortunate misreading of women in the so-called "guilty third tier" as prostitutes by nineteenth-century and current critics alike.[55] In his study of nineteenth-century American theatre, Bruce McConachie points out that working-class women who occupied the third tier were often mistaken for prostitutes.[56] Rosemarie K. Bank likewise refutes the "guilty third tier" premise, noting that such discourse draws not only on classist, but also racist assumptions that conflates working-class women and women of color with the underworld. "While a feminist history rightly notes the injustice of conflating working women with prostitutes," writes Bank, "prostitutes are also working women, and the erasure of the fluid line between the one and the other in these decades only expunges the historical positioning of waged work for women and its poverty, and reinscribes prostitution as a moral issue."[57] Indeed, in the early twentieth century, prostitutes were no longer geographically contained in one part of the auditorium, or in certain kinds of theatres, and thus could leak into the respectable spaces. "The problem for society women," Montgomery observes, "was that the notion of a woman displaying herself was firmly associated with the world of prostitution."[58] Therefore, by 1905, when *Mrs Warren's Profession* premiered, there was very good reason to search for the "hustlers in the house," to use Bank's formation.[59] Now that the geography – as well as the semiotics – of prostitution were no longer clearly contained, one could rub shoulders with a prostitute in the theatre and not always know it. As it became more difficult to distinguish prostitutes from other women, especially from working women, and as borders collapsed, Progressive reform efforts grew significantly to contain and abolish prostitution.

The discursive surveillance of female spectators in the press mirrored the actual investigation of women on the streets by vice commissions like The Committee of Fourteen, which was founded in New York City to investigate the rapid spread of prostitution the very year *Mrs Warren's Profession* opened. The Committee hired detectives to go to clubs, restaurants, dance halls, tenement houses, and other "suspicious" spaces, and collect data. In short, a detective could be anywhere, scrutinizing, and reporting upon, women's behavior. Of course, interpreting these signs proved difficult. Many detectives' notes revealed constant guessing in discerning respectable women from prostitutes.[60] The quintessential conundrum was captured by the protagonist in a short story called *Edna: The Girl of Street* (1919): "A blunt question that hit him a blunt blow: can that pretty girl be a street woman?"[61] As Robert G. Allen has argued, "In the increasingly difficult struggle to distinguish the respectable 'lady' from the woman who was not, bourgeois culture saw all manner of divergence from the rigid norms of 'true womanhood' as whorishness."[62] Sites for working-class leisure were particularly singled out as bawdy houses. Young working-class women were drawn to cheap amusements, Kathy Peiss points out, in an articulation of "an assertion of self, a working-class variant of the 'New Woman.'"[63] Under the aegis of studying the social evil, vice commissions studied the working girl and her leisure habits. The surveillance of suspicious female behavior – whether in

106   WORKING GIRLS

the Garrick Theatre or in working-class cabarets – was thus a regular practice in the Progressive Era, where much energy was directed, often unsuccessfully, into decoding the signs of prostitution.

For the record: Women's reactions

Of the many hundreds of women I interviewed, I never talked with one who was shocked by *Mrs Warren's Profession*. On the other hand, it was most unusual to find a man who was not shocked by it.[64]
                                                    Mary Shaw, "My 'Immoral' Play"

Although there was much ado about how *Mrs Warren's Profession* would affect female spectators, women's reactions were notably absent from the historical record. Indeed, theatre scholarship about *Mrs Warren's Profession* has paid little attention to the ways in which the discourse was gendered.[65] Yet almost a century ago Mary Shaw argued that the controversy over *Mrs Warren's Profession* was split along gender lines, and that women's responses hadn't been heard properly: "This play I knew to be what stage people call a 'woman's play' – one in which the theme appeals more powerfully to women than to men. In all the hubbub, not a woman's voice had been heard; it was simply one vast aggregate of men and their opinions."[66] While Comstock and McAdoo portrayed their censorship of *Mrs Warren's Profession* as upholding the sexual moral order, they also protected male control over sex discourse. Bernard Shaw predicted that most of the objections would come from "the patrons of prostitutes" not "women who are engaged in rescuing women from prostitution."[67] In clarifying the strategy of producing *Mrs Warren's Profession* to Daly, Bernard Shaw wrote: "Get the rescuers into the theatre and keep the patrons out of it; and you need have no fear about the reception of the play."[68]

If many of "the blue-noses," as George E. Wellwarth called those who regulated New York theatre and morality, voiced their opinions publicly, women were more engaged in discussions about sexuality than has been acknowledged.[69] As Mary Shaw pointed out, "Women may not be supposed to know about these things but they do know about them and they take a deep interest in these problems. Women will look at the play in the right way. They are less conventional than men."[70] Indeed, women were more receptive to *Mrs Warren's Profession* not only in New York, but also throughout the United States during the regional tour. One "lady of society," as she called herself, declared in a letter to the *New York Times*: "I shall not take only my daughter, when she has graduated from school, but also my son, to see it, hoping it will make them think and understand a little of the terrible problems of the life of the present day, before they face it and take an individual part in it."[71] As the *New York Telegram* reported, public opinion had changed after another prominent woman, Mrs. Winchell Smith, spoke in favor of the play. She maintained, "I will admit that when I left the theatre, I was not in a very good mind toward the play. But as I thought of it . . . the great lesson seemed to dawn upon me."[72] Smith was one of the few women quoted in the press, however, and may have been included as an exception because she was married to Daly's financial partner.

If women were rarely quoted in the press concerning the issue of censorship, the most flagrant omission was Mary Shaw herself. Given that Shaw was recognized as an outspoken suffragette, this exclusion may have been deliberate.[73] Her feminist politics were visible as early as 1892 when she became a member of the Professional Women's League, a support group for actresses. The lines between the personal, the public, and the political became blurred when, in 1899, she represented American actresses as a delegate to the International Women's Congress in London. She had been advised not to attend by an influential theatre manager, who warned her that an actress should not become involved in politics. But Shaw was committed to the link between politics and theatre, especially the transformational power it held for women. This was evident in her work to create a Women's National Theatre, an early feminist theatre, which eventually folded for lack of resources. Clearly, *Mrs Warren's Profession* fit into her commitment to sustain feminist politics and theatre, a position that fueled much criticism against her, as Ellen Gainor has shown.[74] "More than any other actress in this country," one critic of the time wrote, "Mary Shaw has stood for what is new and daring and experimental in dramatic art. . . . [S]he played *Mrs Warren's Profession* in America, in the face of a storm of criticism and abuse such as probably no other actress has ever confronted in our time."[75] The storm of criticism would both define, and indelibly mark, Mary Shaw's career. Ellen Donkin argues that Shaw's acting career never fully recovered after *Mrs Warren's Profession*'s premiere.[76]

Mary Shaw persevered by using *Mrs Warren's Profession* as a kind of early feminist consciousness-raising theatre. On tour with *Mrs Warren's Profession*, Mary Shaw sought out women's opinions about the play. In every city where they performed she was invited to speak at a women's club, where she presented the case of the play and asked for their cooperation.

Shaw wrote that she was always "cordially welcomed" by women in every city, who were "eager to hear my side of the case."[77] In each city, groups of women – comprised largely of reform-minded women – decided to see the play and vote on their judgment of it. Shaw gave a passionate tribute to these women, whom she felt were "a splendid example of the courage and fine judgment of American women."[78] Shaw's experience with female audiences around the country disputes the claim by the popular press that women were unworthy interpreters of prostitute dramas. Far from being silent about prostitution, or repelled by Bernard Shaw's prostitute anti-type, women all over America were educating themselves about the oldest profession of all.

In censoring *Mrs Warren's Profession*, the authorities made a decided effort to control representations of the girl shop on stage, as well as women's participation in sex discourse. The controversy surrounding the play sprang not only from the provocative script, but also from Mary Shaw's persona, and the dangerous citationality of prostitution, unregulated sexuality, and first-wave feminism. It was too difficult, perhaps, to separate bodies that lobbied for votes or bartered for sex in the streets from those that performed prostitution on the stage. As powerful as the censorship of the girl shop was in *Mrs Warren's Profession*, however, representations of the shop girl continued. Stories, novels, articles, and plays about the working girl who slides into prostitution were not erased entirely from the stage or from popular culture. Indeed, the shop girl had a vital role in the mythical construction of the Progressive Era's understanding of work and prostitution. If Kitty Warren disappeared from the stage for a number of years, the shop girl kept appearing, usually in the seemingly innocuous form of the musical, with its regressive representations of women's work and sexuality. Seen together, the girl shop and shop girl demonstrate the inherent tension for the working girl in early twentieth-century display and consumer culture.

Part III

Opium dens and urban brothels: Staging the white slave

"My God! If I Could Only Get Out of Here!" was, reportedly, "the midnight shriek of a young girl in the vice district of a large city," according to Ernest Bell's popular book, *Fighting the Traffic in Young Girls: or, War on the White Slave Trade*. Bell's sensational tract, appearing in 1910, effectively declared war on the white slave trade: the supposed systematic abduction and prostitution of women.[1] If one could see behind the brick and mortar of the brothel, Bell claimed, if one could peer behind the iron bars and put an ear to the walls, one would hear the desperate cries of captive sex slaves. The fate of so-called white slaves was one of the primary preoccupations of turn-of-the century America. It was the subject of several vice commission investigations, congressional hearings, and legislation typified by the White Slave Traffic Act of 1910.[2] Indeed, the Federal Bureau of Investigation was originally formed to investigate the trafficking in women. White slave hunters took up "the mighty crusade to protect the purity of our homes," as Clifford G. Roe put it in *The Horrors of the White Slave Trade*.[3] As the subtitle of Bell's book made apparent, the fervent refrain made by reformers was "For God's Sake, Do Something!"

In the wake of such urgency, the figure of the white slave began to appear everywhere during the 1910s: in countless novels such as *The Girl Who Disappeared* by Clifford G. Roe (1914); in nonfiction such as Jean Turner Zimmermann's *America's Black Traffic in White Girls* (1912); in films like *Traffic in Souls* (1913) directed by George Tucker; and most relevant of all to this study, in white slave dramas from the 1913–1914 season like *The Lure* by George Scarborough, *The Fight* by Bayard Veiller, and *The House of Bondage* adapted by Joseph Byron Totten. Of the scores of plays about prostitution in the Progressive Era, the white slave play was by far the most popular and ubiquitous. And while some cultural critics of the time sought to clarify "that nebulous term 'white slavery,'" most popular discourse agreed that "the 'white slave' continues to be a popular theme on the stage and in current fiction, and a sort of slogan used in awakening the endeavors of social reformers."[4] What exactly did this phenomenon reveal about Progressive Era culture?

As recent journalistic exposés on the trafficking in women and children make clear, the problem of sexual slavery is far from being eradicated. Peter Landesman reported in the *New York Times Magazine* in 2004, for instance, that as many as 20,000 young women are still trafficked annually into the US and held as sexual slaves.[5] When the cover story appeared, it received both praise and criticism for reporting facts that could not be verified.[6] The controversy surrounding Landesman's piece is strikingly reminiscent of Progressive Era debates about white slavery. The following two chapters take up these debates, showing that while there is evidence of some abduction and trafficking of women during the Progressive Era, such widespread, and often conspiratorial, accounts of white slavery as a vast network were exaggerated. It is essential not to discount those terrible cases of sexual slavery then, or now, but rather to map out the ideological force of white slave discourse. Why did prostitution get reimagined as white slavery during the Progressive Era? What was at stake in representing prostitution during this particular cultural moment as innocent victimization? As the pages below reveal, the white slave panic offers a unique moment in American history in unraveling constructions of sexuality, gender, ethnicity, and race, as well as the theatre's role in staging these conflicts.

6

White slave plays in Progressive Era theatre

What is called white slavery has now become a favorite topic of dinner table conversation in "our best circles." It is not yet being made on the children's games in the kindergartens, but doubtless will be before long. The stage, always looking for new material and new territory to invade, has seized upon this luscious topic with avidity.[1]

James Metcalfe, *Life Magazine*, 1913

If the "luscious topic" of white slavery, as James Metcalfe put it, had invaded upper-class society in 1913, then the emerging white slave drama was a catalyst for this discursive incursion. White slave characters were everywhere in the theatre of the day. "In any city, no matter where," the *Book News Monthly* noted in 1914, "you will see advertisements of the white slave play . . ."[2] Although white slave dramas were penned by celebrated playwrights such as Eugene Walter, Elizabeth Robins, and Rachel Crothers, and were produced in New York's finest theatres, there were also scores of lesser-known playwrights whose white slave plays thrived throughout the country's little theatres. In spite of this prevalence in American theatre, little has been written about the vast array of such plays.[3] As we shall see, although it was a luscious topic, white slavery could only be staged within certain ideological and mimetic parameters.

What is especially fascinating with the white slave tale is the sudden shift in theorizing prostitutes as victims. No longer perceived as a necessary or social evil, prostitution was now seen as being performed, in part, by helpless sexual slaves. Many first-wave feminists and sociologists had, of course, long argued that economic injustice forced women into prostitution – a kind of sexual slavery. Yet, such arguments had largely fallen on deaf ears. The curious arrival of the white slave figure, however, permitted a theory of victimization to enter popular consciousness. This turn of events generated a paradoxical conception of the prostitute. Though she traversed the sexual underworld, she none-theless maintained her moral purity. The notion of the white slave, in other words, offered a strange fantasy of the "virginal" prostitute.

The white slave tale was a thrilling story told again and again with only minor variations. White slave narratives followed a simple melodramatic formula. In most, a white woman is abducted by a cadet (or pimp) and tricked into entering a brothel where she is drugged, beaten, and held against her will as a sexual slave. In such tales, a nineteenth-century melodramatic heroism is resurrected: the white slave hunter, often a vice commissioner or special agent, saves the helpless victim from her malevolent captors. In the white slave world, the victim is always morally, as well as sexually, pure. Indeed, the protection of the heroine's chastity is often the driving force of the drama: the hero must save her before she is sexually ruined.

White slave narratives followed in the tradition of captivity tales dating back to colonial America. By invoking the captivity narrative, white slave tracts drew on racist and sexist ideologies to retool prostitution discourse within familiar semiotics. As Frederick Turner has noted, captivity tales, especially those written by women, were among the most popular American narratives. These stories followed a similar logic to the white slave tale: white women were abducted by "savage Indians" and held against their will, often as sexual partners. Early captivity narratives thus established the ideological framework through which white slave dramas could understand a new sort of captive woman. If the captivity narrative expressed fear that Native Americans were stealing white virgins from colonial homes – a threat not only to racial purity, but also to Western colonization – then white slave tracts expressed related anxieties resulting from immigration, urbanization, and the rise of women in the workforce. In his analysis of the white slave scare, social historian Mark Connelly suggests that this hysteria reflected deep cultural anxiety about the new urban wilderness of the twentieth century. Indeed, Connelly calls the white slave story "the capti-vity literature of postfrontier America."[4] Casting this new tale of abduction in a familiar narrative, the white slave captivity tract appealed to American audiences, who related to the perils of recent frontier days. According to this logic, the urban wilderness, as Upton Sinclair characterized it in his novel *The Jungle* (1906), was no less dangerous than an expedition into the uncolonized territories.[5]

Like Native American captivity narratives, white slave tracts drew upon the inherently central, yet unarticulated, idea of whiteness as normative (and superior). While prostitution involved "not merely white women, but yellow and black women as well," as Emma Goldman pointed out long ago, white slave narratives worried almost exclusively about the prostitution of white women.[6] Connelly has argued that immigrant women figured prominently in virtually all white slave narratives, just as they were the focus of numerous studies and investigations. This was *not* the case with the white slave drama, however. Significantly, in the scores of white slave dramas to appear in New York City, none of the heroines is an immigrant or woman of color. In the transition from novel to stage, therefore, prostitution was whitewashed, its racial complexity ignored, conveying the message that those who were worthy to be saved were white women. In addition, the portrayal of helpless white victims engendered a sense that women should be protected and rescued from the new "frontier" violence of the city. This emerging cultural imperative dovetailed seamlessly with agendas to regulate women's sexuality and gender roles.

In contrast to the "white" victims, the slavers were often "dark" immigrants, especially Jews, Italians, and Eastern Europeans. White slave tracts played upon ethnic stereotypes, recycling jingoistic images dating back to the volatile birth of the nation. The fear of immigrants was indeed one of the primary motivations for much Progressive legislation against, and investigations into, white slavery.[7] Drawing on the emerging eugenics and criminology discourses of the day, white slave narratives suggested that certain foreigners would contaminate the nation in more ways than one. These obvious stereotypes can be seen in characters like the aptly named Mark Diablo from Joseph LeBrant's unpublished play *Escaped From the Harem*. Described as having "a dark olive complexion, [a] wicked scar on his left cheek," wearing "stylish dress with foreign cut," and being "nervous," Diablo is so indisputably foreign that one blind character remarks, "What a musical voice. I'm sure he's dark."[8] Similarly, in *The House of Bondage*, an "alien" named Max, "a young dark curley [sic] headed Greek about 25 – very dark, dressed in the extreme of fashion" and with "dark hands," reveals his method of procuring white slaves: "my business is all right [;] sometimes it's bad – it ain't so easy as you think – You got to find the girls – who haf no money – or on strike – or haf to support a big family – or their folks treat 'em bad."[9] Such portrayals drew on already circulating fears of ethnic others, heightening the tension between supposedly pure white American women and undesirable aliens.

If white slavery adapted familiar scripts from colonial American captivity narratives, it also conjured up two earlier uses of the term "white slave." The first application of the phrase was used to describe racially mixed slaves before emancipation, as portrayed in the play *The White Slave* (1882) by Bartley Theo Campbell.[10] By the middle of the nineteenth century, this version of the white slave functioned as a liminal character who negotiated mixed racial borders. This imagining of white slavery was often used to invoke a sense of injustice, in that "innocents" – those with white blood – were wrongfully forced into slavery.

The term white slave had also been used to describe working conditions in Britain in the 1830s. This economic sense of the term had made its way to America by the mid 1850s.[11] The undercover exposé *The White Slave Girls of Chicago* (1888) by Nell Nelson, for instance, focused on the heinous working conditions of white women in industry.[12] After the turn of the twentieth century, the white slave no longer toiled away simply in factories, but rather in other urban work environments, especially department stores (see chapter 4). White slavery was thus imagined no longer in terms of the drudgery of sweatshops, but now as something that threatened the new urban working woman at the very center of fashionable city life. As Kathleen Barry notes, this new conceptualization of white slavery had popular appeal because "the term eventually embodied all the sexist, classist, and racist bigotry that was ultimately incorporated within the movement dominated by religious morality."[13]

Just as women were entering the work force, fighting for the vote, and lobbying for control of their sexuality, white slave narratives reminded Americans of the dangers of such freedoms. Nowhere was this battle more clearly articulated than in defining the white slave's sexuality. White slave discourse harkened back to the rhetoric of fallenness by splitting prostitution into two archetypes: the innocent white slave and the corrupt prostitute. As I have already suggested, this bifurcated view of women's sexuality was quite common throughout the nineteenth century, but as retooled here, it made sexual purity a quintessential aspect of reimagining prostitution.[14] Though there was by no means a consensus as to what defined white slavery, sexual purity was a consistent feature of its portrayal in white slave dramas. As a special agent in the play *The Girl Who Disappeared* (1914) explains:

> There are many differences of opinion ... as to just what white slavery means. Some people call every woman in a resort a white slave; others call every girl who supports a cadet, a white slave. What I mean by a white slave is a girl who has never been a sporting woman before, who gets deceived and placed in a house of ill-fame.[15]

According to this white slave hunter, only chaste women can count as white slaves. Sexually "impure" women, on the other hand, cannot be considered captives of the brothel, or victims of any other ensnaring circumstances. One regrettable consequence of white slave discourse, as Ruth Rosen writes, was that it served "to deflect attention away from the very real social and economic factors that led women into prostitution."[16] Instead, an ideal of purity and innocence emerged in the figure of the helpless white slave, a white girl whose only crime was that she was too innocent to understand the world of vice into which she stumbled.

During the 1910s, white slave narratives grew in popularity and increasingly took on the quality of true-crime testimonials narrated by white slave hunters. Functioning as sexual confessions, they reaffirmed reformers' impulses to protect – and hence regulate – women's sexuality. One of the most unrelenting white slave rescuers was Clifford G. Roe, Assistant State Attorney in Illinois, who fervently believed "there was a gigantic slave trade in women," a "system of slavery" that had "grown to enormous proportions."[17] Roe stated that "sixty percent [of prostitutes] are led into it by some scheme or entrapped and sold," citing several cases he had experienced first hand in the courts.[18] Confessions of former white slaves, such as "A White Slave's Own Story," were often published by vigilance committees like Roe's or Bell's, and were often formidably persuasive narratives.[19] We can think of such testimonials – particularly those on the stage – as Foucauldian confessionals about sex whereby there is "a determination on the part of the agencies of power to hear it spoken about, and to cause it to speak through explicit articulation and endlessly accumulated detail."[20] Like Native American captivity confessions, these stories incited Bell's readers to war – not only, as his title suggests, on the white slave trade, but also on sex itself.

In addition to provoking its readers to a rhetorical war, white slave narratives also incited more discourse about white slavery. White slave tracts produced, in other words, the very phenomenon they claimed they were documenting. The 1914 *Report of the Commission for the Investigation of the White Slave Traffic, So-Called* in Massachusetts acknowledged that white slave tracts were creating yet more white slave testimonials:

> Every story of this kind has been thoroughly investigated, and either found to be a vague rumor ... or, in a few instances, imaginary occurrences explained by hysteria or actual malingering. Several of the stories were easily recognized versions of incidents in certain books or plays.[21]

In short, a discursive feedback loop had been established. And the stage, it turned out, would play a central role.

Joining the discursive battle on white slavery was the old warhorse Theodore Roosevelt, no longer President, but now serving as New York Police Commissioner. In true rugged, individualist fashion, he proposed that white slavers be whipped, as was the law in England. Declaring that white slavery was worse than murder, Roosevelt suggested that women's rights were in part to blame for this mess: "The women who preach late marriages are . . . making it difficult to better the standard of chastity."[22] As M. Joan McDermott and Sarah Blackstone have observed, comments like Roosevelt's sent the message "that women's sexuality should be controlled and that a lack of such controls would lead to disaster."[23] Because chastity was a requirement for how popular discourse understood the white slave, modern women were perceived as unwittingly placing themselves in jeopardy. The message that white slave discourse had generated was clear: keep your daughters and wives at home.

Not all Progressive reformers understood white slavery in the same way. Just as white slave rescuers and other sexual purity groups argued that there was a vast movement to capture and prostitute white women, there were others who disputed the white slave hysteria, as it became known. Virtually all studies from the period itself concluded that while there was evidence of *individual* cases of white slavery, no grand organized scheme existed, at least not as depicted by white slave hunters. The first substantial study by an American vice commission, The Committee of Fifteen, concluded in its 1902 report that although they had searched for proof of an international white slave ring, they could find "no trace of one."[24] Eight years later, the Rockefeller Grand Jury reported similar results, as did George J. Kneeland's classic study of prostitution from 1913, *Commercialized Prostitution in New York.*[25]

By 1913, cultural critics were publishing their doubts about white slavery. In his article "Is White Slavery Nothing More Than a Myth?" reformer A. W. Elliott emphatically denounced white slavery: "We frankly say that there never was a joke of more huge proportions perpetrated upon the American public than this white slave joke. There is scarcely a simmering of truth in the various stories of so-called white slavery."[26] Another article in the *New York Sun* in 1917 likewise denounced white slave rumors: "All around are heard lurid stories of organized traffic in women . . . New York never held fewer traffickers in women than it does now. Finally, in none of the many investigations to which New York has been subjected has there ever been unfolded straightforward proof that white slavery has been organized here."[27] While Emma Goldman did not dispute the existence of white slavery, she mocked moralists who positioned themselves as newly unearthing it: "Our reformers have suddenly made a great discovery – the white slave traffic ... How is it that an institution, known almost to every child should have been discovered so suddenly? How is it that this evil, known to all sociologists, should now be made such an important issue?"[28] The white slave "panic" was, as Goldman's irony reveals, a rhetorical and ideological construct. As a former prostitute, Madeleine, in her autobiography of the same title, made clear in 1919: "I do not know anything about the so-called white-slave trade, for the simple reason that no such thing exists."[29] What Madeline and Goldman both describe, in other words, is that prostitution is far more complex than the white slave discourse allowed.

In analyzing this discursive phenomenon, contemporary social historians have also concluded that the white slave panic was an ideological construct of the Progressive Era. Based on her extensive research into Progressive Era prostitution Rosen notes that it is unlikely that white slavery comprised more than 10 percent of all prostitution cases.[30] Connelly agrees that white slave narratives "reduced the problem of prostitution to the cardboard dimensions of a modern-day morality play, with beautiful country girls debauched by swarthy immigrants, lurid descriptions of brothels, and last-minute rescues from a fate worse than death. It was an Armageddon with the fate of American womanhood at stake."[31] Connelly is careful to temper his argument, however, with a claim that I wish to stress as well: there *were* instances of abduction and forced prostitution, as well as very real anxieties about country girls being taken advantage of in the urban sphere. To claim that the white slave scare was exaggerated is not to discount those cases, or the very real suffering those women endured. Yet it is important to note that the white slave panic created what Mary de Young calls "a reality of little substance," or a kind of cultural fairy tale.[32]

Given this historical debate regarding white slavery, then, how should we theorize the white slave? Kathleen Barry makes some headway in the right direction, writing, "female sexual slavery ... refers to international traffic in women and forced street prostitution taken together."[33] Barry here makes the leap that Progressive Era reformers did *not* – that is, she deconstructs the binary between the virginal white slave and the common streetwalker. Yet she fails to acknowledge that a woman could very well *choose* to be a prostitute. As Julia O'Connell Davidson notes, such an approach adopts "a zero-sum view of power as a 'commodity' possessed by the client (and/or third-party controller of prostitution) and exercised over prostitutes."[34] As the following pages reveal, not all prostitutes were power-less victims. At the same time, arguing that prostitutes and sex workers command total control over their trades also misses the mark. While such an approach endows prostitutes with the agency that they are deprived of in the victim model, it nonetheless obscures the real abuse and oppression that some prostitutes face. What is needed instead in analyzing the white slave problem is a model that acknowledges that multiple forms of oppression were brought to bear on prostitutes, just as there were various occasions for resistance to that repression. In Davidson's words, "there is no single, unitary source of power within prostitution that can be seized and wielded by third party, client, or prostitute. Rather, prostitution as a social practice is embedded in a particular set of social relations which produce a series of variable and interlocking constraints upon action."[35] White slavery must be understood within the intersecting discourses that constructed it, noting how the white slave signified differently in the diverse terrains in which she appeared. In the white slave drama of the period, she most often appears as a hapless victim, certainly, but she also materializes as brothel fighter, racial border-crosser, hunger-striker, woman-centered brothel-owner, and cunning suffragette.

Of the many "red light" plays, as they were also called, three discernable subgenres can be said to have emerged in the white slave tradition: country-girl white slave plays, urban white slave plays, and the opium-den and harem plays. The remaining part of this chapter explores each of them in more detail.

Country-girl white slaves

Among the most popular plotline for white slave dramas was the melodra-matic story of the country girl being seduced by a man from the city, who proposes marriage and takes her to the city for a bogus wedding. This charade is soon revealed once the girl is whisked away by the cadet and brought to the brothel (usually portrayed as an aunt's house), where she is kept captive. Such narratives portrayed the city as a dangerous urban jungle in juxtaposition to the peaceful countryside. David Burrell's popular novel *The Lure of the City* (1908) captured this anxiety with an emotional anthro-pomorphized chant: "This is the call of the city – the insatiable call of the city for new blood and fresh sinew to make the wheels go round. 'I am the city!' it says. 'Give! Give! Give me the strength of your farms and villages and towns! ... Give me your sons and your daughters!' ... The battle is on!"[36] Burgeoning migration from the country to the city, especially by young women entering the urban workforce, was a central source of Progressive Era anxiety. According to Connelly, "The cutting edge of the white-slave tracts was a question concerning the relationship between these two circumstances: what was happening to the American girl who struck out for the city?"[37] As the United States District Attorney in Chicago warned in 1910, "the best and the surest way for parents of girls in the country to protect them from the clutches of the white slaver is to keep them in the country."[38] The country girl came to stand in for a national yearning for a pastoral ideal that had faded away; in the midst of this mourning, she also signified as especially vulnerable. "Our country girls," Florence Mabel Dedrick wrote in 1910, "are in more danger from white slave traders than city girls" because they are "more truthful, perfectly innocent and unsuspecting."[39] Not uncoincidentally, perfectly unsuspecting heroines make for great melodrama.

Plays like *White Slavery* by Franklyn Casswell (1911), *Why Girls Go Wrong* by W. C. Herman (1915), *Her Road to Ruin* by Fred K. Melville, *Dangers of Innocence; or the Lure of the City* by Charles A. Warren, and *Bess From Peaceful Valley, or The White Slave Traffic*, all portrayed the abduction of a country girl by a slick city cadet. Sometimes the country girl is lured to a false employment bureau in New York, like in Hal Reid's *The Lights of Broadway: or, Breach of Promise* (1905). In all such narratives, the country girl is saved, usually by a young man from back home, and order is restored once she returns home.

Little Lost Sister, by Arthur James Pegler and Edward Rose (1913), was perhaps the best-known country-girl white slave melodrama. A young unsuspecting woman from the country is lured to the big city, where she is betrayed by the cadet posing as a beau. Advertised as a "great white slave play," the plot offered more than the usual country bumpkin tale. The third act featured salacious and sensational scenes from the underworld. As Charles Washburn mused in his account of prostitution in Chicago, "Another crack of the whip; another piercing scream from the off-stage heroine. How could the play fail?"[40] And, indeed, it did not fail; the play toured regionally for three years.[41] As the *Cincinnati Commercial Tribune* noted in 1914, "Of all the many and sundry white-slave plays, *Little Lost Sister* has been the best accepted and most enduring. One reason for this is that it deals with the great vice in a fearless yet wholesome manner ..."[42] It is precisely this last observation that resonates with the white slave genre: while it was salacious in topic, white slave dramaturgy was also intensely regulated.

In yet another form of the country-girl white slave play, a girl is fooled and abducted by a madam posing as a relative. In Elizabeth Robins' unpublished play *My Little Sister* (adapted from her 1912 best-selling novel *Where Are You Going To?*), two sisters journey to see their long-lost aunt, whom they have never met. In a state of interminable naiveté, the girls meet the madam at the train station, travel back to her bordello (which they think is her estate), and do not suspect something is awry until it is far too late. One sister escapes with the assistance of a kind customer, but cannot remember where the brothel is. Robins also takes a stab at police complicity with the sexual underworld, by showing that the boys in blue know precisely where all the brothels are. Given their corruption, and the sister's poor memory, rescue comes too late; the abducted sister has already been transported to Asia. Along with other prominent white slave narratives of the 1913 season, *My Little Sister* tapped into the already substantial anxieties over international white slave trafficking. The fifth International Congress on the White Slave Traffic was held in London in 1913, just as Robins's serialization of *My Little Sister* appeared in *McClure's Magazine*.[43] Though *My Little Sister* was never produced, some critics maintained that Robins was influential in bringing discussion about white slavery into the mainstream.[44] And because audiences did not quickly tire of the subject, a film version of *My Little Sister* appeared in 1919.

Urban white slaves

A second, less frequent, sort of white slave play featured the capture of a young woman already living in the city. Often, an impoverished girl lets her judgment slip out of desperation. For instance, George Scarborough's *The Lure* (1913), which I discuss in detail in chapter 7, portrays the capture of an innocent working girl from a poor tenement housing project. Similarly, in the short-run "underworld play," *The Traffic* (1913) by Rachael Marshall and Oliver Bailey, a poverty-stricken worker in a shirtwaist factory named Agnes is seduced by "a professional 'cadet' of the dance hall variety" and set up in a brothel.[45] When her fourteen-year-old, consumptive sister is also abducted, a police raid ensues and Agnes shoots the culprit. Although exonerated by a court, Agnes discovers reform is not so easy. She "resolutely pushes impossible respectability aside," asking the audience for compassion in a prologue to the play.[46] Two things make *The Traffic* unusual: first, it is one of three plays in the white slave genre penned by a woman (in this case coauthored); and second, it portrayed the interior of a brothel – a point to which I shall return later in the chapter. Like *Mrs Warren's Profession, The Traffic* "prove[d] the claim that girls receiving less than a living wage are easily lured, and often forced[,] into leading a life of shame," as the *Los Angeles Rounder* put it.[47] Running for just eight performances in New York, *The Traffic* may have suffered for its novelties more than it benefited, for white slave narratives which challenged prevailing ideologies were doomed to failure.

The Girl Without a Chance by E. Whitney Collins (1915) shows another popular urban myth: the drugging and capture of young women who ventured into public urban spaces. Though lowbrow establishments like music halls or concert saloons had long been marked as questionable spaces for respectable upper-class girls, *The Girl Without a Chance* portrays respectable sites as perilous too. As one character explains: "Why, they are grabbing sixteen year olds right off the front door steps. They have got needle gangs working in the big theatres."[48] The drugging of young women was considered part of a systematic abduction process, a process that was elaborately illustrated in Roe's *Horrors of the White Slave Trade*. According to one cautionary quote: "Having taken the drugged potion she is now incapable of self-control and is easily led to her ruin. Awaking she will find herself an inmate of a house of shame."[49] While individual cases of drugging must have taken place, such urban myths took on a larger cultural force, weighing upon, and often restricting, young women's freedom in the public domain.

Eugene Walter's unpublished play *The Knife* (1917) put a new spin on this tired story by portraying a doctor who kills white slavers not only to rid society of them, but also to harvest their organs for research. A kind of urban vigilante, the Doctor explains his logic to his victims as follows: "You're [sic] souls are rotten but your bones are whole, and I am going to use them."[50] Even though some audiences were tiring of the ubiquitous white slave formula, *The Knife* was successful because, as Channing Pollock of the *Green Book Magazine* noted, "it has all the appeal of *The Lure* – without its prurience – and the speed and nervous tension of *The Conspiracy*."[51] Arthur Hornblow of *Theatre Magazine* called *The Knife* "the most engrossing melodrama of the season."[52] To take the "bloodcurdling plot," as the *Sun* called it, seriously was not the point. Like all good thrillers, *The Knife* was about the lure of the grotesque and the excitement of melodrama. "You want to leave the scene," the review continued, "but remain rooted to the spot, fascinated by horror and the repulsiveness of it." Though *The Knife* was admittedly melodramatic, audiences seemed to be drawn to the play "that has the old Eugene Walter punch."[53] They were equally drawn to its film version in 1918. Walter understood what audiences wanted: a glimpse into the brothel itself, which, just a few years earlier, was a tabooed space for the stage. As the reviewer for the *Nation* wrote, "what is counted upon to hold the audience is the glimpse into a white-slave den disguised as the rooms of a fortune teller."[54] Eerily predicting contemporary urban legends of organ theft, *The Knife*, long since forgotten in theatre history, goes beyond the predictable melodramatic tale. Well-written and suspenseful, it is one of the best extant white slave plays, and should be included in any critical reception of Walter's work.

Opium den and harem white slaves

A third type of white slave play focused on the fascination with opium dens and harems. A hangover from the Victorian obsession with *chinoiserie*, they recycled elements of nineteenth-century opium-war plays and featured an array of stereotypical Asian characters, usually playing opium smugglers, gang members, and the ruthless abductors of white women.[55] In the simplest terms, these plays enacted the dual fascination and repulsion with the Orient that Edward Said has characterized as orientalism.[56] As Edward Ziter has shown, miscegenist fantasies of the Orient had long played on the Victorian stage and had often dovetailed with imperialist agendas. So it comes as no surprise that the portrayal of the Orient in Progressive Era white slave plays intersected with rising anti-Chinese immigration sentiments in the United States. These Asian characters, representing the very worst stereotyping, are often not even given names. In *Dealers in White Women* by Martin Hurley (1904), the central white slaver, a doctor, is described reductively as a "Hindoo," who runs "an opium joint in Chinatown."[57] Virtually all of these characters speak in broken dialect, such as One Lung in *Queen of Chinatown*: "Me no pay; me no lose," and are almost universally portrayed as kings and queens of drug dynasties, as in the *King of the Opium Ring* by Chas. E. Blaney and Chas. A. Taylor (1900).[58] In addition to being portrayed as members of the opium underworld, Asian characters were depicted as successful businessmen, thus revealing the anxiety that Chinese immigrants were achieving the American dream too quickly, in spite of the Chinese Exclusion Act of

1882. All of these elements come together in the central character from *Slaves of the Opium Ring: The Opium Smugglers of 'Frisco or The Crimes of a Beautiful Opium Fiend* by Billy Getthore. As one character introduces him, "That's Lee Bock Dong. Prince of Opium Smugglers – he has a dozen wives and is the richest Chinaman in 'Frisco."[59] Sometimes Asian gangs are portrayed as at war with one another, as in *The Slave Girl: 20 Minutes in Frisco's Chinatown* by Walter Montague (1913). As Chinatown Mag says, "Stealing slave girls is what causes all these killings in Chinatown, and from the looks of things [they] will be at each others throats."[60] The stealing of white women, we can conclude, is so disruptive that it unravels not only white families, but also the very fabric of the Asian community.

Like country-girl white slave plays, opium-den dramas featured mostly white victims. The insistence on white women is particularly egregious, given that white slave hunters such as Roe had written extensively about "the yellow slave traffic" in the United States. "Deplorable and disgraceful as is the white slave traffic in the Orient," he wrote, "the yellow slave traffic in our own country is infinitely more disgraceful."[61] On occasion, the central white slave at first *appears* Asian, but is eventually revealed, by the play's end, to be white after all. In such plays the highly touted rescue scene involved not only the woman's sexual, but also racial, purity.

One of the earliest plays, *Queen of Chinatown* by Joseph Jarrow (1899), is probably the only drama of this period set in Manhattan's Chinatown (others are predictably set in California). When a beautiful Mission teacher goes missing, forces descend upon Hop Lee's gambling room and opium den, where the girl has been hidden. As a publicity poster advertises, this play is about "a daring abduction and vain attempt at rescue." On another level, the play is fueled by thinly veiled masculinist and eugenicist desires. As Harry, the brother of the abducted girl, puts it: "I want to enter all the opium joints and if possible, I want to penetrate even the houses of Chinamen living with white women" (1.9). His urge to "penetrate" and "enter" these sexualized spaces betrays his desire for the racial Other as well as for forbidden sexual fruits, but it also reveals precisely the opposite: the anti-miscegenist and eugenicist desire to protect "American" blood from Asian contamination. These impulses are underscored by Mary's sale to another Chinese man, Tong-Sing. With such severe stakes, Harry eventually rescues his sister, but not without the help and self-sacrifice of Beezie, the Queen of Chinatown, the familiar hooker-with-a-heart-of-gold.

One of the longest-running white slave plays of the Progressive Era (it ran for 680 performances in 1918) was the smash hit *East is West.*

Although in many ways *East is West* mimicked the traditional white slave tract, it was among the very first to portray the delicate issue of interracial desire. The lead character, Ming Toy, is rescued from a Chinese white slave den characterized as a "love boat whose proprietor sells 'Sing-song Girls' to whomever wants them."[62] While the modern American *Love Boat* "promises something for everyone," this Eastern love boat is clearly not "an open smile on a friendly shore." Rather, *East is West*'s plot reveals both desire and antipathy for the exotic Other. Now in San Francisco, Ming Toy undergoes a Pygmalion-like transformation, but rather than erasing her class markings, she unlearns her Asianness (facilitated, as we later learn, by her true racial identity). Put on the auction block once again in San Francisco, Ming Toy is rescued by an American, Benson, who takes her home to be his sister's maid. When Ming Toy and Benson fall in love, there is, as *Theatre Magazine* put it, "a perilous racial problem to solve."[63] Just when the romance raises the specter of miscegenation, it is revealed that Ming Toy "is a perfectly good white girl, who, when a baby, was kidnapped by Chinese bandits from her American missionary father and her Spanish mother."[64] Passing was never so easy, nor so unbelievable, as the reviewer in *Theatre Magazine* commented: "Would you believe it, the maiden stolen in her childhood, wasn't Chinese at all? Italian blood accounted for her exotic type."[65] That this reviewer mistakenly calls the mother Italian rather than Spanish is quite telling: in the white slave world, nonwhites are marked in the impossible space of representation, conflated as racial Others, always in relation to whiteness, always less than whiteness. While *East is West* purports to be "a tale dealing with love between brown and white," as the *Illustrated London News* observed, "any problem of mixed marriage is conveniently shelved."[66] Made into a film in 1922 and again in 1930 (with Lupe Velez in yellow face), *East is West* raised the possibility of interracial desire, but not without disavowing true border crossings.

Some opium-den plays modified the basic plot by taking the love boat story to exotic locales. In transposing the brothel to a harem in the Orient, playwrights sufficiently distanced audiences from the New York underworld – a mimetic space that proved controversial to stage even as late as 1913. At the same time, the harem was a familiar discursive site to stage imperialist and sexual conquests. "Harem imagery was used," as Ziter notes, "to describe not only the relation between white men and brown women but also the relation between white nations and brown peoples."[67] In *Escaped From the Harem*, for instance, the second and third acts take place in the Prince Agaza's palace in India. In an unusual twist, an American girl,

Mabel, has been lured onto a ship by another (ruined) woman, Cassy, and whisked away to the Prince's harem in India. Mabel escapes with the assistance of a circus owner, who takes her back to America, but the trauma of her escape through the jungles of India amongst "natives" has left her with amnesia. In a bizarre ending which exudes poetic justice, Mabel is rescued by her fiancé, father, and blind sister, while Cassy is trampled by elephants as she tries to get away.

In *Slaves of the Orient* (1909), Theodore Kremer set his harem story in Egypt.[68] Kremer was a popular writer of melodrama, and *Slaves of the Orient* offered all of the "thrills, situations and climaxes," that one would expect from this genre, not to mention "trouble [that] is rampant,"[69] a real camel on stage, and "real Orientals."[70] In addition to the problematic way in which people and animals were staged as exotica, *Slaves of the Orient* contrasted the "barbaric" nature of Abou Hammed, overseer of his harem, with Tom Carter, an American whose battleship has docked in this Egyptian port. Carter, like all heroes in these plays, defends the slave's honor, proclaiming, "It is the duty of every American to protect a lady when in trouble."[71] Tom recovers Zuleka, who was "taken captive by a band of Arabs and sold into slavery," and takes her back to America. When Hammed boards the ship to recapture Zuleka, she resists, stating, "Queen of the harem I never shall be. I am now the wife of Tom Carter, a wife, blessed with the holy bonds of matrimony."[72] Insofar as white actresses usually portrayed these roles in yellow or brown face, "the pleasure of the theatrical harem (at least for the male audience)," Ziter observes of Victorian dramas, "was the opportunity to imagine white European women assuming the position of the compliant and sensual Eastern woman."[73] If this was so in the nineteenth century, it was even more exaggerated during Progressive Era theatre. *Slaves of the Orient* moreover sutures female subservience to the ideology of nationalism and empire building. Its nativist leanings pleased audiences favorably. According to the *New York Dramatic Mirror*, "The gallery arose and yelled at each frequent pulling of the Star Spangled Banner, and shrieked with joy upon the numerous tributes paid to Christianity."[74] With the triumph of the stars and the stripes, *Slaves of the Orient* demonstrates that the harem, like the opium den, proved an ideal site to enact sexual and imperialist fantasies.

As late as 1926, harem and opium-den white slave plays were still popular. One of the raciest and most popular of such plays was John Colton's *Shanghai Gesture*, which ran for 206 performances and featured Florence Reed and John Barrymore. One publicity flier boasted: "*The*

Shanghai Gesture is the most successful drama in the history of the modern theatre. It has broken all records of gross receipts for non-musical shows."[75] Made into a movie in 1941 (starring Gene Tierney and Victor Mature), *Shanghai Gesture* proved that a Chinese brothel, complete with girls in gilded cages, still captivated American audiences. However, it was not uncontroversial and the film was rejected 32 times by the Hays censorship office before it was finally granted approval. These opium-den dramas, then, like all Orientalist narratives, are about East and West. They are about white men controlling, hunting, and rescuing women while simultaneously policing national and sexual borders. But they are also about penetrating those boundaries, if only momentarily. The danger of the opium smoke is not so much that it creates addiction, or that it sparks desire, but that it clouds the rigid parameters of history, nation, race, and gender.

7

Brothel anyone? Laundering the 1913–14 white slave season

Going to the theatres these nights is like going slumming.[1]
Theatre critic Charles Darnton, 1913

The tumultuous Broadway season of 1913–14 was marked by contradictions as perhaps no other. As James Metcalfe, theatre reviewer for *Life Magazine*, mused, "There are white slavers and white slavers. One kind the law can deal with. The other kind lives on in topic."[2] But, in fact, the law dealt with both kinds: the real white slavers hunted by the budding FBI and the mythical kind who made nightly appearances on the New York stage. In September 1913 *The Lure* and *The Fight* were shut down by the New York police and became embroiled in high-profile obscenity cases. Given this precedent, everyone was watching *Ourselves* by Rachel Crothers when it premiered on November 13. Many observers felt that *Ourselves* would determine the future of the brothel genre. Astonishingly, *Ourselves*, the only white slave play penned by a woman that was ever produced, escaped censorship. But the issue was far from being settled. Just weeks after *Ourselves* began what would be a modest and unremarkable run, *The House of Bondage*, adapted and produced by actress/manager Cecil Spooner, became engulfed in a dramatic censorship battle. A casualty of intense regulation, the play underwent forced revision, which led it to flop after just eight performances. What are we to make of these disparate receptions?

These four white slave plays provide insight into a much larger phenomenon that found expression not only on Broadway, but also in countless theatres throughout the United States during the Progressive Era. As *Theatre Magazine* proclaimed in 1913, the Broadway season that year was one defined by theatre censorship.[3] And while the pages to follow trace those censorship battles, it is important to speak about censorship in

tandem with the production of sexuality (literally and symbolically) on the
stage. As the performance histories of the white slave dramas demonstrate,
representations of white slavery on the stage were highly regulated. Yet,
while some were censored and eventually laundered, others were left largely
intact. Indeed, dozens of white slave plays did go uncensored and ran night
after night on Broadway. In spite of the seemingly haphazard production
histories of *The Lure*, *The Fight*, *Ourselves*, and *The House of Bondage*, what
these four white slave plays demonstrate are the limits of staging nontraditional sexualities, feminist politics, as well as the brothel as mise-en-scène.
Yet they also show us unexpected possibilities. The battles surrounding the
white slave play were, therefore, much like the sexuality debates in culture
at large: struggles over which ideologies would be produced as "truth."

Traditional white slave fare? The controversy surrounding *The Lure*

> There is no doubt that girls are decoyed into houses of prostitution, for
> I have known of at least fifty cases of the kind myself.[4]
> Vincent Serrano, leading actor from *The Lure*

Until the opening of *The Lure*, no one had heard of George Scarborough, a
special agent investigating white slavery in Chicago. Deeply moved by one
tragic white slave story, he wrote *The Lure* in just eight days. Scarborough
sent the play to Stanley Finch, Special US Commissioner for the
Suppression of the White Slave Traffic, in late April 1913. Especially
pleased with the characterization of the cadet, Finch's only criticism was
that Scarborough should emphasize "the utter depravity of such creatures."[5]
By May, Scarborough was ready to present the script to Lee Shubert, who
accepted it and put it into production immediately.

  The Lure's plot weaves together several strands of the conventional white
slave categories: a country girl who ventures to the city to earn enough to
purchase medicine for her ill mother. The daughter, Sylvia, works in a
department store, earning only six dollars a week – well below the poverty
standard.[6] Sylvia decides to seek extra work at night to earn more cash. Like
most white slave heroines, she does not suspect that her job interview is
with a madam inside a brothel. Meanwhile, Bob, a "White Slave
Specialist," contacts the family because he is hunting down, as he puts it,
"recruiting officers for the scarlet militia."[7] True to melodramatic form, *The
Lure* advances a love story between Sylvia and Bob.

  Act 3, the controversial act that was ultimately censored, takes place
inside the brothel. Even though Sylvia has been tricked into wearing

prostitute garb and sits nervously awaiting her customer, what this act is really about is sexual innocence. Miraculously, however, Bob enters in disguise while on a mission to save another white slave. Upon seeing Sylvia, Bob suspects that she has already ruined herself and laments, "Oh, hell – I fell for something that had already fallen" (3.6–7). But Sylvia tells Bob that her desperation to save her mother's life led her into the clutches of madam Kate. Her display of virtuous self-sacrifice helps convince Bob that she is still a virgin. He forgives her, saying, "Thank God – the halo's back" (3.8). *The Lure*, in short, reinforces the notion that virtuous women's sexuality needs both rescue and regulation.

The Lure's representation of another white slave, Nell Jordan, further underscores this view of female sexuality. As originally written, Nell appears "half denuded, with her hair hanging down in tangles; her face is bruised, eyes are blackened and blood trickles down her face" (3.19). McDermott and Blackstone have suggested that such semi-nude scenes were found pornographic by audiences, offering a voyeuristic glimpse of the underworld.[8] While *The Lure* did in fact draw upon sexual codes in representing the brothel interior (a point to which I will return shortly), the leading actresses resisted pornographic citationality in their performances of white slaves. Significantly, none of the reviews for *The Lure* referred to nudity or revealing clothing in commenting on Nell, Sylvia, or madam Kate (though some critics were shocked about the transgressing of other social taboos, such as Kate drinking absinthe). Moreover, production photos show Nell (the white slave whom the stage directions suggest should be "half nude") completely clothed in a long-sleeved white frock (see figure 7), perhaps a nightgown, while Kate appears in a beautifully beaded, albeit low-cut, dress. Unlike *Sapho*, where Nethersole's performing body became the central site of controversy, none of the actresses' performances in *The Lure* were found shocking at all, not even before the brothel scene was censored. In fact, the lack of discourse on the white slave's body in brothel dramas seems initially puzzling. Yet, a likely explanation can be found in the symbolic force of white slave discourse itself. Because the white slave was so carefully desexualized throughout white slave narratives, the actual depiction of a half-denuded character as sexual or even pornographic simply became impossible. The white slave could only signify sexual purity.

If the white slave character was rendered sexless, there were nonetheless other volatile aspects to the script. Chief among them was *The Lure*'s unfavorable portrayal of the police. Though this was not the first time that police and politicians had been portrayed as participants in organized

Figure 7. Lola May and Mary Nash as two white slaves in the censored brothel scene from George Scarborough's *The Lure*. Photo courtesy of the New York Public Library.

prostitution, a claim that prostitution studies and vice commission reports were beginning to substantiate, it was the first time that the police reacted to being portrayed negatively in a brothel drama. The second act of *The Lure* referenced the political scandal of 1913, which forced the ruling Democratic Party headquarters (Tammany Hall) out of power. Indeed, police corruption had reached staggering proportions in New York, and by 1913 there were even regular articles on police corruption, including an exposé series in *McClure's Magazine*.[9] As Parke F. Hanley pointed out in 1913, "white slavery and the police always have been linked in investigations."[10] However, New York's own former Police Commissioner General Bingham, who had himself been exposed in a scandal involving bribery and sexual vice, applauded *The Lure* for its disclosure of corruption: "This play presents a wonderful moral lesson. I know these conditions are true and so does everybody in police circles. I wonder how much longer New Yorkers will stand for the white slave trade?"[11]

On the heels of these numerous investigations, articles, and editorials, *The Lure*'s depiction of Captain Jim Wilson was a serious rendering of a corrupt official. In act 4, white slave hunter Bob implicates the Captain for his complicity in organized vice: "You know, the best way to break up a white slave gang is to find out if there's a politician behind the house" (4.10). The complicity of politicians and the police with sexual vice is one controversial theme that several other white slave plays echoed after the stormy opening of *The Lure* and *The Fight*. As we shall see, the controversy would end, and the plays would continue, but only after producers Shubert and Harris conceded to launder *The Lure* and *The Fight* by washing out the so-called offensive scenes.

Although some social purity reformers, members of the clergy, and the police strongly objected to *The Lure*, support from audiences who saw the play could not have been more resounding. Many civic leaders were among those who supported *The Lure*, including "Judge Warren W. Foster, District Attorney Whitman and Justice Gerard, the new Ambassador to Germany."[12] Approximately 600 voting slips were passed out to audiences of *The Lure* on September 6, asking viewers to check a box for either "I approve" or "I disapprove." According to the *New York Times*, "Ninety-eight per cent of the audience approved of the play."[13] There was a sense that *The Lure* had succeeded where *Mrs Warren's Profession* had failed in representing prostitution on the stage (though Bernard Shaw's play had also won the audience vote in a similar audience survey). The *New York Dramatic Mirror* reported the "marked enthusiasm" of opening night, reflecting that "times have changed and we applaud that from which we shrunk in *Mrs Warren's Profession* a few years ago."[14]

At first glance, then, *The Lure* seems standard white slave fare, a melodrama that reinscribed normative white slave ideology while reifying traditional gender norms and sexuality. And, to be sure, it was that in part. If that were *only* the case, however, *The Lure* would not have been shut down by the police; nor would such a view explain why the play ultimately won approval from high-ranking government officials while at the same time winning over radical suffragettes. In fact, *The Lure* appealed to those both from the left and the right precisely because it both reinforced and subverted classical white slave iconography.

Despite the fact that *The Lure* offers much in terms of traditional white slave fare, there is a significant rupture with the formula in act 2. In a controversial scene between the white slave, Sylvia, and the madam, Kate, Sylvia actually *chooses* to become a prostitute when she realizes she has no other option if she wants to save her mother's life. More than this, their dialogue reveals a sympathetic treatment of prostitution, a rare moment in American drama. In contrast to typical white slave tales, then, *The Lure* reveals that women turn to prostitution out of economic desperation. As Kate puts it, "When a woman's up against it like I was – and *like you* are – there's just – *one – way*" (2.17–18; original emphasis). While Kate is the villain of this melodrama, she hints at what Kitty Warren of Bernard Shaw's *Mrs Warren's Profession* makes explicit: economic injustice, not a mythical immigrant captor, forces women into prostitution. Since the sensational American premiere of *Mrs Warren's Profession* in 1905, this was one of the first scenes between a madam and soon-to-be prostitute seen on the American stage. Indeed, prostitution is given unusual sympathy in *The Lure*. Though the Police Captain expresses the dominant cultural view that condemns prostitutes, stating: "Coming voluntarily, the girl ain't entitled to any sympathy – this is no place for sympathy, no how," it is Kate who has the last word, replying: "It's the place women need it the most" (2.25). These lines were apparently not censored from the production.

Because of such ruptures in an otherwise conventional white slave tale, *The Lure* was embraced by leading reformers and women's groups. Support from women led to an extraordinary gathering of around eight hundred suffragettes who held a rally outside The Maxine Elliott Theatre on October 12, 1913. The following influential women all spoke: Dr. Anna Shaw, President of the National Woman's Suffrage Association; Harriet Stanton Blatch, President of the Women's Political Union; Mary Nash, the actress who played Sylvia; and actress Olga Nethersole. Suffragettes saw *The Lure* as an opportunity not only to speak about women's sexuality but also to lobby for the vote. The *New York Times* wryly remarked, "Mrs. Blatch did not forget to prescribe 'votes for women' as the cure for the social evil. A jury of women, she thought, would be the best play censors," suggesting it was unsavory to mix politics with the morally higher ground of reform.[15] These women, however, saw the two struggles as inextricably connected.

At the rally, Olga Nethersole gave an impassioned description of her ordeal during the *Sapho* obscenity trial fourteen years earlier, and asked her audience to engage themselves in the larger struggle for women's rights: "I want to ask you to go next Monday night to hear Mrs. Pankhurst and give a hearty cheer for the little woman who has had the moral courage to voluntarily starve herself for a cause which represents the future welfare of the race and the betterment of conditions for future generations."[16] Mrs. Pankhurst's presence at *The Lure* on October 22 created a media buzz. Most of the press focused on Pankhurst's controversial politics rather than on her response to the play. For example, Pankhurst was described by the *New York Times* as: "the militant suffragette leader of England" and "a stalwart Amazon."[17] One editorial implored "this old lady to confine her riots, harangues, hunger strikes, and anarchy to the United Kingdom" and suggested that if she was found not guilty for her politics that she could be certified as insane.[18] But Pankhurst did have something to say about *The Lure*. After the second act, she addressed the audience: "I think the public is to be congratulated that the stage has at last awakened to its mission as a factor in public education and is presenting the sordid truths of life in a courageous fashion."[19] Unfortunately, the press not only attacked the messenger, but also now the message. The *New York Times* looked down upon any "woman of good character" who involved herself in "such filthy stuff."[20] Unlike their more respectable society sisters, suffragettes were unwelcome participants in this debate. Yet, in spite of such admonishments, suffragettes kept their support for the play.

If *The Lure* advanced a typical melodrama with white slave victims and burly heroes, it also offered, if only temporarily, other possibilities. As the suffragettes' support demonstrates, even conventional white slave fare offered scenes that contained a disruptive political change. Scattered throughout the play, such momentary ruptures clarify the pleasures – and perceived dangers – of the text as experienced by its opponents and supporters. In the midst of this controversy, *The Lure's* future was tied to the opening of another white slave play: *The Fight*.

The Fight: Censored brothel interiors and the female fighter

The controversy of *The Lure* was swiftly grafted onto the premiere of Bayard Veiller's *The Fight*, which "stirred up a veritable whirlwind of protest" just two weeks later.[21] In his memoir, *The Fun I've Had*, Veiller remembered *The Fight* as "a pretty bad play."[22] Yet, this characterization greatly underestimates his drama's strengths. *The Fight* is better written, more innovative, and more politically risky than *The Lure*. This may have been why so much was censored from the text and why *The Fight* was, to use Veiller's words, "ill-fated," running for only half as long as *The Lure*.[23] Its production history – and eventual revision – shows how the stage became a space for resistance – if only for a few moments before the police chief blew his whistle.

The Fight's leading female character, Jane Thomas, stands out among the array of conventional female protagonists usually seen in the white slave drama. Veiller created what the *New York Sun* called "an impossible heroine," replacing the traditional rescuer with an articulate, intelligent, and strong woman.[24] There are very few white slave dramas, in fact, with a female lead who is not herself a white slave, madam, or mother (Rachel Crothers's *Ourselves* is a notable exception, as I explain below). In creating an active female protagonist, Veiller therefore subverted classic white slave iconography, suggesting that women could be active rather than passive agents in prostitution discourse and, indeed, effect change. The evolution of the play's working titles, from *Big Sister* to *Standing Pat* to *The Fight*, also signals Veiller's increasing investment in an active female lead.

Jane, who is running for mayor of her namesake town, Thomastown, and who is a banker by trade, is scoffed at by men for jumping into politics. Her brother-in-law, Edward, remarks, "Nobody wants to marry her now. A woman politician! Huh! Why she's making the whole town a joke, that's what she's doing" (1.3). While Jane's mother is supportive of her career, in 1913 the prospect of women entering politics was on the public mind, as several states had recently adopted legislation allowing women's suffrage. Indeed, *The Fight* is set in Colorado, where women had already won the right to vote in state elections, a right they would not exercise at the national level until 1920.

As invested as *The Fight* is in women's suffrage, the play oscillates between advocating progressive and normative values. Jane is an unusual mixture of independence and traditionalism. On the one hand she has achieved autonomy by running the family bank for five years since her father's death. Her work as a banker shapes her identity. As she puts it, "I'm not a lady – I'm just a business woman" (1.25). On the other hand, Jane often checks her more liberal remarks with conservative afterthoughts. In response to Dr. Root's claim that "you're letting business and politics take the place of a family," Jane first replies, "Oh, no." She then counters, "You don't really think I want to hold office? Don't you suppose I'm like other women, that I want a husband and children? Why, Doc, I'm twenty-eight years old, I've a right to my babies and I want 'em" (1.19). Later in the first act, a similar construction occurs. Jane's opponent Jimmie Callahan quips, "I don't like women mixin' in politics." At first, Jane replies, "women mix in nearly everything now," but then she admits: "I don't like to see women

smoke either" (1.26). Jane's straight-laced rejection of smoking verifies that
she could never be mistaken for a radical suffragette and thus makes her
more appealing to moderates of the time.

Overall, however, Jane is a strong, intelligent character who is a match
for her male rivals. In addition to being a banker, Jane has entered politics
because none of the male civic leaders have addressed the recent problem
of prostitution. Vice and complicity have gotten the best of Thomastown,
and Jane is not going to allow it to continue. As she defiantly tells her
colleagues:

> JANE. [Yo]u tell me your town's all right. How in God's name could it
> be worse? . . . I want to guard all the children and all the young
> girls and that's the reason I tell you your town's all wrong and if
> there's anything in the world a woman can do to make it right,
> I'm going to do it. I won't give up! I won't deal with you! I'm
> going to fight! I'm going to fight! (1.44–45)

In spite of its melodramatic excess, Jane's speech echoes the battle cry of the
women's suffrage movement. Though she displays a motherly desire to
protect children, she also promises to combat failing patriarchal structures.
In spite of the inconsistencies in her character, Jane remains an interesting
contrast to the tradition of women as either victim or villain in the white
slave tract.

Veiller's female heroine, played by Margaret Wycherly, Veiller's wife,
was a new character for the old white slave tale. As the *Stage* put it, "*The
Fight* is uncommonly interesting. This may be due to the fact that a woman
is the personage chiefly concerned."[25] And insofar as Jane subverted the
binary between victim and rescuer – and, indeed, between male and female,
between public and private – her character was one of the most polemical.
The *Morning Telegram* bluntly wrote that Jane Thomas was "almost too
good to be true."[26] The *New York Times* agreed that Jane's character was
unbelievable: "One may reasonably smile at the dubious astuteness of the
young woman candidate, who, with triumph in her grasp, succumbs to the
feminine weakness and talks a bit too much."[27] While the *New York Tribune*
dwelled on the "improbabilities, and even impossibilities," of a plot with a
strong female character, it found the play "good entertainment none the
less."[28] The *New York Sun* likewise characterized Jane's character as "in the
realm of fantasy," but conceded: "Not a human being in the audience
thought for a second of the improbability of all the episodes by which the

heroine confounded, with nothing more unusual than a telephone at her elbow, all the powers of evil arrayed against her. The spectators delighted in her triumphs . . ."[29] In spite of the fact that many other feminist aspects of *The Fight* were casualties of the blue pencil, it seems clear that Jane's strong character remained.

Other critics praised *The Fight* precisely for its feminist politics. Clayton Hamilton from the *Bookman* wrote, "the main theme of *The Fight* is not the white slave traffic but another topic of greater importance to the public – namely, the potential influence of women in politics . . ."[30] Another reviewer claimed, "*The Fight* would come close to being the first real woman suffrage play."[31] While this was certainly not the first suffrage play, the reviewer's focus on "real" implies that it was among the first to be written by a mainstream male author. Indeed, the *New York Press* noted: "It is the best argument for woman's suffrage that we have heard, and the theatre should be packed with [this] party alone if all the women [who] marched in the parade are still in town."[32]

And suffragettes did fill the theatres. A month into the run of *The Fight*, twenty-four women's organizations from New York were invited to view the show and report their findings. At the behest of producer Henry B. Harris, these women were to act "as an unofficial board of censorship" whose recommendations Harris meant to take seriously; he "offered to change any line or eliminate any character if they found it offensive."[33] They did not. As with *The Lure*, an impressive group of women went on the record in support of *The Fight*, including leading suffragettes.[34] These women not only championed the play for their own politics but also became part of the production themselves, running the show one night. In an unusual display of support, these women conducted "everything, from the selling of the tickets to the stage management" by "installing members of their party in the box office, inside the theatre as ushers, and filling every position back of the scenes except that of the electrician."[35] Working literally behind the scenes, the suffragettes' labors demonstrate more than mere support for the play, but rather an intense collaboration of politics and the stage.

In addition to presenting feminist themes, *The Fight* was controversial for its critique of political corruption and its portrayal of the brothel. In act 2, a corrupt senator employs Pearl, the ironically named madam, to procure a white slave for him. Having paid $500 for a young girl, senator Woodford enters the room to have his way with her only to realize that she is his own daughter. One source described this scene as "so shocking that everyone

shuddered. It is hoped that this scene can be cut out of the play . . ."[36] The
New York Sun reported, "altogether this was the most unfortunate part of
The Fight."[37] If this scene portraying "the loathsome crime of incest," as the
Morning Telegram put it, was shocking, it was not altogether unfamiliar.[38]
The Fight borrowed some of its plot from two other white slave plays
produced earlier in the season: *Any Night* by Edward Ellis and *Tiger* by
Witter Bynner. As Clayton Hamilton wrote, "he merely repeated the too
familiar narrative of an unexpected encounter in a brothel between a father
and his own daughter."[39]

Veiller's plot was familiar for other reasons. According to the *Globe*, it
"happen[ed] to be founded upon an actuality recorded in the newspapers
not long ago."[40] Veiller defended his second act by reminding New Yorkers
of its proximity to real life:

> They say that the second act of *The Fight* was unnecessary. Let me tell
> you that within four doors of Fifth Avenue in the neighborhood of
> Forty-seventh Street is a house of prostitution where the women are
> dressed as nurses. Within the last two weeks two girls have been decoyed
> there by advertisements in a prominent morning paper for nurses. And
> this is the paper that is attacking us so much.[41]

While Veiller revised his sentiments about the second act thirty years later
in his memoir, at the time of writing the play, at least, he believed in the
brothel's poignancy as a mimetic space.

Although this scene resonated with audiences because of its borrowed
plot, it also reminded them of fraudulent Tammany politics. As *Theatre
Magazine* observed:

> A little excitement was created during the second act when, at the point
> where the Senator in the play tells the woman reformer that he will "drag
> her through the mire," a loud voice coming from the gallery proclaimed:
> "That is what Charles F. Murphy is doing to New York now." The voice
> was plainly audible all over the house. The audience laughed for a moment,
> and then a wave of applause started. The actors had to stop the scene for
> a moment.[42]

Charles Murphy was the head of Tammany Hall, democratic headquarters
in New York. Murphy was forced to take action against the red-light
districts in 1912 after a scandal, but acted too late and Tammany was
charged in 1913 on numerous charges of corruption. As one reviewer noted:
"Mr. Veiller knows enough of political life to make capital out of the tricks

Figure 8. Publicity flier for *The Fight* portraying corruption. Image courtesy of the Museum of the City of New York.

employed during the election period."[43] A publicity flier for *The Fight* depicts corruption, graft, perjury, filth, and hypocrisy as heads of a dragon-like beast called "Machine Politics" (see figure 8). Such a political monster was not uncommon to New Yorkers, according to the *Globe's* review: "The senator, the district leader, and the brothel keeper are all stewing in the same juice, the political power of Washington 'statesman' resting upon the shoulders of the cadet just as surely as that of any two penny alderman – here is a timely theme and true if ever there was one."[44] Given the portrayal of the police as complicit with graft and prostitution, the *New York Dramatic Mirror* raised the question of "whether the New York police department is intellectually or morally fit to say whether a play shall be produced."[45] None of this was lost on Commissioner Newburger, who, according to the *New York Times*, was in the audience (and who would play a major role in the ensuing censorship case). In spite of some doubts about the police's integrity, they would go on to censor the play, citing the dangerous representation of the brothel.

Brothel, anyone?

How long is New York going to stand for the two bawdy-house plays which outrage public decency at prominent theatres? How long will it tolerate a form of drama which outdoes in nastiness anything previously attempted by local managers?[46]

Editorial in the *World*, 1913

The most pronounced obscenity debates since *Mrs Warren's Profession* surrounded the staging of the brothel in the so-called bawdy-house plays during the 1913–14 season. For the first time, *The Lure*, *The Fight*, and *The House of Bondage* attempted to show the interior workings of the brothel. The brothel was a charged mimetic space, not only because of its potentially salacious details – its red-papered walls, drink, tobacco, music, and garish dress – but also because it revealed to a mixed gender audience a previously unexposed underground terrain that catered to a select male clientele. Yet, what is astonishing about these plays is that while each originally featured significant scenes or entire acts that took place in brothels, *all* of these scenes were eventually censored out. The brothel drama, it turned out, had become a genre without many brothels.

Shortly after the opening of *The Lure* and *The Fight*, both shows were closed by the New York police. Lee Shubert, producer of *The Lure*, and Henry Harris, producer of *The Fight*, were arrested by New York Police Chief McAdoo and charged with violating the obscenity penal code. Commissioner Waldo, who had earlier been the driving force behind police intervention in *Sapho* and *Mrs Warren's Profession*, characterized his opposition to both plays in moral terms: "[T]hese two plays are very rotten. Of course there is a difference of opinion as to how far police power extends in a matter of this kind. My opinion is that such plays as the two in question are offenses against public decency and morals."[47] Waldo was not alone in expressing his repugnance for both plays. As the *New York Dramatic Mirror* reported, "[n]ewspapers gave front page stories and leading editorials, most of them attacking the managers who put on the plays."[48] Harvard professor Hugo Muensterberg argued that the "erotic overflow" of "the red light drama" sullied the very fabric of America "by dragging the sexual problems to the street for the inspection of the crowd without shyness and without shame."[49] One article suggested that there was a "rapidly developing sentiment against the prevailing vogue of plays whose scenes are laid in disreputable resorts and which deal all too frankly with evils ..."[50] Editorials, with titles such as "Away With Brothel Plays," appeared in the New York papers.[51] The morning edition of the *World* forcefully denounced the "vicious melodramas" and pleaded for the censorship of both.[52] *Theatre Magazine* also attacked the genre of the "Red Light drama" for its lowbrow content: "Perhaps we may venture the opinion that the stage is not the place on which to fight such crusades ... Have our dramatists no higher aim than to dramatize contemporary excitements?"[53] Even the *New York Times* took a stand against both plays in an editorial, commenting,

"There is no saving grace about these plays. They are cheap, disgusting, and hopelessly stupid. Their performances should be stopped."[54]

Though Shubert and Harris were charged with violating the penal code for obscenity, neither case was resolved in the courts. After the warrants had been served, both Shubert and Harris voluntarily withdrew their plays. Striking a deal with the police, they were released on their own recognizance. Both plays were suspended until a Grand Jury could view the plays, in specially arranged performances, and then make a decision. If sixteen out of the twenty-three members of the Grand Jury found either play obscene, the producers agreed to permanently withdraw them. However, this was not necessary, as both production teams revised the objectionable material.

As originally conceived, *The Lure* showed the inside of a brothel with what one newspaper called "photographic fidelity."[55] *The Lure* was based on the actual closing of the Everleigh Club, the best-known high-class brothel in Chicago. Opened in 1900 by Ada and Minna Everleigh, the club catered to a rich clientele and was known for its grand furnishings, its $15,000 gold-leaf piano, and extravagant "theme rooms."[56] *The Lure*'s incorporation of the Everleigh story was underscored by the possibility of hiring the real Everleigh prostitutes as actresses. According to a press report, the Shubert organization offered to employ the Everleigh Club prostitutes, described as "a large number of comely young women out of employment," once they had been thrown out into the streets: "Since the young women were out of employment," Charles Washburn recounted, "the Shubert official document immediately proposed that they should turn to the stage for occupation. There was the inference that the *stage was the logical shelter for the Everleigh Club outcasts*" (my emphasis).[57] Claiming the theatre was a logical space for the out-of-work prostitutes reflects the age-old idea of the connection between the stage and prostitution, already implicit in a variety of discourses (see part I). While it appears that the Everleigh prostitutes did not take Shubert up on his offer, the prospect of an actual prostitute stepping foot on the stage, particularly in a brothel scene, was more than enough to pique New York audiences – and censors.

Portraying the brothel interior drew even more criticism. As David Belasco declared, "there is no excuse for any play that has a disorderly house for one of its scenes."[58] Such underworld representations were, as he put it, "vile, nauseating and dangerous." Like other civic leaders, Belasco believed "the brothel should not be shown on the stage, nor painted women and their even worse associates be paraded before the public."[59] Belasco admitted that his position might be perceived as hypocritical, given his celebrated staging of an actress-turned-prostitute in *The Easiest Way* in 1909 (see chapter 3). But his story differed from *The Lure*, he argued, because it "told a serious story that depicted a phase of Tenderloin life without descending to its most vicious depths."[60] This is precisely the point: one could tell a Tenderloin story, but not from the interior of a brothel. Richard Bennett, producer of, and lead actor in, *Damaged Goods*, likewise distanced his pseudoscientific production from those representing brothel interiors:

> [*The Lure* and *The Fight*] are not imitations of *Damaged Goods*, because that does not contain any scene in a brothel . . . In both of the plays under discussion, I believe that the scenes which have created so much comment could have been laid in the dormitory of a young ladies' seminary or an old ladies' home, and have been just as effective.[61]

Rather than causing a scandal that concerned the performing body, then, *The Lure* had transgressed boundaries of proper mise-en-scène. By showing the tabooed brothel interior, the play disclosed to audiences a hitherto forbidden underworld. A space that had been previously known only by prostitutes and their male clients had now been exposed to mixed gender audiences, evoking differing responses from the men and women present. As one unidentified source recounted, "Comes then the scene that shocked many women in the audience – madam's room in what the police term a 'disorderly house.' It was quite true to life, judging by the expressions of recognition that buzzed around many of the male portion of the audience."[62] The *New York Times* likewise reported varied responses among men and women: "Certainly a good many women found themselves asking the question last night, 'Can such things be?' And a good many men found themselves replying, 'Maybe so.'"[63] But, portraying such a space would prove to be too politically sensitive and so out the brothel went.

Shubert preemptively wrote the Grand Jury and offered to "have the offending play rewritten so as to eliminate all the objectionable passages."[64] *Vanity Fair* described the revisions as follows: "In its new form, the second act of the drama takes place in an employment bureau in which the villainess is now the manager."[65] Many thought the change in the setting from brothel to employment agency was absurd, particularly in light of the fact that everyone knew the scene had originally taken place in a brothel. Mrs. Harriet Stanton Blatch, President of the Women's Political Union, ridiculed this and other changes in the script, saying "that the censorship had been laughable; that the principal changes had been the substitution of puritanical mission furniture for the gilt chairs and upholstered couch in the scene representing the interior of a disorderly resort, and the use of tea instead of absinthe as the favorite tipple of the woman manager of the resort."[66] Yet the changes worked. The Grand Jury dropped its charges against Shubert and in its new laundered form, *The Lure* had a respectable run. The *World* reported, "Hundreds of applicants for admittance were turned away after the space allowed for standees had been filled. Speculators worked on the sidewalks and in neighboring doorways, getting big prices for seats."[67]

The Lure's self-censorship and ultimate return to the stage influenced *The Fight*'s critical reception. As originally conceived, *The Fight* provided a vivid portrayal of a brothel interior "with its cigarettes, its red wall paper and its desperate chatelaine" to create a "sufficiently realistic picture of gay life in a small town . . ."[68] In portraying the brothel *The Fight* also transgressed prescribed norms concerning proper mimetic space just as *The Lure* had. "The details of the brothel are spread out in disgusting, nauseating detail," the *Morning Telegram* reported. "The interior of the 'sporting house' is painted in vivid colors – sickening red, to be specific."[69] While Americans had witnessed countless prostitute characters on the stage before, they were unprepared for the portrayal of the array of underworld characters found *in* the brothel itself. Police Chief McAdoo echoed these sentiments: "The main objections to the play centers around the second act which shows the parlor or reception room of a house of prostitution. The more realistic the rooms the more offensive."[70]

There was something potentially perilous, McAdoo's remark suggests, about what might be called brothel realism. Indeed, the brothel drama was thought to have contributed to a rising tide of theatrical realism, leading to what one critic called "the most realistic period" in American drama.[71] In other words, if the prostitute exemplified "the modern narratable," as Peter Brooks has put it, the brothel embodied irrefutable – though volatile – verisimilitude.[72] If the brothel was all too real, McAdoo reasoned, so too were the figures represented there, including "the woman manager of the place, boasting of her wealth, smoking and drinking."[73] As Veiller recalled, one way to get a white slave hit was to incorporate nice-looking whores. As the producer of *The Fight* told him: "What you want, Biddy is a better-looking madam and six prettier whores, and then you have got a hit."[74] Though his remark was flippant, Veiller knew that portraying the ugly side of whoredom was a guarantee of failure. Part of the "nauseating detail," according to the *Morning Telegram*, included "The 'dopey' piano player, general friend of the establishment, and the proprietress, dressed garishly according to her standards . . ."[75] The union of underworld characters, then, and the representation of a brothel were together too dangerous a portrayal for the self-proclaimed moralists.

Even Veiller viewed his original depiction of the brothel scene in act 2 as foul, writing "the only thing I can say about the hoped-for second curtain was that it stank. It was unbelievably bad."[76] Veiller was not alone in critiquing the bordello's stench. The *Morning Telegram* called the brothel "an act of addenda which smelled to the skies with the vileness of its subject . . ."[77] Channing Pollock of the *Green Book Magazine* continued the foul aroma theme, characterizing the second act as having been "dropped into the play as a poached egg is dropped on a plate of corned-beef hash."[78] These critics were right. *The Fight* had originally been produced without the brothel scene (once under the title of *When All Has Been Said* and again as *Standing Pat*).[79] Veiller wrote an entirely new second act before the show opened in New York, which he characterized as "a perfectly innocuous scene in a house of ill fame."[80] He never guessed it would only be temporary.

Before the Grand Jury's special performance of *The Fight*: "a hurried revision was made, and the second act, which had been laid in a disreputable house, was cleansed."[81] According to the *Stage*, the censorship was preemptory, but thorough, cutting out the second act and writing "in some six minutes more of explanatory dialogue for Act III, after which the play was allowed to proceed."[82] Veiller's strategy was effective. After seeing the altered version of *The Fight*, the Grand Jury dropped the charges against Veiller, and *The Fight* opened as a cause célèbre. "The result is that the management cannot accommodate the crowds," reported the *New York Dramatic Mirror*. "On Friday night, with every inch of standing space taken, the fire department would not let another person into *The Fight*, though many demanded admission. The next morning there were thirty-two in line before the box-office opened."[83] Although *The Fight* survived this censorship battle, it would be imprecise to characterize its performance history as triumphant. Even though it was a much better written play, *The Fight* ran only half as long as *The Lure*. While the authors and producers of *The Fight* and *The Lure* removed the brothel from their plays, it was not the only casualty of this laundering.

Excised female brothel fighters

Most white slave plays, this chapter has argued, deployed conventional melodramatic dramaturgy with women as victims and men as rescuers. Yet some white slave plays – *The Lure* and *The Fight* among them – portrayed female brothel fighters: women who fought against captivity. The female brothel fighter was stunningly resourceful; constructing makeshift weapons, going on hunger strikes, climbing fire escapes, and outwitting criminals. And because she appeared in the mythical white slave world, she was also blessed with quasi-mythical powers to keep fighting back the white slavers. Most unusual of all, female fighters sometimes saved other *women*. Unfortunately, the female brothel fighters were excised from both *The Lure* and *The Fight*, right along with the brothel.

In the original version of *The Fight* Jane was one such fighter. Instead of relying on the men to liberate the white slave, Jane did so herself by marching boldly into Pearl's brothel and exclaiming, "You've got a young girl in this house. I want her" (J 2.1).[84] As originally conceived, Jane had the makings of a true action hero. While one critic dismissed this portrayal as "simply the hackneyed material of The Man of the Hour with the sexes reversed," the gesture was nonetheless powerful.[85] The censored version, however, removed Jane's daring rescue, allowing her only the following weak exposition of the event after it had occurred:

> JANE. I did go into that house. I went to that house to rescue a child of
> seventeen who had been tricked into it . . . They'd decoyed that
> child into the house, thrown her into a room and locked the door
> because a low vile beast had offered five hundred dollars – it's no
> use, I can't talk about it. (2.4–2.5)

Doctor Root's next line also rings hollow: "But you saved her." None of the conflict between Jane and the madam, or senator Woodford, survived as staged action. Theatre critic Charles Darnton scorned the revised version of *The Fight* for "the heroine who plays her 'strong' scene with a beer bottle at one house, while at another she comes to rescue – and to talk." Given that much of the action was cut and supplanted by narration, Darnton was "hardly prepared to see her run over to Pearl Haskell's notorious house and search it for an innocent young girl who had been called in from the street and locked in a room."[86] Jane's character was no longer consistent with these heroic actions.

In *The Lure*, a similar moment was excised. Originally, in act 2, while Bob is elsewhere in the brothel rescuing the other white slave, the madam and her cadet, Paul, recapture Sylvia. As Paul approaches Sylvia, she breaks the end off a bottle to use in self-defense, and, echoing Jane's defiant speech from *The Fight*, replies, "I'm going to fight" (3.18). Although this country girl's street acumen has hardly been explained (where *did* she learn that move?), there she is, a weapon in her hand. Just at this instant, in a moment of melodramatic excess, another white slave, Nell, bursts into the room and screams, "For God's sake don't let them beat me any more" (3.19). Sylvia instinctively protects Nell, stepping in front of her with her make-shift weapon.

While the script called for Sylvia to become a female brothel fighter, production photographs show her as weak and weaponless (see figure 7). In transition from page to stage, this moment of resistance was summarily removed. A caption from one production photograph sums it up: "A girl in white enters shrieking, having escaped from her room where she was being beaten. The Cadet and the Madam viciously attack both girls but the detective arrives just time."[87] Fighting, in other words, is better left to the men in the play. With the finesse of a true stage hero, Bob bursts into the room and utters, pithily, "Don't touch that arm – I've just been vaccinated" (3.20). He then fights off the villains, and rushes both women to safety. *The Lure* ends with typical melodramatic resolution: marriage and a retreat to the country where Bob's father, a doctor, can care for Sylvia's mother.

As revised, both *The Lure* and *The Fight* inched closer to typical white slave fare. Their obscenity cases dominated not only the 1913 season, but also determined the future of subsequent white slave dramas ready to take to the stage.

Rachel Crothers's *Ourselves*: Feminist dramaturgy in the brothel drama

"The tireless Rachel Crothers,"[88] as fellow author Djuna Barnes called her, was the only female playwright whose brothel drama was produced during the early 1910s.[89] Given the tumult of previous white slave plays, everyone was watching *Ourselves* when it premiered on November 13, "to decide which way the winds of popular favor were blowing."[90] Though *Ourselves* appeared just six weeks after *The Lure* and *The Fight*, it encountered none of the censorship battles that had dogged their productions. In spite of reviews that praised its writing, however the Drama League refused to endorse it, and the show closed after just twenty-nine performances. What are we to make of this failure given the popularity of this genre?

Most critics of the period suggested that *Ourselves* had poor timing. As *Everybody's Magazine* reported in 1913, "It is too bad it did not come early in the season, before the public's stomach turned against the whole sex morality as a play problem."[91] But was *Ourselves'* failure merely a matter of poor timing, or were there other factors to consider? It is insufficient to conclude that the public had tired of the brothel, for stories about prostitution resurfaced again and again on the New York stage and in silent films during this period. While *Ourselves* is a better play than those by Crothers's male contemporaries of the period – even by the critics' own admission – it was destined to failure not only because Crothers offered what the press called "a feminine viewpoint," but also because she subverted the predictable brothel drama formula.[92]

From its very inception, *Ourselves* was written with a female audience in mind. Crothers had signed a contract with actress Grace Ellison in December 1912 to write a play about prostitution, with a leading part for Ellison.[93] This date is important because it demonstrates that Crothers had begun her play well before the popular swell of white slave plays hit Broadway in 1913. How Crothers approached the task is also noteworthy: while some of her male colleagues capitalized on the popular trend and churned out their brothel plays rather quickly (George Scarborough claimed he wrote *The Lure* in just eight days), she took nearly a year to research, write, and revise *Ourselves.*

In addition, Crothers turned toward a women-centered institution as her source: the Bedford State Reformatory for Women, which she visited several times while researching and writing the play.[94] Such pseudo-ethnographic research was not uncommon in the writing of social problem plays: Mrs. Leslie Carter interviewed Parisian courtesans for *Zaza* (1899); both Mr. and Mrs. Fiske interviewed and photographed people from the Lower-East Side for *Salvation Nell* (1908); and former reporter George Scarborough walked the red-light district of Chicago for *The Lure* (1913). What made Crothers unique was that she was the first playwright to use a girls' reformatory so extensively as a source for writing a play about prostitution (taking, perhaps, her impulse from George J. Kneeland's recently released *Commercialized Prostitution in New York* [1913], for which Kneeland had interviewed prostitutes at Blackwell's Island Hospital).

Moreover, in privileging prostitutes' own testimonies about sexuality, economics, and possibilities for reform (as opposed to the usual testimonies about the so-called sexual fall or the popular white slave captivity narratives), Crothers shifted the discursive focus from sensational portraits of the sexual underworld to a practical reform agenda. In addition, Crothers had transgressed a dramaturgical line, which, taking its impulse from naturalism, dictated that a playwright remain objective. It was acceptable to report about prostitution as a social evil, as The Committee of Fifteen had done, but to portray the prostitute's perspective sympathetically was not in keeping with traditional brothel dramaturgy. This sentiment was expressed in the *Louisville Courier*: "Rachel Crothers social worker has rather obtruded on Rachel Crothers, dramatist."[95] In fact, the social awareness with which Crothers created this project was not unlike what we would now call community-based theatre. Indeed, *Ourselves* should be regarded as an early precursor to this kind of work.

A second indicator of Crothers' feminist dramaturgy is her use of the title. *Ourselves* suggests a subjective story about women, told by a female insider, calling into question the identity of the spectator (who might not be included in the appellation "ourselves"). The trajectory of the title's development suggests that Crothers moved from the typical pseudoscientific approach, which dominated the day, to a more subjective and feminist one. The working title for *Ourselves* was originally *The Social Evil*, according to a contract agreement with the Shuberts, who produced the show.[96] At this time, prostitution was commonly referred to as "the social evil," a term that was popularized by The Committee of Fifteen's 1902 report on prostitution in New York City, *The Social Evil*.[97] Perhaps wanting to distance herself from this kind of regulatory discourse, Crothers dispensed with the working title. Just a month before its premiere, J. J. Shubert had asked Crothers to consider changing the title, writing her, "What do you think of *The Unwelcome Guest* as a title?"[98] While truer to the plot of her play and less entrenched in antiprostitution discourse, this suggested title demonstrates that Shubert had missed one of Crothers's central points: the guest to which he refers (a reformed prostitute working in an upper-class home) was *not* unwelcome. Crothers disregarded Shubert's suggestion, but changed the title nonetheless: in early November, the play was produced in Albany and Providence as *When It Strikes Home*.[99] While this title reflected how prostitution affects middle-class families, it was at odds with the script: rather than suggesting that prostitution is "our" problem, as the play does, *When It Strikes Home* connotes an anxious perspective, the fear that middle- and upper-class families might be hit by a kind of first-wave (sexual) assault. This title may have also alluded to the recently successful *Damaged Goods*, the first drama on the New York stage to explicitly portray the dangers of venereal disease (see chapter 8). To avoid raising false expectations, Crothers changed the title to *Ourselves* just ten days later, when the play moved to New York City's Lyric Theatre. *Ourselves* therefore distinguished itself from the titles of other brothel plays, which suggested either a critical distance between the play-wright and the object of study (*Damaged Goods*), a prurient interest in the sexual underworld (*The House of Bondage*), or the apportioning of blame for a woman's sexual fall (*The Easiest Way*). Crothers's feminist emphasis seems to have confused at least one reviewer who asked: "*Ourselves* has a grip. But where and why the name?"[100] The title engendered a threatening rhetorical hailing of sorts, as another review revealed: "To see ourselves as Miss Crothers sees us is no Christmas gift."[101] Indeed, *Ourselves* "hit them, as the saying goes, where they live," according to the *Bulletin*, which continued, "It is well named *Ourselves*."[102] Crothers's title subverted both objectivity and objectification and can be seen as a strong a feminist intervention in the male-controlled discourse about prostitution and the regulation of sexuality.

A third aspect of Crothers' dramaturgy is that her brothel play featured no brothel. While *The Lure* and *The Fight* each featured a brothel scene that was later was removed, Crothers steered clear from the brothel altogether. Even though the press repeatedly characterized *Ourselves* as a white slave play, it eliminated the classic elements of the white slave melodrama, including the brothel interior, white slave abduction, and rescue scenes. As one review noted, in *Ourselves* "the white slave is shown once removed from the stage brothel, which was her accepted rendezvous of the early season."[103] It is possible that Crothers's choice to eliminate the brothel was motivated by the high-profile obscenity cases involving *The Lure* and *The Fight* in September. After all, the Shuberts had also produced *The Lure*, and Lee Shubert himself was arrested in that case. Shubert may have instructed Crothers to refrain from portraying such an inflammatory scene in *Ourselves*. However, no record of such an instruction exists in the corres-pondence file at the Shubert Archive, and the Shuberts were known for keeping meticulous records.

While it is impossible to solve this conundrum, it is interesting to examine the choices that Crothers made beyond the brothel. Switching from a site of sexual encounter or abduction to one of reform, *Ourselves* privileges a female-centered space, focusing not on the problem, but rather the *solution*. By taking the whore out of the brothel, Crothers short-circuits the voyeuristic interest in the sexual underworld. In comparing *Ourselves* with *The Lure* and *The Fight*, a reporter from the *Morning Sun* wrote, "The first act of the play contained no scene of the kind which the police have already interrupted in two notable cases. It was a revelation of this same milieu carried a power higher. There was no parlor. But there was the sitting room of a 'reform home' for girls."[104] One review remarked that

Crothers's switch in emphasis served her well: "The reform home itself, with its inmates, is put on the stage with all the terse vividness with which it might be described by a good police reporter and all the deeper understanding which would be supplied from the experience of a Miss Maude Miner or a Jane Addams."[105] This change in focus allowed Crothers to circumvent melodramatic formulas and dwell on the realities of prostitution as told from a female perspective.

One of the most striking aspects of *Ourselves* is that it centers on women's relationships, telling the story of prostitution from a female point of view. And as such it initiates a new perspective on the topic of prostitution as represented on the New York stage. Reminiscent of Cecily Hamilton's *Diana of Dobson's*, act I reveals the women of the reform house interacting with one another beyond the confines created by the male gaze. "They are allowed," one review noted, to act "themselves in other ways inevitable when there was no masculine society present."[106] Indeed, the girls' behavior only changes when they are either conscious of men watching them (the chauffeur outside, whom we never see), or when they are discussing how to appeal to men once they leave the home. Otherwise, we see the women as themselves (ourselves?), attending to their daily chores, arguing about certain privileges, or entertaining themselves with song and dance.

Run by the efficient and liberal-minded Miss Carew, the "hen coop," as it is called by one of the girls, can be seen as a feminist space. The home is visited by Beatrice Barrington, an upper-class woman interested in reform efforts. Here she encounters Molly, a fine-spirited girl who was lured into prostitution, and whom Beatrice convinces to work in her home. The reform house trains the women with job skills and provides day care for those who have children. Significantly, *Ourselves* is the only prostitution play that actually proposes a solution to the inevitable problem of pregnancy and childcare. Crothers's inclusion of a female-operated day-care center is both radical and utopian.

Other than *Mrs Warren's Profession*, no other play from this period devotes so much dramaturgical space to women discussing the problem of prostitution. In most prostitute dramas, debates about prostitution were left to men of action (Burke in *"Anna Christie"* or Madison in *The Easiest Way*), and, increasingly, to experts in medical and juridical domains (as with the Doctor and senator in *Damaged Goods*). It is quite right that, as the *Woman's Journal* put it, Crothers "showed women grappling as a group for the first time with an age-old problem which they had hitherto avoided as something too dreadful for discussion."[107] Act I, therefore, establishes that women can engage in prostitution discourse – and not merely as *objects* in the study, but as enlightened subjects themselves.

In addition to the female-centered first act, female bonding occurs between Molly and Wilson, the head housekeeper of the Barrington home. Molly has promised that she would try to work honestly at Barrington's for one month and not see her pimp, Leever, who seeks to lure her back to the old life with false promises. After one month, Leever visits the Barrington home, but his courtly façade soon crumbles and he becomes violent. He steals Molly's wages, accuses her of hooking on the side, and threatens to kill her if she doesn't return to him. Just as things escalate toward physical violence, Wilson intervenes. Here Crothers does not resort to typical white slave fare and offer a melodramatic rescue by a white slave hunter. Rather, Wilson simply picks up a bell and rings it; her presence and the threat of backup is enough to halt Leever's abuse. He "slinks out," leaving Molly heartbroken (3.19).[108] At this time of devastation, Molly turns *not* to her upper-class patron, Miss Barrington, but rather to co-worker Wilson for comfort (see figure 9). In Molly's words: "I'd a' run away long ago if it hadn't been for you, Mrs. Wilson; she is good – but you're human. You kinda know." Wilson replies: "Know? I ain't worked with my two hands since I was ten years old, without *knowin'*" (3.19).

This scene between two working-class women is particularly noteworthy because it demonstrates that Molly and Wilson have different perspectives – and indeed, bodies of knowledge – from their bourgeois employer. It also shows that Molly is no dupe; she is skeptical of Miss Barrington's friendship. With this scene, Crothers was critiquing the reformist impulses of privileged white women, impulses that often backfired against their working-class sisters.[109] As Miss Carew says to Beatrice in the first act: "We have a lot of dabblers who do more harm than good, you know" (1.4). Though Crothers is careful not to idealize the relationship between Molly and Beatrice Barrington, she nonetheless believed that some kind of female support system was important for female delinquents once they were released. In writing about this topic, Crothers argued for the creation of an auxiliary board patterned on the Big Sisters' program: "Every girl who is released from the institution should have an interested sympathetic woman to look out for her. It would do the woman just as much good as the girl, too."[110]

Crothers continues this analysis in the final act of the play – where Molly and Beatrice resolve their differences. Beatrice's brother has made repeated passes at Molly – who is naïve enough to believe his promises. What's unusual about the final act is that instead of blaming Molly for breaking

Figure 9. Jobyna Howland as Beatrice Barrington and Grace Ellingston as Molly from Rachel Crothers's *Ourselves* (previously titled *When it Strikes Home*). Photo courtesy of the New York Public Library.

up her brother's marriage, Beatrice realizes her own complicity in the problem (the "our" in *Ourselves* includes, in other words, all sections of society). In response to her brother's reproach that she had caused the whole problem with her "confounded [reform] ideas," Beatrice replies, "[t]here's only one thing to blame me for – and that's for . . . not defending her before you all – and telling her *then* that I *did not* hold her responsible for all that's happened – but *you* entirely" (4.10; emphasis in original). *Ourselves* therefore ends uncharacteristically with female bonding and surprisingly unsentimental bonding at that. Molly's next line reveals her guarded appreciation: "That means more than all you ever said to me put together. I never thought I was a real human being to you before. I always thought you was just experimenting on me" (4.10). With a realistic look at the uneven power balance between these women, *Ourselves* concludes with women supporting other women, even across class lines.

Yet, Crothers's focus on women was a central reason the show flopped. Writing in *Harper's Weekly*, Norman Hapgood complained that the part of Bob "exhibits masculine nature with a harshness and cruelty unfamiliar to me."[111] Alan Dale noted the dearth of male parts: "In the cast of twenty-one persons there were only four men."[112] And the *New York Dramatic Mirror* delivered an uncharacteristically acerbic review, also mourning the absence of men.[113] In spite of the reviewer's claims that Crothers slights her male characters, in the male-dominated theatre of the day, female characters were routinely underdeveloped or missing altogether. When Crothers subverted this paradigm, she was attacked for breaking not only unwritten dramaturgical rules, but also for challenging the very foundational premises of patriarchal logic, offering instead what the press repeatedly called "the feminine view."

Not only did *Ourselves* privilege female bonding; it also advocated feminist ideas about sexual responsibility and legislation. For example, when discussing the lopsided policy of incarcerating prostitutes, Miss Carew states: "What's the use shutting up a few hundred girls a year, while the men are running around loose looking for more? Once we take to locking up man – we'll get somewhere, not before" (1.17). Critic Alan Dale rejoined: "Why not lock up the men? This feminine view appeared to be rather pleasing, and sympathetic hands applauded it."[114] When Miss Carew delivered this line at the Bedford State Reformatory for Women, "such a wild storm of applause burst forth that the whole cast was temporarily disabled. One of the women was unable to speak her lines, Molly turned her back and wiped her eyes, and another [actress] . . . had to retire precipitately from the stage . . ."[115] As the *New York City Tribune* reported, "The Bedford girls got the point," suggesting that the play resonated with them far more successfully than with Broadway audiences.[116]

Although Miss Carew suggests holding men accountable, Crothers did not lay the blame solely at men's feet, even though several critics believed otherwise. Rather, Crothers argued that women should take responsibility for the double standard. While other playwrights had tackled this issue before, what Crothers introduces is the idea that women must get involved in the sex debates.

> BEATRICE. [N]ow that I understand the horrors of what we call the social evil, I know that good women are terribly to blame

for it all – because of their indifference towards the whole
thing. It's we – we ourselves who are responsible for conditions – ourselves. If we don't care – if we don't demand
the highest morality in our own men, how are we going to
get it? Or do anything for anybody else? (2.4)

Molly underscores Beatrice's point with a sense of urgency: "Are you blind
as bats? Don't you live in this world? Don't you know what's going on? If
you feel like this about it, why don't you stop it? If this is the worst thing
your men can do why do you let 'em? Why do you stand for it and – and
there wouldn't *be* any of us" (3.19). Molly's words are an important inclusion
in the sexuality debates, which were often dominated in public discourse by
the middle and upper classes. Molly's speech also argues that women should
take an active stance, a point Crothers echoed in an interview in the *New
York Tribune*: "the thing women must do to help is to insist on high
standards of morality in the men they know. Women can no longer be
indifferent to this thing."[117]

While early in *Ourselves* Crothers argues that women should uphold
high morals, she does not resort to familiar platitudes by portraying women
as morally superior or sexually repressed. She rather combines the critique
of male sporting with an assertion of female heterosexual desire. When
Molly is seduced and falsely promised love by Beatrice's own brother, Bob,
he callously defends his "animal nature," as the *Morning Telegraph* called
it.[118] "We're not to blame for how we're made," he tells his wife Irene. "Do
you think for a minute if you had the same amount of animal passion in
your make-up that I have – you'd blame me so – for this? You don't know.
Your pulses beat evenly and slowly" (4.8). Irene dismantles this common
view by asserting an active female sexuality:

> IRENE. Don't count so much on the slow, even pulses of a woman –
> don't be so sure of the cool blood in her veins. I've kept myself
> for you – because I married you. I've made you the one man –
> not because no one else has ever stirred me – not because I'm not
> just as strong and healthy an animal as you are – but because of
> *you – you*. (4.8)

In addition to portraying upper-class female sexual desire, Crothers also
represented working-class girls' sexual cravings. One of the new points that
Ourselves made is that some women turn to having sex outside of marriage

for pleasure (a choice that sometimes leads them to prostitution once they
are ruined on the marriage market). Crothers made the unpopular point
that "the girl problem," as it became known, had as much to do with
acknowledging sexual desire and thirst for entertainment as it did with
economic hardship or moral weakness.[119] As she put it in an interview,
"Poverty is only indirectly the cause ... Every girl craves affection."[120]
Molly, described in one review as "a vital healthy, active bundle of animal
spirits," echoes this view in act 3:[121]

> MOLLY. I give up my fella. I don't want him, but I want somebody.
> What am I goin' to do? What am I goin' to do? Stay here and
> dry up in this straight-jacket of a dress – watchin' the good
> people dancin' and makin' love for the rest of my love? What
> am I goin' to do? I'm lonely. (3.19)

While this articulation of female desire was not entirely new to modern
theatre, in the context of white slave plays, which tended to idealize
bourgeois women's sexual purity, this scene brought a "clarity that was
quite unusual on the American stage in the teens," according to theatre
historian Brenda Murphy.[122]

   In order to understand Crothers's radical gesture here, we need to
understand the nature of typical brothel dramaturgy. Usually, the prostitute
is saved (either by reform, God, or a man) and then renounces "the life"
forever. In *Ourselves*, by contrast, Molly is reformed, but she still wants
to have sex – not for money – but sex just the same. Because the two
ideas were incompatible in the Progressive imagination, *Ourselves* defied
conventional dramaturgy and sex discourse. But not until we examine its
critical reception can we fully grasp why so much was at stake for this
production.

Critical reception: A "woman's show"

While white slave plays of the 1913 season encountered varied receptions,
Crothers was the only playwright who was derided for her gender in the
press. Recent scholarship about Rachel Crothers, however, has not fully
explored the ways in which Crothers was attacked for her feminist dramaturgy or even the failure of the play itself. For example, Colette and James
Lindroth's *Rachel Crothers Production Sourcebook* summarizes the critical
response to *Ourselves* as "generally positive."[123] In her influential book on

Rachel Crothers, Lois Gottlieb wrote, "most critics applauded the play's straightforward expression of the problem."[124]

While several critics of the time praised *Ourselves*, many others revealed a distinct gender bias, even when they acknowledged that Crothers had written a good play. For example, the *New York Dramatic Mirror* commented, "Womanlike, Rachel Crothers has tried to have the last word on that much press-agented subject, the white slave. Note that she has only tried. The final word remains to be spoken."[125] The *New York Herald* suggested "to have called the play *The Woman's Point of View* might better have fitted the text," lamenting that "when the final curtain dropped the voting half of the species had all the worst of it."[126] "It is a woman's show," declared the reviewer of the *Telegram*, "One had only to watch the part of the audience which voiced its white gloved approval to decide the theme would not be a popular one with the men folk."[127] Alan Dale gave his usual dig at his least favoured playwright or actress of the moment, calling Crothers "a spinster" and declaring, "she errs in her reasoning, and . . . the feminine view – if this be it – is absurd."[128] And perhaps the most anxious review was the following: "Any man who takes his wife to that play will never again be able to convince her he is on the square."[129] The *Morning Telegraph* agreed: "Some of those in the audience last night wondered if the producers hadn't staged *The Guilty Man* under a new name."[130] As Doris Abramson has shown in her research of Crothers, "standards of excellence were inevitably masculine."[131]

Although much of the press offered the same view of Crothers's "peculiarly feminine play,"[132] as one review put it, the *New York City Tribune* defended it, claiming, "The spectator may not share these ideals; he may object that the play is special pleading, but he cannot escape the fact that here is work of unusual distinction."[133] The *New York City Review*'s observations also seem quite relevant in this regard:

> The criticisms of *Ourselves* have been so amusingly transparent. Said they: "It's a woman's standpoint." . . . And . . . why not? There isn't a reason in the world why the woman's standpoint should not be propounded as well as the man's . . . Heaven knows the man's standpoint is idiotic enough standing alone.[134]

Perhaps the most revealing comment was made in the *Baltimore News*: "If Rachel Crothers had produced her latest play, *Ourselves*, under a man's name or even anonymously, it would have had very different treatment at the hands of the critics, and might have proved a success."[135] The *Baltimore News* got it right: in spite of Crothers's other successes, the brothel drama could only go so far in the hands of a woman. As *Munsey's Magazine* put it bluntly, "it failed."[136]

Although *Ourselves* was unsuccessful in Broadway venues, it excelled in alternative performances that were devoted to raising women's consciousness.[137] It is the only white slave play that actually played to an exclusive audience of former prostitutes and delinquent women. In true community-based theatre spirit Crothers continued her relationship with Bedford and its chief administrator, Dr. Katherine Davis, a major figure in prostitution reform work, throughout the production process. Performing *Ourselves* at the Bedford State Reformatory for Girls in December 1913 was, in Crothers's words, "a very daring experiment" by Davis.[138] As the private showing at Bedford proved, *Ourselves* resonated with its female inmates. Described by Crothers, this performance was one of the highlights of her career:

> The most impressive thing I have ever seen, without any exception, was the effect the play produced upon the girls when it was given for them in the little hall at Bedford, and without hesitation, I say that the way in which they received the play filled me with more gratitude than all the response which has come from all the rest of my work put together.[139]

Although Crothers and company never made it back to Bedford for another performance, they did present *Ourselves* on December 9 "as a benefit performance to raise money for a new and valuable line of rescue work for women, under the auspices of a special committee of the Woman's Civic Federation."[140] These two instances of *Ourselves* being used as a vehicle of consciousness-raising for women reveal how distinctly gendered prostitution discourse was. Its success in these two venues parallels, and clarifies, its failure at the Lyric.

While *Ourselves* was not censored for its racy brothel scenes, it also had little to offer mainstream audiences that were not invested in female-centered plots. As the private showing at the Bedford State Reformatory for Girls showed, however, *Ourselves* did resonate with female audiences. But as for the Drama League, the male critics, and the Shuberts, who eventually closed the show, *Ourselves* would remain a woman's story, too feminist, and too bitterly close to home.

The short-lived *The House of Bondage*

The House of Bondage is so scarlet it screams.
                                    New York Telegram, 1914

In December 1913, just five weeks after the opening of *Ourselves*, the same issues surfaced again in Joseph Byron Totten's adaptation of

Reginald Wright Kauffman's white slave novel, *The House of Bondage*. By now some critics, like the reviewer from *Munsey's Magazine*, felt that the white slave drama had become tiresome: "The short-lived *House of Bondage* ... hesitated in New York just long enough to prove our contention of some months ago that Broadway is indeed through with the vice drama ..."[141] Yet, as demonstrated in the proliferation of white slave films and dramas as late as the 1940s, this was not entirely true. What is intriguing about *The House of Bondage* is how it suffered by arriving, as it did, in the wake of *Ourselves*. Although *The House of Bondage* was also temporarily censored, as were *The Lure* and *The Fight*, it experienced police brutality and intervention on an unprecedented scale.

No other producer of a white slave play was harassed by the police as was actress/manager Cecil Spooner. Not only was Spooner's brutal treatment unprecedented, but her arrest was ghosted by the performance of prostitution itself. Just moments before the opening night perfor-mance, approximately thirty police waited in the theatre. Shortly before the curtain went up, "they descended, hood and hide, buckle and strap, clubs and badgers, upon the playhouse, with all the parade of bumptious authority in vogue when a gambling house or a resort of gunmen and thieves is about to be raided."[142] It is difficult to recall such an aggressive display of police power in the early twentieth-century American theatre. The *New York Times* reported "many in the audience shouted protests at the action of the police." Not even allowing Spooner time to change out of her costume, the police hauled her into Night Court in a paddy wagon like "a common brothel inmate."[143] Women's Night Court was notorious for trying prostitutes. Insofar as Spooner was arrested for playing a prostitute, while still in costume, and forced to undergo jur-idical process like a prostitute, she was hailed, to use Althusser's forma-tion, as a hooker.

But why did the police react with so much acrimony against Spooner? Why wasn't she released, like Shubert and Harris, on her own recogni-zance? Why was she hauled into Night Court like a prostitute? The performance by the police (for we should regard it as a performance) disciplined Spooner for her actions as a transgressive woman, one who had stepped outside the boundaries of proper behavior (both as actress, and as actress-playing-a-prostitute). Spooner had a reputation for playing fallen women. As Channing Pollock noted in 1911, "In Brooklyn it used to be a common thing to hear that Cecil Spooner was much better than Mrs. Leslie Carter as *Zaza*."[144] There was a way in which Spooner's fallen woman repertoire ghosted her public persona, and the police may have been unwilling, or unable, to disengage from that performance history.

Spooner was also an influential actress/manager and one of the few women in this powerful position during her day. Part of the Spooner Stock Company, created by her mother, Mary, and featuring her sister, Edna, Cecil Spooner had long had a reputation as a formative female force in the theatre. She then formed her own company, and, as Mari Kathleen Fielder notes, "The Cecil Spooner Stock Company became the toast of the Bronx."[145] It was here that Spooner staged *The House of Bondage*.[146] Given such an overstated arrest scene, the police seemed vindictive after taking such a beating in *The Lure* and *The Fight*. Spooner's harassment suggests that women were not allowed to produce brothel plays; that domain was left to the men who could launder their plays and be released on their own recognizance. The *New York Dramatic Mirror* was especially outraged at this show of "raw police power" and "brutality" directed at Spooner.[147] The *Mirror*'s editorial argued that such treatment was unfairly accorded Spooner, and that Shubert and Harris "were not put to the indignity of riding to a station in a police van with an escort of thirty blue-coats."[148] Though she "was dragged like a felon through the streets," Spooner became an instant hero.[149] Part of the audience followed Spooner to the police station, where they cheered her from outside. According to the *New York Times*, Spooner announced that she would file a complaint against Police Sergeant Quinn for the manner in which she was arrested, though it is unclear if she ever did so.[150]

The rigorous supervision of Spooner's censorship of the script was also unprecedented. In order to get around the obscenity code, Spooner had *The House of Bondage* "rewritten and expurgated."[151] At the December 10 opening of the revised play, "twenty-five hundred persons packed the building to the doors and thousands were turned away," the *New York Times* reported.[152] At first, Spooner changed very little in the script: "Miss Spooner appeared in the second act in a blue dress instead of a red one," the *New York Dramatic Mirror* noted, "and as far as could be ascertained, about a dozen lines were altered, but in other respects the play seemed about the same."[153] Unfortunately for Spooner, Deputy Police Commissioner Newburger was in the audience that night and "said that [the play] had not been revised enough to make it come within the law, and that he would apply for a fresh warrant" for Spooner and her manager, Joseph Cone.[154] More revisions were made.

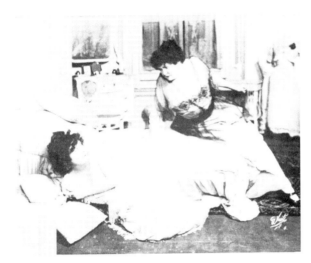

Figure 10. Lucille La Verne as the Madam threatens Cecil Spooner as the white slave in the censored brothel scene from *The House of Bondage.* Courtesy of the New York Public Library.

Spooner's persecution was also linked to how the police were portrayed as corrupt in the play, a now volatile feature of brothel dramas, and all but guaranteeing censorship. In a tear-filled speech after the third act, Spooner denounced the outrageous police brutality that she had endured. A man in the audience stood up, and, according to the *New York Times*, "said he had been investigating vice in the city on his own responsibility for more than a year, and that he knew that the 'police grafters' were after Miss Spooner because she was 'showing up police methods in the play.' Both Miss Spooner and the man speaker were applauded by the audience."[155] This outburst no doubt sat poorly with the police representatives in the audience. Spooner continued revisions. By December 17, the *New York Dramatic Mirror* reported "there has been no direct police interference since, and the indications are that the play will move down-town."[156]

By the time *The House of Bondage* made it to the Longacre Theatre, the changes had rendered it "ridiculous" and "idiotic," according to Alan Dale.[157] The *New York Dramatic Mirror* noted, "the play has not been improved since it was recently produced," suggesting that it was so offensive that "the audience hissed roundly."[158] Indeed, production photographs show the madam rendered so ineffective that instead of physically threatening the white slave as originally planned (see figure 10), she waves a large wooden spoon about her head. Another reviewer agreed the play was the worse for wear: "For its downtown appearances certain lines, it is said, have been softened and the cast has been refurbished."[159] The *New York Globe* wondered, "It is supposed to have been rewritten and expurgated since it was suppressed by the police at an uptown theatre. What on earth can the original have been like?"[160] As Dale put it, "anything as badly written as *The House of Bondage* couldn't live on upper Broadway."[161] He was right; the new version lasted only eight performances. Pressured by the police, Spooner had no choice but render the play ridiculous through extensive revision.

Although it is quite clear that poor writing as a result of censorship caused *The House of Bondage* to be called "quite the most absurd, preposterous and impossible of the so-called white slave melodramas," there was also a feeling that Broadway was tiring of the white slave drama.[162] "As a lesson," one critic lamented, "it is at least six months behind the times. The things it has to tell of the alleged white slave traffic have been told before."[163] Another critic claimed, "Its scenes and incidents have become commonplaces both of the printed page and the acted word.[164] Even when it was revived under the auspices of the *Medical Review of Reviews* in late January 1914, James Metcalfe called it "a bore."[165] *Munsey's Magazine* observed that its failure proved "that Broadway is indeed through with the vice drama that has nothing better than the vice theme to sustain it."[166]

In spite of these declarations of boredom with white slavery, however, a number of white slave plays continued well after the ill-fated red-light drama season. Although "white slavery melodramas played a critical role in social control," as McDermott and Blackstone have noted, not all white slave plays functioned in the same way.[167] A critical eye to Progressive Era white slave discourse demonstrates that the stage was both producer *and* censor of this phenomenon within a larger matrix of sexual discourse. The fates of *The Lure*, *The Fight*, and *The House of Bondage* all reveal the dangers of staging corrupt politicians as well as the brothel interior. Brothel dramaturgy required the white slave play to adhere to melodramatic formulas, conventional gender norms, and notions of sexual and racial purity. Yet, while most red-light plays promulgated regressive sexual politics and racist stereotypes, others advanced feminist politics and interracial desire, even if only for brief moments. This unexpected tension, therefore, underscored by uneven receptions of the dramas, demonstrates that this genre resisted certain forms of social control at the very same time it reinscribed them. The rather unspectacular run of *Ourselves* shows how unpopular a feminist alternative view could be, even when well rendered. Similarly, Cecil Spooner's brutal arrest exposes the reaction to women producing white slave plays. The white slave phenomenon, therefore, offers a most interesting case study of how power and resistance flow in and out of each other, where the stage is the central site on which these battles are waged.

Part IV

The legitimation and decline
of the brothel drama

This project began by discussing two plays (*Zaza* and *Sapho*) that featured performing women who were perceived as prostitutes, and that premiered in New York on the cusp of the turn of the century. Just as *Zaza* and *Sapho* had divergent performance histories – the former was celebrated while the latter was brought up on charges of obscenity – so too the plays from the 1913–14 season encountered a similar ambiguity. If the white slave brothel-drama season was dominated by censorship – and irregular censorship at that – then what became of the sex hysteria? This last section focuses on plays featuring prostitutes that sought, and, in some cases, received, unexpected legitimation. The very season that white slave plays were battling censorship, Eugène Brieux's *Damaged Goods* (*Les Avariés*) was, after encountering some resistance, ultimately deemed a great sermon and given as a command performance at the White House.

Nine years later, the 1921–22 season featured plays that focused on the issue of respectability within prostitution. Eugene O'Neill's *"Anna Christie"* received the Pulitzer Prize, garnering an uncanny kind of respectability. On the other hand, Sholom Asch's *The God of Vengeance*, which portrayed a brothel owner who seeks respectability for his daughter, became the first play in thirty years to be deemed immoral by the obscenity penal code. Paradoxically, the same year that O'Neill captured his accolade and *The God of Vengeance* was halted over obscenity charges, another play featuring a prostitute seeking salvation, *Rain*, became one of the longest-running productions of 1922 (running for 648 performances). What are we to make of these seemingly erratic performance histories?

Seen together, these plays show both the decline and the legitimation of the brothel drama. More than this, they demonstrate the irregular politics of staging the prostitute. Much like rising industrial modernity itself, which was both seduced and repulsed by the image of the prostitute, so too

Progressive Era theatre expressed profound ambivalence about the prostitute in the very midst of antiprostitution reform on the one hand, and two decades of brothel dramas on the other. While *"Anna Christie"* and *Rain* both feature redeemed, repentant prostitutes, *Damaged Goods* and *The God of Vengeance* portray prostitutes who are far more unsettling: the *prostitute fatale* and the lesbian prostitute. These characters' presence – or absence – from the stage is an index of the cultural imperative to simultaneously speak about and censor sexuality discourse. And just as the red-light districts were being closed for good, displacing but not eradicating prostitution, so too certain brothel dramas were still being staged during the genre's decline.

   These next two chapters explore these paradoxical tensions, and show that when certain brothel plays portrayed a repentant prostitute, or when they advocated sexual politics in line with emerging sexual science, they met with success. But plays like *The God of Vengeance*, which unsettled expected brothel dramaturgy by reintroducing the brothel interior and portraying lesbian sexuality, were ultimately found obscene. These contrasting production histories show the Progressive Era's ambivalence regarding whoredom. With all its beauty and peculiarity, prostitution was indeed produced in certain venues if it adhered to hegemonic sexual discourse. The stage can be understood in such moments as a literal producer of sexuality. As the production history of *Damaged Goods* shows, at times the theatre even worked in tandem with the US military to promote sex hygiene. So, too, the watchdogs of Broadway policed those plays that rivaled conventional sexual wisdom. What these plays' Pulitzer prizes, command performances at the White House, and obscenity charges reveal, in other words, is the complex web of sexual discourse that was operative on the New York stage, which, at times, reinforced the regulatory ideal of sex and which, at times, subverted it. The decline of the brothel drama was marked, therefore, by the paradoxical desires that spawned it: legitimation and censorship.

8

Damaged Goods: *Sex hysteria and the*
prostitute fatale

In 1913, the play characterized in the popular press as "unquestionably the most widely discussed play of a decade," was not a brilliant interpretation of a classic, one of Bernard Shaw's problem plays, or one of David Belasco's realist inventions. The production that took the country by storm, Eugène Brieux's *Damaged Goods* (*Les Avariés*), was the first play on the American stage to deal openly with syphilis, and use it as a central theme. Though celebrated at the time as "The Greatest Contribution Ever Made by the Stage to the Cause of Humanity,"[1] this play merits the modern scholar's attention not only because its immense popularity has been overlooked or because it broke what turn-of-the century narratives called the "conspiracy of silence." Rather, this chapter will argue that the performance history of *Damaged Goods*, far from marking a threshold-crossing freedom in sexual discourse in Progressive America, reveals how Progressives utilized the stage to normalize and reinforce the social centrality of bourgeois marriage, reproductivity, and traditional gender norms, much as they had wielded other discourses to study, contain, and discipline sexuality for decades before. While this regulation of sexuality rested upon a conservative agenda that the ostensible liberalism of the play obfuscated in its own (and even our) day, the play's portrayal of prostitution demonstrates a rather clear, though vexed, relationship between contagion and the dangers of unsanctioned sex.

From its very first private performance in March 1913, *Damaged Goods* managed to do what no sex play before it had. At a time when plays were regularly yanked off Broadway for containing sexual themes, this play was enthusiastically supported by public figures who saw it as promoting an important social cause.[2] Significantly, after its premiere, *Damaged Goods* was given as a command performance for President Wilson, his cabinet, both houses of Congress, members of the United States Supreme Court, diplomats and "the most distinguished audience ever assembled in America, including exclusively the foremost men and women of the Capital."[3] When it moved to New York City in April, *Damaged Goods* was likewise endorsed by leading medical scientists, legislators, clergy, suffragists, and reformers, including John Rockefeller, Jr., chair of the Bureau of Social Hygiene and leader of many antiprostitution investigations, reformer Maude E. Miner, and New York City's mayor, William J. Gaynor. Though it captured the attention of the social elite, the play appealed across political and class lines, as this newspaper account noted: "Many of the most prominent people in the city were present, numbering representatives not only of sociological and medical interests, but members of society, leaders in the world of fashion, of the drama and of education, well known first nighters and not a few just plain people."[4] The chief administrator of the Metropolitan Life Insurance Company was so impressed with *Damaged Goods* that he offered, "if someone could be found who would treat the same subject properly in book form[,] his company would publish it and distribute it free to the Metropolitan's seven million subscribers."[5] The *New York Evening Mail*'s drama critic, Burns Mantle, emphatically judged *Damaged Goods* "the biggest, the most meaningful, the most vital, the most impressive and the most terribly true drama we have ever seen played."[6] In short, while *Damaged Goods* had been banned from the legitimate stage in France and England, it received the ultimate stamp of legitimacy in the United States.[7] What, precisely, fueled the unprecedented success of this venereal disease play?

One answer would be that *Damaged Goods* represented a watershed moment in sex discourse, signaling a new level of public discussion about venereal disease, sexuality, and prostitution. Certainly, this was the prevailing view of the day. As a *Current Opinion* article in 1913 observed, "A wave of sex hysteria and sex discussion seems to have invaded this country. Our former reticence on matters of sex is giving way to a frankness that would even startle Paris. Prostitution . . . is the chief topic of polite conversation. It has struck 'sex o'clock' in America . . ."[8] The American premiere of *Damaged Goods*, the article continued, marked the beginning of "an epoch of new freedom in sex discussion," challenging the boundaries of public sexual decorum and instigating what many perceived to be a flurry of public discourse on sex.[9] As the title of Jane Addam's 1912 book on the Chicago sex trade made clear, America had developed "a new conscience" regarding sex and the social evil.[10] Everyone, it seems, was suddenly talking about sex.

Leading this fervent discussion, George Bernard Shaw applauded Brieux for mentioning "the most unmentionable subject of all – the subject of the diseases that are supposed to be the punishment of profligate men and worthless women."[11] An article in the *New Republic* likewise praised Brieux for "expos[ing] the conspiracy of syphilis and silence."[12] By all accounts, then, the 1913 production of *Damaged Goods* signaled a major shift toward an openness in American public discourse on sexuality.

This view of *Damaged Goods* still prevails among the few scholars who have given attention to the play. Allan M. Brandt, in his otherwise stunning social history of venereal disease in the United States, *No Magic Bullet* (1997), for example, claims that *Damaged Goods* "became a symbol of a new sexual openness. A financial success, it spawned a series of dramas on sexual themes."[13] Dramas on sexual themes, however, had long been performed on the New York stage. These were often at the very center of sex debates, igniting censorship and obscenity cases, riots in Times Square, and a profusion of discourse by newly emerging sex "experts." Claiming that *Damaged Goods* was "unprecedented in its open confrontation of sexual issues," and that it "attack[ed] hypocrisy and silence," Brandt replicates the logic of 1913 in reading *Damaged Goods* as a "transformation in sexual attitudes and practice."[14] It is this logic that I now wish to interrogate.

The popular view that the American premiere of *Damaged Goods* had broken the "conspiracy of silence," or that public discussions about venereal disease and prostitution (the two topics were often related) had reached a new level is simply incorrect. Although *Damaged Goods* initiated detailed discussions of venereal disease on the American stage, the United States, like many countries in Europe, had a long history of studying, legislating, and regulating sexuality in other cultural realms. Prostitution and venereal disease were hardly absent from public debate. On the contrary, as Michel Foucault has shown in his *History of Sexuality*, sex was meticulously studied, discussed, and regulated ad infinitum both in pseudoscientific and in official discourses while nonetheless "exploiting it as *the* secret."[15] As one reviewer remarked in 1913, "They thought they were removing a taboo. How they chattered between acts about the taboo! The taboo! George Bernard Shaw *raved* about the taboo! ... As a matter of fact there was not one fact mentioned that the average citizen doesn't know" (original emphasis).[16] Given these perspectives, how is it, then, that so many perceived *Damaged Goods* as breaking a taboo?

I propose three reasons why *Damaged Goods* functioned as "sociological propaganda" (as the *New York Times* put it) between 1913 and the end of the

First World War for groups as diverse as the social hygiene movement, antiprostitution reform, the White House, and the US military.[17]

First, *Damaged Goods* promoted a social hygiene agenda that advocated sexual responsibility and premarital health examinations to prevent needless infection of spouses (primarily women) by their sporting mates. These goals were linked to a perceived national panic (or, "hysteria," as the *Current Opinion* article claimed) about the threat of venereal disease to the so-called purity of the race. Maintaining the social hygiene of individual goods – within the marital frame – was part of a larger national ideology of purifying the national goods, a strategy that increasingly became allied with eugenics and antiprostitution efforts.

Second, *Damaged Goods* escaped censorship because its dramaturgy and mise-en-scène rendered the unseemly topic of venereal disease in a non-threatening manner. Pedagogically driven (though certainly not in Brecht's sense), *Damaged Goods* resembles a lecture more than a problem play. Maintaining a scientific distance from its subject, the play focuses on message rather than dramatic conflict. Most important, however, *Damaged Goods* anchors the central conflict not in the contested site of the brothel but rather in the sanctified, bourgeois settings of a doctor's office and an upper-class home. Marriage is the adhesive that holds together – as well as distorts – the dramatic action of the play. Accordingly, the main characters of this play are not the typical figures of the underworld (no Kitty Warrens or Anna Christies here), but rather people from the upper and professional classes. This dramaturgical framing, I suggest, protected bourgeois audiences from direct contact with the rank underworld.

Third, *Damaged Goods* advocated "proper" (that is, reproductive, marital) sexuality by juxtaposing social hygiene with its nefarious counterpart – prostitution – in ambivalent terms, a framing characteristic of modernism itself. The play's ambivalence results from, on the one hand, demonstrating a social hygiene agenda and sympathy toward the plight of prostitutes and other women contaminated by men, yet, on the other hand, characterizing the prostitute as what I call the *prostitute fatale*. Like her filmic descendant the *femme fatale*, the *prostitute fatale* represents the deadly part of pleasure, the evil side of the flower (as Baudelaire famously put it), the dangerous potential of unchecked female sexuality. A construct of the Progressive imagination, the *prostitute fatale* represents the dialectical tension between Eros and Thanatos – desire encased by necrophilia. Desired, yet feared, the *prostitute fatale* resides in an impossible space of ambiguity. Constructed since Dumas *fils' La Dame aux Camélias* in 1852 as a hooker-with-a-heart-of-gold, she reappears in the 1910s as a deadly source of contagion. Though a marginal or liminal figure, the *prostitute fatale*, paradoxically, becomes central to the definition of other subject positions: parent, wife, husband, national subject, innocent victim, and john.

Social hygiene takes the stage

While Bernard Shaw and others saw *Damaged Goods* as breaking the conspiracy of silence regarding sex, America had a long history of sex debates clustered around the topic of prostitution (see introduction). Rather than being silent about the topic of sex, the theatre was in fact the site of intense discursive activity. Yet, as I have been arguing throughout this study, the fate of the brothel drama was quite erratic. In the fall of 1913, just months after *Damaged Goods* played at the White House, the tide turned once again toward censorship. Three brothel plays, *The Lure, The Fight*, and *The House of Bondage* were shut down by the New York police (see chapter 7). However, the New York police did not touch *Damaged Goods* when it opened in New York for a commercial run, though it was not without its detractors. Considering censorship's presence on the New York stage, the American premiere of *Damaged Goods* is, at first glance, perplexing. Yet, in what follows, further scrutiny soon reveals why this sex play captivated the nation. In *Damaged Goods*, the forces of social hygiene, Progressivism, and pseudoscience struggled to control sexual discourse through the figure of the prostitute.

As perhaps no other play before it, *Damaged Goods* was literally produced by sexual science. Initially privately staged under the auspices of the Sociological Fund of the *Medical Review of Reviews, Damaged Goods* was part of what Foucault has termed the Western *scientia sexualis* – the scientific discourse which produces the "truth" of sex, and (I would add) of gender.[18] To ensure that his dramatic depiction of syphilis was medically accurate, Brieux asked Alfred Fournier, noted venereologist and author of *Syphilis and Marriage* (1880), to assist him.[19] Their collaboration was so intense that Brieux dedicated the play to Fournier, crediting him with most of the ideas for the plot.[20] Fournier lent scientific credibility to the text and *Damaged Goods* became known for its accurate, if shocking, medical information about venereal disease. As Brieux described it in the stage directions, the play's opening scene establishes the Doctor as the medical authority, his office literally basking in the light of morality (from "a large stained-glass window representing a religious subject"), and filled with emblems of knowledge including "a large glass bookcase."[21] Portraits and busts of the founders of modern science make up a mini-pantheon in the background. Unlike the British production, which portrayed a state-of-the-art scientific examination room, the American doctor's office resembled an upper-class parlor with plush leather furniture, rich hardwood paneling, and an ornately carved Edwardian desk. Flanked not only by the authority of science and religious morality, but also bourgeois respectability, the Doctor is unquestionably the voice of knowledge and the mediator of the "truth" of sex and gender.

Damaged Goods was successful on so many fronts because it promoted a pro-social hygiene agenda by advocating a healthy and clean body politic, sexual education, and a single sexual standard for men and women. These three threads are woven into the moral fabric of the play. As act 1 unfolds, the protagonist, George DuPont (played by Richard Bennett), is at his doctor's office, despondent at learning that he has contracted syphilis.[22] George seeks a quick fix to his problem, since he is soon to be married. At first denying that he has done anything to put himself in contagion's way, George eventually confesses that he has had two mistresses while he was engaged, one the wife of his best friend (a woman "of the most rigid morals") and the other an unsuspecting country girl (1.189). Misinformed about the nature of contagion, George chose both women because he believed that they were "clean." Ironically, George had frightened one mistress into being faithful to him by exaggerating the extent of venereal disease in the city. He boasts to the Doctor, "I kept her in absolute terror of this disease. I told her that almost all men were taken with it, so that she mightn't dream of being false to me" (1.189). This critique of George's reprehensible behavior – and, in effect, of male sporting in general – was interpreted as radical when the play premiered. As an article in the New York Independent noted, "Les Avariés, when it was first presented in 1901, shocked all Paris, less apparently because of its disgusting subject than because of its stern condemnation of the double standard of morality."[23] Twelve years after its French premiere, American audiences were receptive to a denunciation of male sporting, largely due to public debates instigated by the social hygiene movement. Damaged Goods therefore delivered an important critique of the male double (sex) standard, a critique that was very much in sync with American reform rhetoric.

Like a social hygiene pamphlet, Damaged Goods presents its message by reporting "facts" through the Doctor, who educates both the other characters in the play and the audience. As the Doctor tells George "Out of every seven men you meet in the street, or in society, or at the theatre, there is at least one who is or has been in your condition. One in seven, fifteen per cent" (1.188). Social hygienists and other reformers made similar arguments about the escalation of venereal disease. According to Dr. Prince Morrow, leader of the social hygiene movement and founder of the American Society for Sanitary and Moral Prophylaxis, up to 80 percent of all New York City males had contracted gonorrhea at some point, and he concluded, "fully one-eighth of all human suffering comes from this source."[24] In addition, *Damaged Goods* brought gory and sensational details about venereal disease to light. In the opening scene, for instance, the Doctor recounts, "I have seen an unfortunate young woman changed by this disease into the likeness of a beast. The face, or I should rather say, what remained of it, was nothing but a flat surface seamed with scars" (1.202).

In advocating clean sexual hygiene and rejecting a double standard for sexuality, Brieux's play echoed another tenet of social hygiene ideology: its sanctification of marriage and reproductive sex. As a pamphlet advertising *Damaged Goods* proclaimed, "The object of this play is a study of the Sex Problem in its bearing on marriage."[25] While the threat to marriage through infidelity was a staple theme in nineteenth-century theatre and literature, never had the institution of marriage been so drastically imperiled by venereal disease on stage as it was in this play. Indeed, the central dramatic conflict hinges on George's tenacious refusal to postpone his marriage until he takes the full cure. Disastrously, George ignores the Doctor, visits a quack, marries on time, and infects his wife and newborn child.

This depiction of George dovetailed with the Progressive preoccupation with protecting "venereal insontium": the infection of innocent women and children, by their husbands and fathers, with venereal diseases.[26] Defending the health of the innocent ones was taken up most publicly by Dr. Prince Morrow, who viewed venereal disease as a threat to the existence of the family, which he saw as the reproductive organ of the national body. Morrow's *Social Diseases and Marriage: Social Prophylaxis* (1904) argued not only that venereal disease was dangerous for the institution of marriage, but also that it struck "at the very root of nature's process for the perpetuation of the race."[27] Seeing the social body as an extension of the individual healthy body, social hygienists like Morrow directed many of their educational materials at women. In *Good Housekeeping*, Morrow wrote: "From the socio-political standpoint children are the only excuse for marriage – not offspring merely, but children born in conditions of vitality, health, and physical vigor, and capable of becoming useful citizens to the state. This gives a new and more exalted conception of the responsibilities of parentage."[28] In Morrow's view, reproductivity was not only a parental virtue, but also a national responsibility – sentiments vital to the plot of *Damaged Goods*. This national quest for vital offspring manifested in the baby shows of August 1913, which awarded cash for the healthiest babies in welfare neighborhoods.[29]

The central trope of the play, that of "damaged goods," demonstrates the play's investment in marriage and nation building. John Pollock's transla-tion of Brieux's title *Les Avariés* ("The Syphilitics") as *Damaged Goods* – which William Dean Howells thought "a very vulgar misnomer" – renders the problem quite literally as an economic matter.[30] What is damaged in this play is, on one level, a family. Because the central victims are George's unsuspecting wife and child, *Damaged Goods* seems to take the first-wave feminist insight about marriage as a business transaction, where women are exchanged as goods between men, and to overlay nationalistic and pure race agendas upon it. In George's mind, postponing his marriage would be "absolutely disastrous," since he is marrying into money which he needs for business purposes (1.196). While the Doctor is quick to rebuke George for acting recklessly, he does so by refashioning the economic metaphor so that the goods are gendered male: "Marriage is a contract. If you marry without saying anything, you will be giving an implied warranty for goods which you know to be bad. That is the term, isn't it? It would be a fraud which ought to be punishable by law" (1.198). Here, we see Brieux's plea for premarital venereal disease testing and for men like George to assume responsibility; yet the Doctor's rhetoric privileges a male economy wherein men have power over the goods, indeed, where they *are* the goods. According to the logic of the play, George's mistake is not that he callously views his wife as investment capital, but that he is a bad businessman. He allows his goods – his semen and, eventually, his genetic stock – to be damaged.

As the play's title reveals, then, *Damaged Goods* problematized real damage: the needless infection of wives and newborns by their husbands/ fathers. Yet, in spite of its critique of sporting male sexuality, the figurative framing of the problem as a business problem (i.e. as damaged goods) contributed to national anxieties about racial purity. This becomes evident through the Doctor's rhetoric. Unable to convince George to wait three years before marrying in order to undergo a proper cure, the Doctor changes his strategy and appeals to George's patriotism through the rhetoric of race suicide: "For the moment I will not think of you or of [your wife]: it is in the name of those innocent little ones that I appeal to you; it is the future of the race that I am defending" (1.204). Healthy, reproductive bodies – or goods – were increasingly theorized as integral to nation making and the preservation of white middle-class supremacy over the lower classes and ethnic minorities. Morrow echoed this anxiety: "the chief social danger of venereal diseases comes from their destructive effects on the health and the productive energy of the family. The office of the social hygiene . . . embraces . . . those who are destined to continue the race. This protective duty extends to the unborn children."[31] This view is articulated at the end of *Damaged Goods*:

> DOCTOR. [Those who contract syphilis] ought to be made to under-
> stand that the future of the race is in their hands and to be
> taught to transmit the great heritage they have received from
> their ancestors intact with all its possibilities to their descen-
> dants. (3.249)

The gravity of George's mistake then, is that he has damaged not only his "goods" but also his reproductive legacy.

At the conclusion of *Damaged Goods*, pure race ideology is fused with a reinscription of patriarchal order. In order to protect the DuPonts' ancestral legacy, the Doctor suggests that George's wife, Henriette, should forgive him and rescue their marriage. He tells Henriette's father, "If your daughter consents to forgive and forget, he will not only respect her, he will be eternally grateful . . . As for the future, we will make sure that when they are reunited their next child shall be healthy and vigorous" (3.242). Above all, this scene suggests, marriage and hetero-reproductivity (in the upper, "clean," classes) need to be salvaged for the greater good of the nation. In offering marriage as denouement, however, *Damaged Goods* resorts to very old dramaturgy indeed. It was far too late in the millennium for Henriette to marry her (diseased) man and forget all. Ibsen's Nora has already walked out of that door. Indeed, New York City's mayor, William J. Gaynor, found "that the ending of the play, where the husband and wife reunite (the danger having passed), ruined the impact of the play as a whole. As far as he was concerned, the ending aided the cause of men who sought out prostitutes."[32]

As committed as *Damaged Goods* was to marriage and eugenics, Brieux staunchly advocated education for women as well as men – a broadminded stance at the time. As Brieux put it, in a prologue read to the audience before the curtain rises, *Damaged Goods* "may be witnessed by everyone, unless we must believe that folly and ignorance are necessary conditions of female virtue."[33] Women like Mrs. Helen Brent of the New York Legislative League agreed: "The women of this country certainly owe Mr. Richard Bennett a debt of gratitude."[34] Indeed, female theatre-goers attended *Damaged Goods* in notable numbers, as the *New York Dramatic Mirror* reported: "Women if anything were in the majority. They seemed to belong to the better class and applauded vociferously such lines as had a more or less direct bearing on social conditions and evil."[35] Other reviewers commented not only on the reaction of the female members of the audience (no mention is made of the reactions of their male counterparts), but also speculated about their politics. The *New York Independent*, for example, noted that the Fulton was packed with an audience that included "suffragists,"[36] while another reviewer (somewhat disparagingly) reported, "Hundreds of women (with a 'mission'), applauded vociferously."[37] A particularly nasty review in the *New York American* not only insulted the playwright, but also objectified female theatre-goers: "Its only remarkable feature was its audience. That, made up of extraordinary-looking women, was worth looking at."[38] Though it is unclear just how seriously women were taken in 1913, both as audience members and as political subjects, it is noteworthy the extent to which dominant culture sought to make sense of their presence and reactions.

At the same time that *Damaged Goods* advocated a certain liberal view regarding sexual education for both men and women, it also recycled traditional notions regarding gender, especially in its celebration of maternity, pure womanhood, and sexual propriety. As a flier advertising the New York production boasted, "Women Hail Brieux' Play as a Champion of Motherhood."[39] Brieux capitalized on maternity as a metaphor, saying that "health is a form of virtue, that it is the mother of virtue[,] that each one of us should be in good health."[40] In promoting a new, morally hygienic national identity, Brieux, like others in the social hygiene movement, reconstructed residual Victorian notions of pure womanhood. Like their nineteenth-century counterpart, the "Angel in the House," Progressive Era women were encouraged to cultivate hygienically, and morally, clean domiciles. Indeed, the angelic image was used on a British poster for *Damaged Goods*, which depicted the Virgin Mary presiding over the weeping Henriette and her infected child. In Progressive Era culture, maternity – a woman's "highest destiny," according to Prince Morrow – was valued above all else.[41] Doctors in particular stressed this view. "The supreme importance of woman," wrote one physician, in the *Journal of the American Medical Association*, lies in "her roll [sic] as the nourishing mother; her place as the very foundation stone of every hearth and home, and her life as the vital center about which cluster families and tribes and nations."[42]

As if in response to the cultural impulse for what Bernarr Macfadden in 1918 characterized as "vigorous motherhood," *Damaged Goods* validated the institution visibly through the character of George's wife.[43] "Poor innocent little Henriette," as George calls her, is innocent not only because she and her baby are unknowingly infected with syphilis but also because she has been kept innocent about venereal diseases and about sexuality outside of marriage (2.211). Henriette does not participate in the dialogue concerning venereal disease – Brieux leaves those matters to the men in her life, who have lengthier scenes – and on hearing the grim reality that she and her baby are infected, Henriette can only "shriek like a mad woman" and scream, "Don't touch me!" (2.234). Resorting to the old trope of female madness, Brieux locates national sex hysteria in Henriette's shrieking female body. Significantly, this hysterical scene is her last moment in the play: Henriette does not deal with the consequences of infection (as do George and the Doctor); she does not discuss the pros and cons of anti-prostitution reform (as do Loches and the Doctor); nor does she lament that her monogamy was all for naught (as, with inverted logic, does George). Rather, Henriette is consigned to a brief mad scene and then silenced for the remainder of the play. Even so, this scene was tellingly described by the *New York Times* as the "most powerful and affecting" of the entire play.[44]

Just as Progressive America ambivalently relegated sexual regulation largely to medical, juridical and legislative domains (the regulators of sexuality in the Foucauldian sense), so *Damaged Goods* struck "sex o'clock" in a similarly ambivalent way. On the one hand, the play advocated a liberal social hygiene agenda that struck down the double standard for sexuality, sought to bring women into sex debates, and tried to eliminate venereal contagion. On the other hand, however, the play invested heavily in marriage, motherhood, eugenics, and an ideology about gender roles that both commodified married sexuality and served nation building.

Dramatic sermons

In addition to its advocacy of social hygiene, the sermon-like dramaturgy used in *Damaged Goods*, a characteristic that was both applauded and condemned, helped it escape the censor's wrath. Dramatic critics faulted the play as "hardly drama in its accepted conventional form."[45] Indeed, the *Dial* called it "a thesis without a play."[46] The *World* noted that while "few more instructive or beneficial works have been written . . . to call it a play is equally ridiculous."[47] H. E. Stearns of the *New York Dramatic Mirror* maintained *Damaged Goods* was "a preconceived intellectual thesis" with "morbidly unreal" characters and compared Brieux's dramaturgy negatively to Ibsen's: "*Ghosts* is the work of a dramatist; *Damaged Goods* of a discussionist."[48] James Metcalfe of *Life Magazine* suggested that the play was nothing more than a "medical treatise sugar-coated for general consumption by its background of scenery, impersonations and a semblance of story."[49] The *New York Times* observed, "the third act is more in the nature of an exhibit, a summoning, as it were, of the arguments in concrete tangible symbols with no positive definite association with the dramatic structure that has gone before."[50] The *New York American* joined the chorus of reviewers who faulted *Damaged Goods* for its "discussionist" dramaturgy, finding the "long dissertations" of the actors "tiresome" and unimaginative.[51]

Promotional brochures proclaimed *Damaged Goods* "More Powerful than [the] Greatest Sermon," and they were not alone in viewing the stage as a pulpit.[52] According to an editorial in the *New York Globe*, "*Damaged Goods* is a tract, a pamphlet, a sermon – one of the most awakening and hard-hitting we have ever read or heard. It proves, more completely than any other play we can remember, that the theatre can be the most influential pulpit in the world."[53] The play's "campaign of education" was supported by "the most progressive bodies of social workers," clergy, and Progressive reformers.[54] "It's a moral lesson so strong," added another review, "that it should be given at some theatre gratis, by the city, so that all may witness it."[55] As late as 1915, Brieux continued to defend the mix of pulpit and stage, calling for "drama as an instrument of reform, not as a form of art or a means of recreation."[56]

If there was a discernable sermon-like aesthetic to the play, the hygienic mise-en-scène certainly contributed to it. Brieux located scenes in proper, bourgeois settings: the Doctor's office and the DuPont's upper-class home. By contrast, other prostitute plays from the 1913 Broadway season were required to cut out scenes portraying the brothel before the New York Grand Jury and police dropped charges. Benign in its own dramaturgical framing, however, *Damaged Goods* never ventured into the underworld proper and escaped censorship. Brieux's "discussionist" dramaturgy and the sanitized mise-en-scène allowed certain kinds of knowledge to be represented – epistemologies with hegemonic framings. Yet, into this socially hygienic framework, the underworld seeps like a slow, yet none-theless dangerous, leak in a cracked dam. Enter the *prostitute fatale*.

The *prostitute fatale*

In celebrating innocent reproductive female bodies, *Damaged Goods* vilified their counterparts: the wretched bodies of the underworld. In *Damaged Goods*, the prostitute-figure provoked a kind of sex hysteria. Though it attempted to bring closure to this terror, *Damaged Goods* is itself an ambivalent text, indelibly marked by the polarities of modernity. On the one hand, the play demonstrates sympathy for the plight of prostitutes and other women contaminated by men. On the other hand, it perpetuates stereotypes of the infectious creature of the night: the *prostitute fatale*. This bundling of inconsistent representations demonstrates the ambivalence of Progressive culture, and indeed of modernity itself, in characterizing the underworld.

While a prostitute does not make an entrance on stage until the last act of *Damaged Goods*, there are constant allusions to her. In the first act, when George learns he is infected, for example, he protests, "I didn't take a woman off the streets, you know" (1.193). Since George has not slept with a prostitute, he thinks he is safe from contagion, subscribing to the one-way contamination theory that dominated the day: venereal disease could be transmitted only by women from the sexual underworld to men of the upper class. When this theory proves wrong, George articulates his unfulfilled desire for the prostitute:

> GEORGE. But for nothing! nothing! I have cut myself off from all pleasures. I have resisted attractions as you would the devil. I wouldn't go with my friends to places of amusement: ladies I knew actually pointed me out to their boys as an example . . . Oh, I should have liked to come home at four o'clock in the morning with my coat-collar turned up, smoking a cigar lit in some ballet-girl's rooms! I've longed as much as anyone for the taste of rouged lips and the glitter of blacked eyes and pale faces! (1.191)

George's regret that he hadn't tasted the rouged lips of a prostitute or ballet girl reveals the conflicted cultural response to women who were (or were presumed to be) sexual – imagined as the corporeal site both of pleasure and of infection. As the Doctor puts it at the conclusion of the play, "The whole problem is summed up in her: she is at once the product and the cause" (3.253).

On the surface, *Damaged Goods* rallies sympathy for the plight of prostitutes. In the final scene, George's enraged father-in-law, Loches, wants to do away with prostitution:

> LOCHES. I realize now that what is needed is to attack this evil at its
> source and to suppress prostitution. We ought to hound out
> these vile women who poison the very life of society.
> DOCTOR. You forget that they themselves have first been poisoned.
>
> (3.249)

Indeed, this is true of the final patient, a prostitute who, while working as a domestic at the age of seventeen, was raped by her boss and subsequently became pregnant.[57] After losing her position, she turned to prostitution: "[W]hen you're hungry and a jolly young chap offers you a dinner, my word, I'd like to see the girl who'd say no. I never learnt any trade you see" (3.252–53). Though this character is no Kitty Warren, and her speech is relatively brief, it is nonetheless a rare moment in early twentieth-century drama and gives voice to a figure otherwise criminalized and censored on the stage.

Damaged Goods also argues against regressive antiprostitution legislation, such as the Page Act of 1910 (and, later, the America Plan) which incarcerated large numbers of allegedly infected prostitutes in medical prisons "until cured" – which, according to social historian Ruth Rosen, was 365 days on average.[58] This lopsided practice of interning prostitutes and not their johns is alluded to in *Damaged Goods* by the streetwalker: "These beastly men give you their foul diseases and it's me they stick in prison" (3.253). When Loches, a city official, continues to argue that new laws are needed to regulate this vice, the Doctor urges tolerance and education, rather than legislation: "No, no! We want no new laws: there are too many already. All that is needed is for people to understand the nature of this disease rather better" (3.240). The correlation between these lines and Brieux's own beliefs was exact. "Brieux," explained one critic, "is not one who believes that social evils are to be cured by laws and yet more laws. He ... urges education."[59]

While most vice reports in the nineteenth and early twentieth centuries expressed sympathy for prostitutes and the conditions that drove them to their trade (Sanger, The Committee of Fifteen, The Committee of Fourteen, and Kneeland), they nonetheless proposed solutions that launched vigorous antiprostitution movements intimately linked to anxieties about urbanization and the commercialization of vice. As Brandt has shown, venereal disease became a social symbol of contamination, a sign of decaying social order perceived as out of control, dirty, and untidy: "The very term which the venereal disease control movement took for itself in the twentieth century – social hygiene – makes explicit this association."[60] Similarly, Sander Gilman argues that the desire to distance oneself from disease is an expression of a larger fear of chaos, disintegration, and collapse, which gets mapped onto an Other.[61] The presence of venereal disease in the upper and middle classes at the turn of the century was painful proof that intercourse with the lower-class, damaged Other, the prostitute, was taking place. The new logic of social hygiene asserted that damaged goods must be cured – even if they belonged to the underworld – but only as part of a national strategy to save the national goods. As L. Duncan Bulkey put it in 1906, venereal diseases could never be eliminated until "the lowest levels of society are influenced toward their prevention."[62] Such sentiments drove aggressive antiprostitution efforts until most red-light districts were eradicated toward the end of the second decade of the twentieth century.

Despite its progressive views, *Damaged Goods* perpetuated these lingering myths about prostitution and contagion. Although the beginning of the play suggests that venereal disease can be contracted from anyone and not just prostitutes (George is infected from his friend's wife), the remaining scenes suggest otherwise. In the last act, for example, when Loches expresses the irreparable damage George has done to his family, his complaint is not just that his daughter has been infected, but that through bodily fluids, she has come into contact with a prostitute:

> LOCHES. This man [George] has inflicted on his wife the supreme insult, the most odious degradation. He has, as it were, thrust her into contact with the streetwalker with whose vice he is stained, and created between her and that common thing a bond of blood to poison herself and her child. Thanks to him, this abject creature, this prostitute, lives our life, makes one of our family, sits down with us at the table.
>
> (3.238–39)

In this passage, Brieux echoes Morrow's point that the Angel in the House and the fallen woman were often linked through men's intercourse with them: "It is with this fatal gift," Morrow wrote of venereal disease, "that the courtesan repays her virtuous sister for the scorn and contempt which are heaped upon her, and by a strange irony of fate the husband is made bearer of this venom, and administers it to his family."[63] Though men are bearers of this venom, this logic tells us, prostitutes are its source.

The conclusion of *Damaged Goods* repeats this view. Three patients keep appointments with the Doctor during Loches's visit: a widowed upper-class woman, left bankrupt and infected by her husband; a young college student; and a domestic-turned-prostitute. Each provides a kind of Foucauldian confession about unregulated sexuality. Though these three characters are meant to represent various stations in life and that venereal disease affects everyone alike, the first two locate the source of contagion with a prostitute (and the last, of course, is herself one). The upper-class widow became infected and was unable to bear children as a result of her husband's exploits with prostitutes while in the army. As she explains, "I couldn't ever bring one [baby] to birth, sir. My husband was taken at the very beginning of our marriage, while he was doing his time as a reservist. There are women that hang about the barracks." (3.247). Brieux clearly suggests that these women haunt not only soldiers, but also the civilians, as the account of the father of the college student patient (now paralyzed by venereal disease) demonstrates: "It was at the very college gates that my poor boy was got hold of by one of these women. Is it right, sir, that that should be allowed? Aren't there enough police to prevent children of fifteen from being seduced like that? I ask, is it right?" (3.247–48).

The most incriminating evidence, however, comes from the prostitute herself in the final testimonial. Her confession begins (as we have seen) with a sympathetic account of her fall into prostitution, but concludes with her transformation into the *prostitute fatale*, a ruthless killer, not unlike the contemporary mythic "Patient Zero":[64]

> GIRL. Oh, I had my tit for tat! ... I took on everyone I could, for anything or for nothing! As many as I could, all the youngest and the best looking – well, I only gave 'em back what they gave me! Now somehow I don't care any more. (3.253)

As Sander Gilman has shown, locating the prostitute as the central source of blame evoked a long and rich tradition of representing the syphilitic as a sexually corrupt female.[65] Referencing this iconography, this scene established a kind of melodramatic urgency behind eliminating the prostitute. When *Damaged Goods* toured in Boston in December 1913, the part of the streetwalker was the only part cut when the mayor found the play "disgust-ing."[66] And indeed, such avenging behavior is more typical of a *femme fatale* in film noir. Just as the *femme fatale* was a figure to be contained and even eradicated, so the "diseased whore" sparked a national war on prostitution – an action that dovetailed with the First World War.

When America began to prepare for war, *Damaged Goods* was once again enlisted to educate the nation, this time under the aegis of the United States Army. In 1917, the War Department asked Richard Bennett, who had co-produced the New York version of *Damaged Goods* and starred as George, to tour with the filmed version of the play, to help educate service-men about venereal disease.[67] In order to reach as many soldiers as possible, the military sent Bennett, along with the film, to France to give lectures. Here, quite literally, the army was producing sexual scripts. The film and its use by the army provide a celluloid epilogue to my discussion of the *prostitute fatale*.

Just as *Damaged Goods* was created with support from sexual science as well as political and juridical agencies, so too the film recycled existing antiprostitution sentiments regarding venereal disease and infection. Even so, panic about venereal disease peaked during the war years, as its threat to the nation's health reached what were perceived to be epidemic propor-tions. Indeed, according to military sources in 1917, "venereal diseases ... are the greatest cause of disability in the Army and present the most serious communicable disease problem of the war."[68]

If venereal disease was perceived as the greatest liability to the nation at war, then the prostitute was viewed as the primary contaminator. Her body, considered public property, was once again the site of regulation. War was declared not only abroad, but also at home as "the antivice movement developed into a full-scale repressive movement against the prostitute," with the United States government at its head.[69] The military launched a two-pronged attack: to educate soldiers about venereal disease, and to regulate a five-mile zone around each military camp in which any suspicious woman could be arrested as a prostitute, tested for venereal disease, and detained until "cured." Known as the America Plan, this effort by the War Department's Commission on Training Camp Activities has been called by Timothy J. Gilfoyle "the most aggressive attack on prostitution in the nation's history."[70]

As part of its new approach to sexual morality, the military made it clear that interacting with prostitutes was, quite literally, sleeping with the enemy. One pamphlet stated, "Women who solicit soldiers for Immoral purposes are usually disease spreaders and friends of the enemy."[71] Another pamphlet cautioned, "You wouldn't eat or drink anything that you knew would weaken your vitality, poison your blood, cripple your limbs, rot your flesh, blind your eyes, destroy your brain. Why take the same chance with a whore?"[72] Hundreds of posters like this one, "A German Bullet is Cleaner Than A Whore," equated prostitutes with the foreign foe.[73] Perceived as the enemy, the *prostitute fatale* was represented in popular culture as so fatal that she herself must be obliterated. The ensuing antiprostitution campaign was so successful that, by 1920, prostitution had declined and been driven underground. As Gilfoyle notes, "New York's century of prostitution had ended," though not without serious consequences for prostitutes.[74]

In the interest of constructing a hygienically pure national identity, the film and stage versions of *Damaged Goods* located disease in the body of the prostitute – a familiar target for sexual moralists and reformers. As the first venereal disease drama to take center stage, *Damaged Goods* occupies an important position in American theatre and film history. Embraced by the social hygiene movement, the US government, and the military, *Damaged Goods* might be the most officially sanctioned drama about sex in American history. It is perhaps one of the most flagrant examples of (mis)educating the nation about gender, sexual hygiene, the sanctity of marriage, and the purity of the race. In a theatre season otherwise characterized by censorship, the American success of *Damaged Goods* in 1913 reveals a deployment of sex discourse that must be read closely. As a response to the threat of venereal disease and its imagined counterpart, the prostitute, *Damaged Goods* is a polysemic text marked by the ambivalent characteristics of modernity itself. Important for the awareness it generated about venereal disease and male sporting, the play offered its knowledges within distinctly pseudoscientific, bourgeois, and heteronormative framings. The *prostitute fatale* appears in this play not because Brieux wished to demonize the whore, but rather because she is unimaginable other than as the allegorical "flower of evil." In the end, *Damaged Goods* dramatized conflicting cultural desires concerning commercialized vice, but remained unable to conjure problems, or solutions for them, without the prostitute-construct – a figure it both desired and despised.

9

The repentant courtesan in "Anna Christie" *and the lesbian prostitute in* The God of Vengeance

> The theme of "Anna Christie" is an inversion of that old French thing, the repentant courtesan. Every promising playwright since Augier and Dumas *fils* has had his whack at it, so that it comes into twentieth century drama like a tin can kicked down the street by a parcel of vigorous schoolboys, and bearing the dints made by individual legs.
>
> James Agate, *Saturday Review*, April 21, 1923

The repentant courtesan, as James Agate reminds us, had been resurrected by scores of playwrights ever since Dumas *fils* penned the character of Camille in 1852. If the so-called repentant courtesan was a figure so familiar to the theatrical canon that she could be tossed down the theatrical row, then it was hardly shocking that Eugene O'Neill would, to use Agate's metaphor, put his dent in the old tin can. After all, one of O'Neill's very first plays, a one-act called *The Web* (1913), involved a prostitute character as did several of his later full-length plays (see, for example, *Great God Brown, Welded, Ah, Wilderness!, The Moon for the Caribee*, and *Long Day's Journey Into Night*).[1] As Arthur and Barbara Gelb point out in their biography of O'Neill, "a total of fourteen streetwalkers ply their trade in seven other of his published plays; additional prostitutes figure as offstage characters in another five plays."[2] While much has been written about O'Neill's fascination with prostitutes, the most common interpretation of O'Neill's *"Anna Christie"* is that he recycled the familiar French courtesan plot with an American twist, adding, as Agate put it, "a new milieu, a new setting and something that looks like a new technique to tell us an old and moving story."[3] Most critics agreed with this British reviewer, who claimed O'Neill had reinvented the fallen figure "so that this poor lost Anna Christie is not a stock type but a live creature, whose

183

common little woes are for the given hour the all-important."[4] But was Anna more than a stock type?

If it were true, as Francis Hackett remarked in 1921, that "[a] prostitute to him [O'Neill] has great romantic values," then it was especially important that this character had to be what Hackett called "the right kind of prostitute."[5] O'Neill's reinvention of the courtesan figure emerged at a significant cultural moment: just as red-light districts in most major American cities were being closed. Perceived as a victory for reformists, the prostitution problem appeared, in the early 1920s, to have been solved. After 1920, as Timothy Gilfoyle has noted, "the public decline of prostitution, with its increasing marginalization, reflected the rise of new institutions of leisure, changing heterosexual relations, and new boundaries of acceptable behavior. New York's century of prostitution had ended."[6] But while commercialized vice was thought to have been effectively eradicated from the streets, it was still playing on the New York stage, created by the country's most prominent playwrights.

What is most noteworthy about *"Anna Christie,"* given the history of the censorship of prostitute plays on the New York stage, is that O'Neill achieved a kind of strange respectability by garnering the Pulitzer Prize for the 1921–22 season. Yet, unlike *Mrs Warren's Profession* and many other brothel plays, *"Anna Christie"* not only escaped the attention of New York's censors, but also captured one of the most legitimating prizes in the theatre. By 1921, the prostitute play had become uncannily respectable in mainstream theatre.

As Sheila Hickey Garvey has shown, Anna Christie is "one of the most poignant of dramatic literature's 'fallen women,'" a character who has followed in the footsteps of countless courtesan figures that harken back to Camille.[7] While *"Anna Christie"* is unique in being one of the first prostitute plays on Broadway in which the courtesan or fallen woman does not suffer some kind of negative ending – whether it be death (*Camille, Olympe*), societal scorn (*The Deluge, The Easiest Way*), or personal loss (*Sapho* and *Mrs Warren's Profession*) – the play offers a mixed dramaturgical victory, visible in two points. First, although O'Neill does create a kind of "sentimental sympathy for whores,"[8] as the Gelbs put it, by breaking away from the tragedy of Camille-like narratives, he does so by recycling the old "tin can" of dramaturgy in prostitute plays. Though I arrive at my conclusions by different means, I quite agree with Zander Brietzke's assessment of *"Anna Christie"* when he writes, "O'Neill attempts to transcend nineteenth[-]century melodrama but lacks the means to do it."[9] Second, part of what made *"Anna Christie"* palatable to New York audiences was the curious response to actress Pauline Lord's unconventional looks. Coupled with Lord's positioning of herself as naïve and respectable, Anna's character was ghosted, to use Marvin Carlson's term, by a kind of innocence that rendered her nonthreatening.

With these two points in mind, this chapter argues that the mainstream acceptance of *"Anna Christie"* echoed the containment of the prostitute figure in the Progressive Era. Anna is, in fact, the embodiment of reform. That the play garnered the Pulitzer signals not just that Anna is a "repentant courtesan," as Agate would have it, but more than this a *reformed* prostitute. She is not Kitty Warren, who proudly defends her profession, nor is she a hooker-with-a-heart-of-gold, nor merely a victim of desperate circumstances. The centrifugal force of Anna's story spins toward what Andrew Parker and Eve Kosofsky Sedgwick call "the force field of the marital proscenium."[10] Such a story made great sense to Progressive reformers in what we might call the zenith of their work in 1921, when the battle against prostitution appeared to have been won.

But the question still remains: at what price does this reform come?

In the early twentieth century, there was significant slippage between women who worked the counter and those who worked the street. As Barbara Meil Hobson's research reveals, many women supplemented their jobs with part-time prostitution or hooked for a short period, rather than devoting their lives to it.[11] What is striking, then, is the repeated effort in the theatre, just as in popular culture, to fossilize the fluid nature of this work and to indelibly mark prostitutes as separate. In *"Anna Christie,"* we see a similar slide from working girl to whore in the development of Anna's character. As originally written in an earlier version called *Chris Christophersen* (often called *Chris* by critics and O'Neill himself), Anna was "a respectable British typist," as Travis Bogard notes, "whose greatest oath was 'By jimminy,' and who eagerly refreshed herself after the fatigues of an Atlantic crossing with a cup of her father's tea."[12] In the change "from typist to trollop" in the development of the script, "Anna's decline and fall was as rapid as it was remarkable."[13]

Initially, it may appear that as a typist Anna had more independence than her harlot counterpart. For instance, in *Chris*, rather than being defeated by life, Anna arrives with a sense of optimism about being a career girl: "I dreamed of the big opportunities for a woman over here in America," she says (CP1 825).[14] Like many women who were then entering the work force, this earlier Anna can make "enough to live on my own and be myself," as she puts it (824). This Anna is also not dependent on her father, but rather intends to support *him*. "There'll be no excuse for you keeping this position, once I'm at work," she remarks, "It's time you had a good rest. Let me do the working from now on" (828). Yet, in spite of Anna's initial independence in *Chris*, her character soon loses interest in her former independent life: "My old plans and dreams," she says, "seemed too dreadful – and stupid – and such a waste of life" (879).

While in *Chris Christophersen*, Anna appears as a tea-sipping typist, in *"Anna Christie"* she is streetwise and much stronger for it. In locating the character on the American side of the Atlantic and the other side of the underworld, O'Neill not only creates a compelling native character, but also does so by using the gritty Tenderloin – like many writers of the day – to authenticate her. Because the revised Anna has experienced more than her share of trauma (rape by her Minnesota cousins, prostitution, and illness) she also has more depth. Consequently, the lead character in *"Anna Christie"* has more interesting things to say than her prototype in *Chris* (such as the rather banal "I'm a full-fledged typist now, Father," 823). O'Neill, like other playwrights before him, realized that prim stenographers make less interesting subjects than their brothel sisters.

In *"Anna Christie,"* from her first entrance, Anna is portrayed as an independent, though exhausted and rough-edged, woman (see figure 11). Freshly released from a medical prison, Anna enters a waterfront saloon, uttering the lines made memorable by Garbo in the 1930 film version: "Gimme a whiskey – ginger ale on the side . . . And don't be stingy baby." Here, Anna meets Marthy, described by one critic as "the drink-soaked mistress of [Chris'] domicile."[15] This setting, complete with the separate ladies' entrance (that likely borrowed from Harrison Grey Fiske's staging of Edward Sheldon's *Salvation Nell* in 1908), was dubbed "the acme of realism."[16] Designed by Robert Edmond Jones, the ladies' section of a bar is, in short, a perfect setting for two fallen women to meet and discuss their lives. In this scene, Anna comes across unlike previous prostitute figures on the stage. Rather than expressing love for, or dependence on, men, as was common for the repentant courtesan prototype, she instead reveals her bitter hatred of them:

> ANNA. It was all men's fault – the whole business. It was men on the farm ordering and beating me – and giving me the wrong start. Then I was a nurse, it was men again hanging around, bothering me, trying to see what they could get. (*She gives a hard laugh.*)

Figure 11. Anna's entrance in "*Anna Christie*" as portrayed by Pauline Lord. Photo courtesy of the New York Public Library.

And now it's men all the time. Gawd, I hate 'em all, every mother's son of 'em! Don't you? (CP1 972–73)

However, Anna's rage is quickly checked by Marthy, who responds more temperately with, "Oh, I dunno. There's good ones and bad ones, kid. You've just had a run of bad luck with 'em, that's all. Your Old Man, now – old Chris – he's a good one" (973). As Ann Hall points out, Marthy functions as a defender of patriarchy, "someone to rescue it and Anna from anti-male sentiments."[17]

Just as female anger was only allowed a small amount of dramaturgical space, so too Marthy and Anna are given only a brief scene together. In *Chris Christophersen* this bar scene was originally written as a conversation between Chris's sailor friends, and Marthy and Anna exchange just one or two lines. In *"Anna Christie,"* however, the two women have a meaningful, if short, conversation about "the life" from their differing perspectives as wizened sea hag and worn-out twenty-something prostitute. Yet, like other dramatists who featured scenes with prostitutes (Eugene Walter and Edward Sheldon, for instance), O'Neill is less interested in creating lengthy scenes between two women of the streets than those in which the women interact with the men in their lives. Marthy therefore makes her exit just as Chris arrives, allowing the action to center on the triangular relationship between the principal characters: Anna, Chris, and Mat.

Critics like Barbara Voglino have pointed out Anna's independence and her "surprisingly militant assertion[s] of feminism."[18] These two aspects of Anna's character are seen perhaps most clearly when her wrath at patriarchy erupts in act 3, after Mat and Chris fight over her as if she were a possession. As Mat tells Chris, "She'll do what I say! You've had your hold on her long enough. It's my turn now" (CPI 1006). Upon hearing this, Anna stops their brawl by laughing wildly and exclaiming,

> ANNA. You're just like all the rest of them – you two! Gawd, you'd think I was a piece of furniture! . . . You was going on's if one of you had got to own me. But nobody owns me, see? – 'cepting myself. I'll do what I please and no man, I don't give a hoot who he is, can tell me what to do! I ain't asking either of you for a living. I can make it myself – one way or another. I'm my own boss. So put that in your pipe and smoke it! (1007)

Anna's denouncement of men's desire to own her was not lost on critic Maida Castellun of the *New York Call*, who described the scene as follows: "an electric thrill passed through the audience. It was like an echo of Nora in *The Doll's House* – this cry that she, who had sold herself many times, at least would not be 'owned' by any man."[19] Percy Hammond lauded this monologue as "a fine speech with a wallop in every syllable, spoken in the racy lingo and flat monotonous tones of the Minnesota underworld . . ."[20]

And Ernest Boyd of the *Freeman* praised both the writing and the acting: "This third act is one of the most effective pieces of dramatic writing I have seen in the modern theatre, and Miss Pauline Lord rises to the situation with the art of a great actress."[21]

Anna's monologue is indeed an important moment in the representation of prostitution in American drama, showing a strong woman who is her "own boss," as she herself puts it. Unfortunately, however, Anna too quickly gives up her anger and independence and, unlike Nora, does not walk out of the door. After her "frenzy of disgust," as Boyd called it, it is the *men* who walk out to bury their burden in drink, leaving Anna alone. Though this was not O'Neill's intention, as Hall notes, "any resistance to convention is suppressed by the heterosexual happy ending."[22] In spite of O'Neill's desires to have the ending function like a comma in a larger sentence yet to be completed, his dramaturgical grammar was riddled with syntax problems. Brenda Murphy writes, "O'Neill had not yet found a way to take his audience beyond the introductory clause and into the larger rhythm of the sentence."[23]

This brings us to the problematic fourth act. While the majority of reviews from the original production called *"Anna Christie"* a success, most also agreed that the last act was "full of bogus things."[24] As the reviewer for the *Dial* put it, the end of act 3 "is where good plays end. This one goes on to a so-called happy conclusion."[25] Another review likewise criticized "that wretched and illogical last act," faulting it for "the Broadway happy ending taint," claiming "the last act was quite unworthy of O'Neill and sounded as though it had been evolved in a Broadway manager's office."[26] Robert Benchley of *Life Magazine* mused, "The author would have done well to put that fourth act in an open boat with food and water for three days and turn it out into the sea off Provincetown before sending the play into New York."[27] Maida Castellun found the ending disastrous: "Such an ending to such a beginning is tragic beyond expression. It is worse than a blunder. It is a crime against artistic truth as well as against life."[28] American critics were not alone in the denunciation of the last act. As G. H. Mair of the *Evening Standard* put it, "*'Anna Christie'* had no business to have a happy ending any more than *King Lear.*"[29] Indeed, the last act seemed so dispensable that when the script was reprinted in *Theatre Magazine* in 1922, the editors simply summarized the final act in a paragraph.[30] As the performance history of *"Anna Christie"* suggests, the play encountered modest success (running for 177 performances at the Vanderbilt Theatre). In fact, O'Neill considered *"Anna Christie"* one of his failures and resisted publisher's efforts to include it in a collection of his plays.

Some critics, like James Agate of London's *Saturday Review*, disagreed: "Happy endings are not necessarily bad art. This play called for a happy ending, though perhaps not in the particular manner devised by Mr. O'Neill." Agate stressed that "If Anna had not been taken to her lover's arms at the end, I believe that every member of that crowded audience would have left the theatre in genuine distress."[31] Francis Hackett agreed that it was necessary for O'Neill to "cheat" with the inferior fourth act with its "somewhat inglorious happy ending."[32]

While much has been written about the "inexcusably banal" ending, as one reviewer from the *New York Call* put it, I wish to interpret it somewhat differently.[33] What is problematic with the "unsatisfactory last act," as Walter Prichard Eaton called it, is not just that it offers contrived drama-turgical closure, but rather that it relies so extensively on Anna's submission to patriarchal authority.[34] That the play revolves around the men in Anna's life is hardly surprising. We must remember that this is a story that was not originally about Anna at all, but rather her father. As Bogard notes, O'Neill "reluctantly gave up the old man as the central figure" as Anna assumed more dramaturgical importance.[35] What is intriguing is not that the fourth act resorts to anticlimax, but rather that the climax and denouement are negotiated by the men in Anna's life. As Boyd observed: "Anna Christie becomes a mere bone of selfish contention over which these two animals snarl and fight."[36] She is an object of exchange between men, to use Eve Kosofsky Sedgwick's words. Indeed, Pauline Lord, the actress who origi-nated the role, observed, "her situation is both touching and dreadful, between those two ranting self-centered men who never think of anything but their own feelings."[37] In the final scene, Mat appears back at the boat, drunk and with "an expression in his eyes of wild mental turmoil, of impotent animal rage baffled by its own abject misery." He announces, "'tis well you know I'd have a right to come back and murder you" (CP1 1017). Of course, the threat to murder fallen women was hardly new (in fact, whores regularly died on stage, just as they did in real life, at the hands of lovers or johns). Mat has already threatened to kill her in the previous act, shrieking, "You slut, you, I'll be killing you now!" (1010). The audience had to wonder whether Anna would indeed meet the fate of her tragic courtesan predecessors.

One surprising twist in the action is that when Mat returns, Anna confronts him with a gun and a cold, callous tone, asking, "What are you doing here?" (1018). In spite of this potentially powerful moment, Anna's credibility is dubious, given that there are so few female predecessors in drama who have ever wielded a weapon against a man (Hedda uses it on herself, after all). One reviewer saw through this contrived moment, commenting, "The pistol which was dragged into the last act was merely a stage toy."[38] And Alexander Woollcott wrote that Anna "brandish[ed] a revolver for no other conceivable purpose than that of jouncing the nervous playgoer into a state of receptive agitation."[39] Tellingly, the gun is missing altogether from the 1930 film version. If this was (and is) a world in which men kill fallen women (the shocking pistol scene in *Olympe's Marriage* is just one example), it is no less true in the drama when O'Neill was writing. Mat's threats, of a kind of violence that many prostitutes and other women suffered at the hands of their lovers, are quickly forgiven by all characters in the play, including Anna. After just a few lines of dialogue she gives in, *"letting the revolver drop to the floor, as if her fingers had no strength to hold it"* (1018–19; original emphasis). The gun, defying Chekhov's old rule, slips into oblivion, as the action becomes centered around the question of Anna's love for Mat. If Anna loved only him, Mat says, then he could absolve her: "If I was believing – that you'd never had love for any other man in the world but me – I could be forgetting the rest, maybe" (1023).

At this point, Anna's character assumes some characteristics of what Lesley Ferris calls "the penitent whore." This courtesan figure must not only recant her previous sins, but also suffer, often by sacrificing her desires to the needs of patriarchal authority, a road usually leading to her death. Such a narrative, Ferris writes, "rewards and celebrates such self-sacrifice."[40] Just like Camille, Anna must prove that her love is "pure," not something to be bought and paid for (though unlike Camille, she does not die). The play hinges, in other words, on whether Anna can be recuperated – and in a sense become "virginal" again, as Gary A. Vena maintains – by her love for Mat.[41] Anna demonstrates her unequivocal love by swearing "a terrible, fearful oath" on Mat's crucifix (CP1 1023). Only then does Mat believe her – even after discovering that Anna is not Catholic and that he will "have to be taking [Anna's] naked word for it" (1025). Anna is thus "redeemed by the purity of her love for him," as the reviewer for *Variety* noted, cleansed not only by the fog, but more importantly, by her lover's forgiveness.[42] Anna's "gesture of humility with which, at the end, she abased her head before her lover," Agate observed, "was one of the most beautiful I have ever seen."[43] This one-sided repentance – or, to use Agate's words, abasement – is noteworthy, for Mat does not swear upon the bible, even though he has frequented none too few port-side brothels himself. I therefore disagree with Ann Hall's interpretation that Anna wants Mat on

her own terms and that Mat must make compromises as well. This dramaturgical framing requires *female* repentance, a redemption that only the
whore undergoes. While Anna's future is dubious at best, it is not punishment but rather penance that characterizes her journey, and this atonement
is not constituted by being left *alone*, but rather by being ensnared in the
"inevitable – if overworked – comedic conclusion" of marriage.[44]

What follows is a kind of "superstitious dread," as O'Neill put it, not
only because of the old devil sea, but also because Anna and Mat's union is
framed, if not eclipsed, by Chris and Mat's feuding and intense relationship.[45] While on the surface *"Anna Christie"* is about the two heterosexual
lovers (Anna and Mat), the play in fact portrays a love triangle in which
male bonding between Chris and Mat factors prominently. For if it is true,
as Doris Nelson has written, that O'Neill's "female characters, with few
exceptions, are defined only by their biological roles – in other words, by
their relations to the men in their lives," then it is extremely clear in the
final scene of *"Anna Christie."*[46] Directly after Anna and Mat reconcile,
Anna says to her father, "it's about time for you and Mat to kiss and make
up" (CP1 1025). The drama cannot conclude, in other words, before the
men in the story reconcile. What's more, both men, unbeknownst to each
other, have signed up as shipmates on the same vessel, which soon sets
sail for a long journey at sea. While Anna is destined to wait alone on
shore, it appears as if the two men will have a honeymoon. Anna therefore
assumes the role of a woman whose men belong to the sea – setting up
house for them. This peculiar closure is even remarked upon by Chris in the
final few lines of the play: "It's funny. It's queer, yes – you and me shipping
on same boat dat vay. It ain't right" (1026). And it isn't right – not only
because it is a queer (in both senses of that term) kind of happy end, but
also because it first requires Anna's repentance and reformation to
respectability.

But why, precisely, was O'Neill invested in respectability? O'Neill never
intended the trope of purity to factor so prominently in Anna's character. In
response to winning the Pulitzer for *"Anna Christie"* O'Neill commented,
"When the Police Dept. isn't pinning the Obscenity Medal on my Hairy
Ape chest, why, then it's Columbia adorning the brazen bosom of Anna
with the Cross of Purity. I begin to feel that there is either something all
wrong with me or something all right . . . 'It's a mad world, my masters!'"[47]
Yet, critical reception reveals that audiences did seize upon the "cross of
purity," unable to shake the old repentant courtesan theme. While O'Neill
introduced some innovative aspects to the characterization of a prostitute,

"Anna Christie"'s "commercial success," noted Variety in 1921, "will depend upon whether the public is prepared to accept a heroine who is a graduate from a brothel."[48] But, by all accounts, they did accept her, partly because, as Agate observed, "we know from the actress's face that Anna is no essential prostitute . . ."[49]

If "Anna Christie"'s commercial success depended upon whether audiences embraced this prostitute character, it depended equally on the actress's ability to appeal to audiences. Key in understanding how Anna was perceived are Pauline Lord's acting style, body performativity, and her efforts to construct a respectable public persona. As Ronald Wainscott has noted, "It was Lord's interpretation of Anna, however, which stamped this production with unusual power."[50] Indeed Pauline Lord made her mark with the role of Anna, achieving new heights in naturalistic acting. The Independent's Robert Allerton Parker wrote that Pauline Lord was "the ideal interpreter" of the role, reminiscent of "great continental actresses."[51] Robert Benchley of Life Magazine likewise praised Lord's acting, writing: "Every once in a while Pauline Lord comes along and shows us what real acting is like."[52]

Not surprisingly, reviewers compared Lord's Anna to another reformed figure: Fiske's charwoman from Salvation Nell (1908). Kenneth Macgowan of Vogue Magazine commented: "Miss Lord's "Anna Christie" is the most perfect piece of naturalism I have ever seen on the American stage. Mrs. Fiske's Salvation Nell comes no where near it in the suggestion of reality."[53] This comparison was not accidental. Associating these two actresses made great sense given that both characters – and, both plays – shared the interconnected themes of prostitution and salvation. What is most interesting about these reviews is that they compare Mrs. Fiske's acting style with Lord's, two performances separated by an interval of thirteen years. Of course, Fiske's performance was legendary, one to rival, but I believe that the press was getting at something else: a shift in acting iconography.

One noticeable aspect of this shift can be seen in how the press characterized Lord as "plain." British reviewer Sydney W. Carroll, for instance, called Lord an actress "with a homely face . . . and a liberal supply of Yankee technique."[54] What is interesting is not Carroll's derision of Lord's "Yankee" acting style, but rather his description of Lord as "homely." Other reviewers also noted Lord's plain features, like May Herschel Clarke of the Picture Show, who wrote bluntly: "Pauline Lord is not a beautiful woman, or a handsome woman, or even a pretty woman. She is undeniably what her countrymen call 'homely.' All the critics have said so, she has remarked the same thing herself – thousands of times. And it is true."[55] Lord did remark the same thing herself: "'I am not at all sure that I am suited to film work. You see' – and here she smiled a little – 'I am not good looking, not pretty.'"[56] As Lord tells the story, O'Neill wrote *"Anna Christie"* "with a different girl in mind. She was to be big, with magnificent hair . . . an Olympian beauty." Lord added, "I am not exactly that way . . . She was to be a goddess of the flesh, of deep bosomed strength and golden hair. I couldn't manage that."[57] The Gelbs describe Lord as anything but an Olympian goddess: "thirty-one, delicate, almost fragile, with a tiny waist, small hands and feet, a pale oval face, and tragic brown eyes."[58] In fact, O'Neill was not initially happy with Lord in the role, although the Gelbs report that he was ultimately "delighted with her."[59] In another interview, Lord described how she compensated for her appearance:

> I wasn't the type wanted to fill the big leading parts, I wasn't very beautiful . . . and I had no physique worth speaking about . . . So I had to work hard to make up for all my deficiencies . . . My advice to young actresses setting out on the same road is: "Study and work hard, and above all, be yourself."[60]

Another review underscores this point: "She has learned her business as an actress, and has been compelled to, for she cannot rely on good looks in a conventional way."[61]

Whether Pauline Lord was beautiful or not is less interesting than why there was so much discourse about her looks, especially by Lord herself. It seems apparent, as Margaret Ranald has observed, that "As an actress, she is said to have lacked self-confidence."[62] What is to be gained by interrogating beauty, by denouncing beauty, by rejecting one's "to-be-looked-at-ness" in a profession that has always placed women center stage as visual spectacles?[63] One answer is that Lord's unconventional looks freed her from some of the traps of representation in which many other actresses found themselves. For an actress playing a prostitute, this freedom worked surprisingly well. Unlike Olga Nethersole, whose sexuality was explosive – and thus needed to be contained – Lord's plainness subdued the role of Anna. Just as Mrs. Leslie Carter's maternal body type worked against Zaza's sultry character, so too Pauline Lord's "homeliness" diffused the potential for unchecked female sexuality (she was playing a prostitute, after all). Instead of being objectified, Lord could be taken seriously as an actress.

And Lord did take her work seriously as an actress. As part of her research for the role of Anna, she ventured into the red-light district. Just as

Mrs. Leslie Carter researched French music-hall actresses for her role of Zaza, so too Lord observed real prostitutes on 10th Avenue. As she recounted, "I thought I ought to meet some of these women and find out what they are like."[64] Lord's research was not unlike the work of Progressive Era reformers, who relentlessly sought to understand the workings of the underworld. What is especially intriguing is how Lord spun her research, acting choices, and public persona, as *respectable* even while immersed in the underworld. After interviewing prostitutes while researching the role of Anna, Lord eventually "modeled the character on a department store clerk who waited on her and who projected a 'beaten soul ... tired to death.'"[65] Why a shop girl, we might ask, and not a prostitute? In early twentieth-century American culture, the shop girl signified ambiguously as one who might work either (or both) sides of the counter (see Part II). Lord's choice to model Anna on a shop girl suggests a desire to distance herself from prostitution proper.

In fact, Lord consciously downplayed her investment in playing a prostitute both on and off the stage. This was especially important, for Lord had previously played the role of a prostitute in the doomed production of *The Deluge* in 1917. Actresses regularly represented themselves as conforming to middle-class notions of domesticity and ideal womanhood in the nineteenth century. While this kind of identity construction was not uncommon, what is unusual is that Lord worked so hard to distance herself from the stigma of performing prostitution well into the 1920s. In one interview, for instance, Lord revealed that she was shocked when she first read O'Neill's script: "and even now there are times when I feel I must run into a corner and hide my face at the thought of portraying such a character. Especially when I see some venerable lady in the stalls."[66] With this remark, Lord not only consciously infantilizes herself; she also suggests her affinity with esteemed women, the very benchmark for respectability (even for theatres themselves). "Then I notice the venerable lady is having a little cry," Lord continued, "and I know that the essential nobility of Anna's nature has 'got' her as it has 'got' me, and won her whole-hearted sympathy."[67] It is not, therefore, Anna's plight that awakens sympathy, but rather Anna's "essential nobility."

The commercial success of *"Anna Christie"* depended not so much upon whether the public was prepared to accept a heroine who was a graduate from a brothel, but rather whether she was respectable or noble enough once she left it. As Brietzke points out, by the end of the play "the 'sign' of the prostitute has been erased from her."[68] As we consider, then, why *"Anna Christie"* won the Pulitzer in a season of "sex plays," according to

Robert Benchley, we can see that its success had more to do with respect-ability than with the underworld.[69] Focusing on Anna's integrity was a way of displacing a critical examination of prostitution as a systemic socio-economic problem. Passing out of the Progressive Era, and its tedious reform policies, American audiences wanted, perhaps, to believe they were "post-prostitution." Lord's positioning of herself as respectable and even naive redeemed Anna's character – much as Carter had done with *Zaza*. All of these factors contributed to the resurrection of the repentant courtesan, because although it may have appeared that O'Neill gave the prostitute-figure a dramaturgical face-life, in many respects Anna is the same repentant courtesan-figure audiences had seen so many times before. Her moments of female rage and independence are important ruptures in the American theatrical canon. Yet, like her dramaturgical sisters in sin, Anna swallows her anger and self-determination to live with Mat (who has threa-tened to kill her) and Chris (who has abandoned her). With such grim realities framing the heterosexual closure, I quite agree with O'Neill that audiences misunderstood the happy ending. But what the plot confirms is not only a contrived resolution featuring marriage, but also a triangular love story which includes men who will feud, but eventually bond, while on a voyage on "dat ole davil sea."

The lesbian prostitute in *The God of Vengeance*

While O'Neill was basking in the glow of his Pulitzer, another brothel play, Sholom Asch's *The God of Vengeance*, met a different fate in 1922 and 1923. Although several brothel dramas had been brought up on charges of obscenity almost a decade before, *The God of Vengeance* was the first play in thirty years whose producer and lead actor were actually found guilty of obscenity (though eventually they would win an appeal).[70] Asch's drama, originally entitled *Gott fun Nekoma* in Yiddish, had played throughout Europe after its premiere in 1907 at Max Reinhardt's *Deutsches Theater* in Berlin. *Gott fun Nekoma* had also played successfully in the United States for seventeen years in Yiddish. And, once translated into English, it was still untouched by controversy when it ran at the Provincetown Theatre in the Village. Only when the English version moved to an uptown venue (the Apollo Theater) did Asch's creation encounter problems.[71] Why, on the heels of O'Neill's success, did this drama meet so much controversy?

Like *"Anna Christie,"* respectability is a key motif in *The God of Vengeance*, albeit with a twist. A Jewish brothel owner, Yankl (spelled in

Goldberg's translation as Yekel), and his former-prostitute wife, Sarah, seek to raise their daughter without her being tarnished by the sex trade going on in the basement. In order to facilitate a middle-class marriage (and thus gain respectability) for his daughter Rivkele, Yankl buys a Torah scroll for his home. His attempts at separating vice from home are futile, however, when Rivkele mingles with the girls below, becoming especially enchanted with one prostitute, Manke, who seduces her. Asch's unique plot incorporates virtually none of the staple elements of the brothel genre: there's no white slave in need of rescue, no hero to rescue her, no heterosexual love story, and no self-sacrificing whore. Asch did not, in other words, put his dent in the old tin can of repentant courtesan symbolism, to recall James Agate's phrase. In fact, the play utilized some startlingly unconventional aspects of dramaturgy that were inconsistent with previous brothel plays.

Alisa Solomon claims that *Got fun Nekome* "sparked a spate of melodramatic prostitution plays," yet she mistakenly inverts the genealogy of the brothel genre.[72] As this study has repeatedly argued, prostitution dramas had long played on the New York stage. What Solomon correctly identifies is that *The God of Vengeance* was one of the first serious Yiddish dramas that made it to a Broadway venue.

While other scholars have addressed how *The God of Vengeance* sparked charges of anti-Semitism from the Jewish community, my interests lie elsewhere.[73] In addition to the ways in which *The God of Vengeance* transgressed perceptions of normative Jewish identity, the play's remarkable controversy can be further explained by looking at three additional points. First, unlike O'Neill's Anna, who repents and achieves respectability through marriage, the characters here are hopelessly trapped by the commercialized vice from which they profit. Second, unlike other censored brothel plays from the white slave season, which excised the brothel altogether, *The God of Vengeance* firmly resituated the brothel back into the heart of the drama – literally into the foundation of home. And third, and most importantly, *The God of Vengeance* features a lesbian romance on stage. This play gave, as Curtin Kaier notes, "New Yorkers their first play with a lesbian love scene."[74] Given these mimetic transgressions, it is no wonder that *The God of Vengeance* was charged with obscenity.

Two key motifs from *"Anna Christie,"* repentance and respectability, are barely recognizable in *The God of Vengeance*. Instead Asch makes the father, Yankl, the seeker of respectability – a kind of Jewish Mrs. Warren who strives to promote his daughter with the profits from his brothel. The somewhat unbelievable plot suggests that Rivkele has not been affected by the busy brothel in the basement. She remains pure, chaste, and a fine catch for marriage. However, her isolation and her father's strict and abusive treatment has produced the very curiosity that will be her eventual undoing. She befriends Manke, a prostitute living and working in the basement brothel, for whom she exhibits great affection. As much as Yankl and Sarah try to keep their daughter from mingling below, they inevitably fail. Manke eventually seduces her (a point to which I will return shortly) and the "fallen" daughter loses her currency on the marriage market. This is a play that not only avoids contrived happy endings and clichéd dramaturgical framings, but one that also radically questions the intersection of gender, sexuality, and respectability. As Solomon notes, "even as respectability is the prize Yankl values above all, Asch reveals how untenable it is for women." Indeed, the increasing violence and abuse in the play – Yankl's battering of his wife and daughter even astonishes an abusive pimp – demonstrate that "for any young woman," Solomon continues, "joining the realm of the respectable means enduring violence, or at best, being confined like a Torah scroll."[75]

Portraying respectability as untenable, then, *The God of Vengeance* opens up a space for alternative sexual desire. What is astonishing about *The God of Vengeance* is its unique portrayal of lesbian love between Manke and Rivkele. Rivkele (spelled in Goldberg's translation as Rifkele) sneaks downstairs into the brothel one night, where Manke offers to comb her hair "as if she were a bride." Pursuing the marriage metaphor further, Manke whispers:

> MANKE.   Then we come close to one another, for we are bride and bridegroom, you and I. We embrace. (*Places her arm around Rifkele.*) Ever so tightly. And kiss, very softly. Like this. (*Kisses Rifkele.*) And we turn so red – we're so bashful. It's nice, Rifkele, isn't it?
>
> RIFKELE.   Yes, Manke . . . Yes.
>
> MANKE.   (*Lowering her voice and whispering into Rifkele's ear.*) And then we go to sleep together. Nobody sees, nobody hears. Only you and I. Like this. (*Clasps Rifkele tightly to herself.*) Do you want to sleep with me tonight like this? Eh?
>
> RIFKELE.   (*Looking about nervously*). I do . . . I do . . . (original ellipses).[76]

While this is a "frank and sensual scene of lesbian lovemaking," as Kaier claims, it is hardly one "the like of which has never been repeated in a

Broadway play."[77] Yet, it is a stunningly sensual scene that is unprecedented in brothel dramas, as well as most American drama of the day. In stark contrast to white slave melodramas, this well-written dialogue also demonstrates Asch's naturalistic talents as a writer.

Manke and Rivkele's desire is neither romanticized nor demonized, but it also does not go unchallenged. When Yankl confronts Rivkele about her night with Manke, asking "are you still as pure as when you left this house? Are you still a virtuous Jewish daughter?" Rivkele can only reply "I don't know."[78] With this line, Rivkele may be articulating sexual innocence, but it is more likely that she, and therefore Asch, is questioning whether her lesbian affair is impure. She also attacks Yankl's, and indeed, dominant culture's, hypocrisy in moralizing sexuality. As Rivkele puts it, "It was all right for mamma, wasn't it? And it was all right for you, wasn't it? I know all about it!"[79] While Asch is vague about what it is that Rivkele knows, it seems clear that efforts to protect Rivkele from sexual knowledge and desire have backfired. Asch subverts proscribed sexual morality, demonstrating, as Solomon observes, "there's only one thing that's kosher: the illicit love between Rivkele and Manke."[80]

The site for both kosher and aberrant sex in *The God of Vengeance* is the basement brothel in Yankl's home. Asch's location of the brothel could not be more immediate or threatening to the family. While other brothel plays featured limited excursions to a brothel, usually to far away sites to rescue white slaves, *The God of Vengeance* integrates the brothel into every scene and literally within the home. The play implied, as John Houchin has written, that "the respectable 'upstairs' was supported by the sordid 'downstairs.' "[81] It is the literal foundation upon which the family is built. "The play uncomfortably foregrounds," writes Harley Erdman, "the extent to which bourgeois respectability is maintained economically by a system of sexual exploitation, as well as the way that middle class propriety is balanced on a shaky foundation of repressed, shadowy desire."[82]

It is no wonder, then, that critics of the day like Heywood Broun were made "distinctly uncomfortable" and "a little sick" by *The God of Vengeance*.[83] Many critics could not bring themselves to write explicitly about the lesbian scene or other brothel commerce, using euphemisms such as "the perversion of a young girl."[84] This was not dissimilar from the press's reaction to the "foreignness" of the piece. Unnamed, yet central, both the prostitute and Jewish immigrant were displaced beyond Progressive notions of nation and sexuality, as well as outside the parameters of traditional brothel dramaturgy. *The God of Vengeance* was alien, in other words, not only because of its "Yiddishness," but also because of its portrayal of lesbian desire and a brothel in, of all places, a bourgeois home. Given these departures, this "foreign" (perverted?) play could only be scorned by legitimating structures such as the Grand Jury. In presiding over the obscenity indictment, Judge McIntyre expressed a desire for more traditional sexual mores and dramaturgy, writing, "The people of the State of New York are anxious to have pure drama. They are anxious to have clean plays."[85]

Were audiences anxious to have "pure" plays?

As we have seen with a variety of brothel plays, there was intense anxiety – even a kind of sex hysteria – regarding the staging of prostitution, but certainly there was no uniform desire for pure plays, nor even an agreement about what constituted pure (or obscene) theatre. These debates continued well after the decline of the brothel drama. In the meantime, audiences still flocked to see their Kitty Warrens and Anna Christophersens, eager to see how each playwright would put her or his dent in the old tin can. During the 1920s, most red-light districts had closed throughout the United States and the brothel drama had virtually disappeared. The Progressive Era had ended. What was left in the wake of this intense reform effort is not a tidy trajectory of native drama or a surgical excision of prostitution, but rather lingering ambivalence regarding prostitution, sexuality, censorship, and women in the public sphere. The legacy of brothel dramas and the regulation of sexuality would find articulation in other sisters in sin (from Mae West to Madonna), both in popular culture and the theatre itself. If the popularity of modern material girls (found in *Leaving Las Vegas*, *Pretty Woman*, or *Moulin Rouge*) is any indication, audiences still want to see their hookers-with-a-heart-of-gold. But that is a story for another book.

Notes

Introduction: The brothel drama

1. Scholars bracket the Progressive Era differently, depending on their scope of study. I agree with social historian Ruth Rosen's definition of the Progressive Era as the time of intense American reform movements from the turn of the century until 1918. See Ruth Rosen, *The Lost Sisterhood: Prostitution in America, 1900–1918* (Baltimore: Johns Hopkins University Press, 1982); Mark Connelly's *The Response to Prostitution in the Progressive Era* (Chapel Hill: University of North Carolina Press, 1980) and David J. Pivar, *Purity Crusade: Sexual Morality and Social Control, 1868–1900* (Westport, CT: Greenwood Press, 1973).

2. Rebecca Schneider, *The Explicit Body in Performance* (London: Routledge, 1997), 24.

3. Peter Brooks, "The Mark of the Beast: Prostitution, Melodrama, and Narrative," in *Melodrama*, edited by Daniel Gerould (New York: New York Literary Forum, 1980), 135.

4. See Robert L. Sherman, *Drama Cyclopedia, a Bibliography of Plays and Players* (Chicago: Robert Sherman, 1944), and Library of Congress Copyright Office, *Dramatic Compositions Copyrighted in the United States, 1870–1916* (Washington: Government Printing Office, 1918).

5. Laurence Senelick, *Lovesick: Modernist Plays of Same-Sex Love, 1894–1925* (London: Routledge, 1999), 2. I am grateful to Laurence Senelick for sharing clippings and titles from his private collection.

6. Charles W. Collins, "White Slave Drama," *Inter Ocean*, November 24, 1913.

7. In scholarship on prostitution in America theatre, most work focuses on mid to late nineteenth century. See Rosemarie K. Bank, "Hustlers in the House: the Bowery Theatre as a Mode of Historical Information," in *The American Stage: Social and Economic Issues from the Colonial Period to the Present*, edited by Ron Engle and Tice Miller (Cambridge: Cambridge University Press, 1993). See also Rosemarie K. Bank, *Theatre Culture in America, 1825–1860* (Cambridge: Cambridge University Press, 1997); Claudia D. Johnson, "That Guilty Third Tier: Prostitution in Nineteenth-Century American Theaters," *American Quarterly*, 27 (1975), 575–84; M. Joan McDermott and Sarah J. Blackstone, "White Slavery Plays of the 1910s: Fear of Victimization and the Social Control of Sexuality," *Theatre History Studies*,

202

NOTES TO PAGES 3–7

16 (1996), 141–156; and Gary Luter, "Sexual Reform on the American Stage in the Progressive Era, 1900–1915," Ph.D. dissertation, University of Florida, 1981. Gerald Bordman has one of the most complete references to prostitute dramas, though he does not characterize them as such (or as a genre). See Bordman, *American Theatre: a Chronicle of Comedy and Drama, 1914–1930* (New York: Oxford University Press, 1995). Walter J. Meserve lists three prostitute dramas, but he includes them in a section called "Immorality on the Stage." See Meserve, *An Outline History of American Drama* (Totowa, NJ: Littlefield, Adams & Co., 1965), 166.

8. Barbara Meil Hobson, *Uneasy Virtue: The Politics of Prostitution and the American Reform Tradition* (New York: Basic Books, Inc., 1987), 140.

9. Rosen, *The Lost Sisterhood*, xii.

10. John Corbin, "The Drama of the Slums," *Saturday Evening Post*, March 20, 1909, 15.

11. Jacob Riis, *How the Other Half Lives: Studies Among the Tenements of New York* (1890; reprint, New York: Dover Publications, 1971).

12. "The Rising Tide of Realism in the American Drama," *Current Opinion*, 55 (October 1913), 250.

13. For the relationship between high and low culture see Lawrence W. Levine, *Highbrow/Lowbrow: the Emergence of Cultural Hierarchy in America* (Cambridge, MA: Harvard University Press, 1990).

14. Here I draw on Joseph Roach's idea of "genealogies of performance." See Roach's *Cities of the Dead: Circum-Atlantic Performance* (New York: Columbia Press, 1996), 25.

15. Marvin Carlson, *The Haunted Stage: the Theatre as Memory Machine* (Ann Arbor: University of Michigan Press, 2001), 85.

16. Michael Quinn, "Celebrity and the Semiotics of Acting," *New Theatre Quarterly*, 4 (1990), 154–61.

17. Sos Eltis, "The Fallen Woman on Stage: Maidens, Magdalens, and the Emancipated Female," in *The Cambridge Companion to Victorian and Edwardian Theatre*, edited by Kerry Powell (Cambridge: Cambridge University Press, 2004), 222–36.

18. Amanda Anderson, *Tainted Souls and Painted Faces: the Rhetoric of Fallenness in Victorian Culture* (Ithaca: Cornell University Press, 1993).

19. Lesley Ferris, *Acting Women: Images of Women in Theatre* (Hampshire and London: Macmillan Education Ltd., 1990), 79–95.

20. Howard Bronson, *The Autobiography of a Play* (New York: Columbia University, 1914), 27–28.

21. Ellington's text is otherwise sympathetic toward women of the underworld. George Ellington, *The Women of New York: or the Under-World of the Great City* (1869; reprint New York: Arno Press, 1972), 172.

22. George J. Kneeland, *Commercialized Prostitution in New York City* (1913; reprint, Montclair, NJ: Patterson Smith, 1969), 107.

23. William Acton, *History of Prostitution* (1857; reprint, New York: Rederick A. Praeger, 1969).

24. William W. Sanger, *The History of Prostitution: Its Extent, Causes, and Effect Throughout The World* (1858; reprint, New York: Eugenics Publishing Company, 1937), 489.

25. Ibid.
26. Hamilton Mason, *French Theatre in New York: A List of Plays, 1899–1939* (1940; reprint, New York: AMS Press, Inc., 1966), 21.
27. Stephen S. Stanton, ed., *Camille and Other Plays* (New York: Hill and Wang, 1957), xlii.
28. "The Newest Camille and Some Famous Ones," *Theatre Magazine*, 27 (February 1918), 95.
29. John Chapman and Garrison P. Sherwood, ed., *The Best Plays of 1894–1899* (New York: Dodd, Mead and Company, 1955), 19.
30. Review of *Camille, New York Spirit of the Times*, November 13, 1894.
31. Review of *Camille, Theatre Magazine*, 4 (May 1904), 109.
32. Review of *Camille, Theatre Magazine*, 4 (June 1904), 135.
33. Mason, *French Theatre in New York*, 21.
34. Susan Griffin, *The Book of Courtesans: A Catalogue of Their Virtues* (New York: Broadway Books, 2001), 5, 96.
35. Leigh Woods, "Two-a-Day Redemptions and Truncated Camilles: the Vaudeville Repertoire of Sarah Bernhardt," *New Theatre Quarterly*, 10 (February 1994), 15.
36. Burns Mantel and Garrison P. Sherwood, eds., *The Best Plays of 1899–1909 and the Year Book of the Drama in America* (Philadelphia: The Blakiston Company, 1944), 432.
37. Cornelia Otis Skinner, *Madame Sarah* (Boston: Houghton Mifflin Company, 1967), 148.
38. "A Vivisection of Sarah Bernhardt's Art," *Current Opinion*, 53 (October 1912), 452.
39. Skinner, *Madame Sarah*, 167.
40. Mantle and Sherwood, *Best Plays of 1899–1909*, 403–04.
41. Mason, *French Theatre in New York*, 20.
42. Don B. Wilmeth, *Staging the Nation: Plays from the American Theater, 1787–1909* (Boston: Bedford Books, 1998), vi.
43. Shannon Bell, *Reading, Writing, and Rewriting the Prostitute Body* (Bloomington, IN: Indiana University Press, 1994), 40.
44. Charles Baudelaire, "Allegory," in *Les Fleurs du Mal*, translated by Richard Howard (Boston: Godine, 1982), 155.
45. Walter Benjamin, "Central Park," *New German Critique*, 34 (Winter 1985), 32–58, at 41.
46. Ibid., 40.
47. Schneider, *The Explicit Body*, 24. Schneider is quoting Benjamin. As feminist critics have shown, there are limitations to Baudelaire's and Benjamin's analyses, a critical viewpoint with which I agree. However, while I take issue with the ways in which Benjamin and Baudelaire direct their allegorical gaze at the prostitute, I believe that they correctly identify the prostitute as a central figure of urban modernism of the late nineteenth and early twentieth century.
48. Schneider, *The Explicit Body*, 24.
49. Timothy J. Gilfoyle, *City of Eros: New York City, Prostitution, and the Commercialization of Sex, 1790–1920* (New York: W. W. Norton & Company, 1992), 157.

50. Committee of Fifteen, *The Social Evil with Special Reference to Conditions Existing in the City of New York* (New York: G. P. Putnam's Sons, 1902), v.
51. Ibid., 172.
52. Ibid., 172–76.
53. Ibid., 179.
54. Gilfoyle, *City of Eros*, 304.
55. Rosen, *The Lost Sisterhood*, xi.
56. Gilfoyle, *City of Eros*, 112.
57. Ibid., 202.
58. Allen Churchill, *The Great White Way: A Re-Creation of Broadway's Golden Era of Theatrical Entertainment* (New York: E. P. Dutton & Co., 1962), 12.
59. Marvin Carlson, *Places of Performance: The Semiotics of Theatre Architecture* (Ithaca: Cornell University Press, 1989), 110–112.
60. Churchill, *The Great White Way*, 12.
61. The Page Act was declared unconstitutional by the New York Court of Appeals in June, 1911. See Rosen, *The Lost Sisterhood*, 35.
62. See Morris L. Ernst and Alan U. Schwartz, *Censorship: The Search for the Obscene* (New York: The MacMillan Company, 1964), 29–33; and John H. Houchin, *Censorship of the American Theatre in the Twentieth Century* (Cambridge, Cambridge University Press, 2003).
63. James Shelley Hamilton, "The Sex-Tangled Drama," *Everybody's Magazine*, 29 (July 1913), 676–87.
64. Olga Nethersole, "Sex Dramas To-Day and Yesterday," *Green Book Magazine*, 6 (January 1914), 35.
65. Houchin, *Censorship of the American Theatre*, 1.
66. Michel Foucault, *The History of Sexuality. Volume I: An Introduction*, translated by Robert Hurley (New York: Vintage Books, 1990), 91.
67. Jon McKenzie, *Perform or Else: From Discipline to Performance* (London: Routledge, 2001).

Part I The female performer as prostitute

1. William Winter, *The Life of David Belasco*, 2 vols. (New York: Moffat, Yard & Company, 1918), vol 1, 463.
2. There were many articles written by actresses, including a five-part series called "Advice to Stage-Struck Girls" in *Leslie's Weekly* during 1910 and advice columns in the *Green Book Album* that ran for several years.
3. For more than a hundred articles about actresses see the *Cumulated Dramatic Index, 1909–1949*, 2 vols., edited by Fredrick Winthrop Faxon, Mary E. Bates, and Anne C. Sutherland (Boston: G. K. Hall & Company, 1965).
4. See chapter 2 of Linda Mizejewski, *Ziegfeld Girl: Image and Icon in Culture and Cinema* (Durham and London: Duke University Press, 1999). See also Kristen Pullen, *Actresses and Whores On Stage and In Society* (Cambridge: Cambridge University Press, 2005).

5. Dates given refer to New York City premieres.
6. John A. Degen, "The Evolution of *The Shop Girl* and the Birth of 'Musical Comedy,'" *Theatre History Studies*, 7 (1987), 42.
7. George Ellington, *The Women of New York; or, the Under-World of the Great City* (1869; reprint, New York: Arno Press, 1972), 528–29.
8. James Metcalfe, "Forward!" *Life Magazine*, May 10, 1917, 817.
9. William Sanger, *The History of Prostitution: Its Extent, Causes, and Effect Throughout The World* (1858; reprint, New York: Eugenics Publishing Company, 1937).
10. George J. Kneeland, *Commercialized Prostitution in New York City* (1913; reprint, Montclair, NJ: Patterson Smith, 1969), 230.
11. Ibid., 241.
12. Ibid., 257.
13. Tracy Davis, *Actresses as Working Women: Their Social Identity in Victorian Culture* (London: Routledge, 1991), 78.
14. Sanger, *History of Prostitution*, 550.
15. Maureen Montgomery, *Displaying Women: Spectacles of Leisure in Edith Wharton's New York* (New York: Routledge, 1998), 117.
16. Ibid., 120.
17. Peter G. Buckley, "Introductory Essay," *Inventing Times Square: Commerce and Culture at the Crossroads of the World*, edited by William R. Taylor (New York: Russell Sage Foundation, 1991), 286.
18. Ellington, *Women of New York*, 527.
19. Charles Baudelaire, *My Heart Laid Bare and Other Prose Writings*, edited by Peter Quennell, translated by Norman Cameron (London: Soho Book Company, 1986).
20. Lauren Rabinovitz, *For the Love of Pleasure: Women, Movies, and Culture in Turn-of-the Century Chicago* (New Brunswick, NJ: Rutgers University Press, 1998), 8.
21. Davis, *Actresses as Working Women*, 98.
22. Ibid., 107.
23. "The Stage Struck Girl," *Theatre Magazine*, 22 (1915), 249.
24. Rabinovitz, *For the Love of Pleasure*, 5.

1 *Zaza*: That "obtruding harlot" of the stage

1. Review of *Zaza*, *New York Telegram*, January 3, 1899.
2. Carter revived the role of Zaza in numerous productions up until 1915. For a brief overview of the stage and film versions, see "Zaza," *Stage* (December 1938), 28–29; and "Zaza," *Life Magazine*, January 9, 1939, 37–39.
3. Pierre Berton and Charles Simon, *Zaza* (Paris: Librairie Charpentier et Fasquelle, 1904).
4. Gabriele Réjane, *The One Correct Version of My Plays Translated & Printed From My Own Prompt Books* (New York: F. Rullman, 1904).
5. John Corbin, "The Two *Zazas* – French Drama and American Melodrama," *New York Times*, November 27, 1904, IV, 1.

6. William Winter, *The Life of David Belasco*, 2 vols. (New York: Moffat, Yard & Company, 1918), vol. 1, 463.
7. Hillary Bell, "Genius the Word for Mrs. Carter," *New York Herald*, January 10, 1899.
8. "A Night of New Plays," *New York Times*, January 10, 1899, 7.
9. Alan Dale, "An Opinion of Mrs. Leslie Carter's Performance," *New York American*, January 10, 1899.
10. Kathy Peiss, *Cheap Amusements: Working Women and Leisure in Turn-of-the-Century New York* (Philadelphia: Temple University Press, 1986), 141–42.
11. Robert C. Allen, *Horrible Prettiness: Burlesque and American Culture* (Chapel Hill: University of North Carolina Press, 1991), 76.
12. *Mrs. Leslie Carter in Zaza*, 1899, otherwise unidentified booklet. Billy Rose Theatre Collection.
13. David Belasco, "Zaza", unpublished play, Billy Rose Theatre Collection, 1898, 5.4.; original emphasis. Subsequent references will be included parenthetically in the text.
14. Peter G. Buckley, "Introductory Essay," in *Inventing Times Square: Commerce and Culture at the Crossroads of the World*, edited by William R. Taylor (New York: Russell Sage Foundation, 1991). See also M. Alison Kibler, *Rank Ladies: Gender and Cultural Hierarchy in American Vaudeville* (Chapel Hill: University of North Carolina Press, 1999); and Kathryn J. Oberdeck, *The Evangelist and the Impresario: Religion, Entertainment, and Cultural Politics in America, 1884–1914* (Baltimore: Johns Hopkins University Press, 1999).
15. "The Easiest Way," *Theatre Magazine*, 9 (1909), 81–84.
16. "Mrs. Carter's Latest Portraiture is a Triumph," otherwise unidentified clipping. Billy Rose Theatre Collection.
17. "Drama," *Harper's Weekly*, January 21, 1899.
18. *Mrs. Leslie Carter in Zaza*, 1899, otherwise unidentified booklet. Billy Rose Theatre Collection.
19. *cocotte* is French for prostitute; see Corbin, "The Two *Zazas*," 2.
20. Edith Sessions Tupper, "Camille was Bad, Zaza Only a Woman," *New York World*, January 15, 1899.
21. Berton and Simon, *Zaza*, 5.278–9. Special thanks to Jonathan A. Strauss for translating this last act from the French script.
22. Corbin, "The Two *Zazas*," 1.
23. Ibid.
24. Ibid.
25. Lewis C. Strang, *Famous Actresses of The Day in America* (Boston: L. C. Page and Company, 1902), 201.
26. Bell, "Genius."
27. "This Much is Sure," otherwise unidentified clipping. Billy Rose Theatre Collection.
28. Mrs. Leslie Carter as quoted in Tupper, "Camille was Bad."
29. Strang, *Famous Actresses*, 204.
30. Ibid., 213.
31. "The Evolution of a Star of the Stage," otherwise unidentified clipping. Mrs. Leslie Carter clipping file, Shubert Archive.

32. David Belasco quoted in Bell, "Genius."
33. Bell, "Genius."
34. Unidentified clipping. *Zaza* clipping file, Billy Rose Theatre Collection.
35. Norman Hapgood, "Mrs. Leslie Carter in *Zaza*," *New York Commercial Advertiser*, January 10, 1899, reprinted in *The American Theatre As Seen By its Critics, 1752–1934*, edited by Montrose Moses and John M. Brown (New York: Norton & Company, 1934), 157–58.
36. Ethan Mordden, *The American Theatre* (New York: Oxford University Press, 1981), 43.
37. "Mrs. Marie Wilmerding, of the '400'," *New York Journal*, January 22, 1899.
38. Dale, "An Opinion."
39. "Mrs. Leslie Carter Freed From Debt," October 5, 1899, otherwise unidentified clipping. Clipping file, Billy Rose Theatre Collection.
40. Ibid.
41. Mrs. Leslie Carter, "Mrs. Leslie Carter Discusses *Zaza* and Morality," *Broadway Magazine*, December 1899, 183.
42. Mrs. Leslie Carter, "What My Career Means to Me," otherwise unidentified clipping. Mrs. Leslie Carter Folder, C & L Brown Collection, Billy Rose Theatre Collection.
43. Archie Bell, "Celebrated Actress, Once a Cleveland School Girl, Tells Why She has Played the 'Bad Women of the Stage,'" April 13, 1913, otherwise unidentified clipping. Mrs. Leslie Carter Scrapbook, Billy Rose Theatre Collection.
44. Hapgood, "Mrs. Leslie Carter in *Zaza*."
45. "*Zaza* at the Garrick," *New York Times*, September 12, 1899, 6.
46. See "Mrs. Carter Back in New York"; "Belasco and Mrs. Carter End Their 25-Year Feud," *New York Telegram*, April 10, 1931; "*Zaza* at the Garrick," 6; and "The Real Mrs. Carter," press release. Mrs. Leslie Carter clipping file, Shubert Archive.
47. "Belasco 'Find' Made Real Hit," *Philadelphia Record*, January 25, 1925. The quote refers to nineteenth-century English Pre-Raphaelite painters Dante Gabriel Rossetti and Sir Edward Coley Burne-Jones.
48. "The Real Mrs. Carter."
49. "Mrs. Leslie Carter and Her Temperament," press release. Mrs. Leslie Carter clipping file, Shubert Archive.
50. Hapgood, "Mrs. Leslie Carter in *Zaza*."
51. Tracy Davis, "The Spectacle of Absent Costume: Nudity on the Victorian Stage," *New Theatre Quarterly*, 5 (1989), 326.
52. "A Night of New Plays," 7.
53. Dale, "An Opinion."
54. Michael Quinn, "Celebrity and the Semiotics of Acting," *New Theatre Quarterly*, 4 (1990), 154–61.
55. "Belasco and Mrs. Carter End Their 25-Year Feud," *New York Telegram*, April 10, 1931.
56. "Was Mrs. Leslie Carter Taught to Act?" undated press release (likely from 1907). Mrs. Leslie Carter clipping file, Shubert Archive.
57. Jane Dixon, "Put Motherhood Above All, with Work and Love on One Plane, Says Mrs. Carter," *Evening Telegram*, November 6, 1921.

208   NOTES TO PAGES 41–47

58. "Mrs. Leslie Carter," *Notable Women in the American Theatre: a Biographical Dictionary*, edited by Alice M. Robinson, Vera Mowry Roberts, and Milly S. Barranger (Westport, CT: Greenwood Press, 1989), 114–17.
59. Bell, "This Much Is Sure."
60. "Drama," *Harper's Weekly*.
61. Buckley, *Inventing Times Square*, 291.
62. "Belasco 'Find' Made Real Hit."
63. Here I am referring to J. L. Austin's work on the performative nature of speech acts. See J. L. Austin, *How to Do Things With Words*, edited by J. O. Urmson and Marina Sbisà (Cambridge: Harvard University Press, 1955).
64. Bell, "This Much is True."
65. Ibid.
66. Kibler, *Rank Ladies*, 9.
67. Bell, "This Much is Sure."
68. *Mrs. Leslie Carter in Zaza*, 1899, otherwise unidentified booklet. Billy Rose Theatre Collection.
69. Ibid.
70. Lawrence Levine, *Highbrow/Lowbrow: the Emergence of Cultural Hierarchy in America* (Cambridge: Harvard University Press, 1988), 207.
71. Bell, "This Much is Sure."
72. Winter, *The Life of David Belasco*, vol. 1, 458–63. Patchouly was a scent used both by actresses and prostitutes.

2 That "sin-stained" *Sapho*

1. See Joy Harriman Reilly, "A Forgotten 'Fallen Woman,' Olga Nethersole's *Sapho*," in *When They Weren't Doing Shakespeare*, edited by Judith L. Fisher and Stephen Watt (Athens: University of Georgia Press, 1989); and Anne Everal Callis, "Olga Nethersole and the Sapho Scandal," Master's Thesis, Ohio State University, 1974.
2. Abe Laufe, *The Wicked Stage: A History of Theater Censorship and Harassment in the United States* (New York: Frederick Ungar Publishing Company, 1978), 24.
3. "The *Sapho* Case," *New York Times*, March 8, 1900, 7.
4. Yopi Prins, *Victorian Sappho* (Princeton: Princeton University Press, 1999), 15.
5. Margaret Reynolds, *The Sappho Companion* (London: Chatto & Windus, 2000), 258.
6. Appleton quoted in Reynolds, *The Sappho Companion*, 284.
7. Prins, *Victorian Sappho*, 17.
8. C. Hayward, *Dictionary of Courtesans: An Anthology, Sometimes Gay, Sometimes Tragic, of the Celebrated Courtesans of History from Antiquity to the Present Day* (New York: University Books, 1962), 393–94.
9. "Olga Nethersole Arrives," *New York Times*, October 2, 1899, 7.
10. Clyde Fitch, Letter to Minnie Gerson, May 14, 1898, *Clyde Fitch and His Letters*, edited by Montrose J. Moses and Virginia Gerson (Boston: Little Brown & Company, 1924), 136.

11. W. E. Davies, Letter, *New York Times*, February 24, 1900, 7.

12. T. Allston Brown, *A History of the New York Stage From 1732 to 1901* (New York: Benjamin Blom, Inc., 1903), 363.

13. Review of *Sapho, New York Sun*, February 6, 1900.

14. "The Play Defended," Letter, *New York Times*, February 24, 1900, 7.

15. Michel Foucault, *The History of Sexuality, Volume I: An Introduction*, translated by Robert Hurley (New York: Vintage Books, 1990), 17.

16. Bruce MacDonal, "*Sapho* Seen By Mr. Devery," *New York Telegraph*, February 6, 1990.

17. Ibid.

18. Foucault, *History of Sexuality*, 24.

19. John H. Houchin, *Censorship of the American Theatre in the Twentieth Century* (Cambridge: Cambridge University Press, 2003), 40–42. See also Houchin's "Depraved Women and Wicked Plays: Olga Nethersole's Production of *Sapho*," *Journal of American Drama and Theatre*, 6 (Winter 1994), 40.

20. Murray Sachs, *The Career of Alphonse Daudet* (Cambridge, MA: Harvard University Press, 1965), 131.

21. Timothy J. Gilfoyle, *City of Eros: New York City, Prostitution, and the Commercialization of Sex, 1790–1920* (New York: W. W. Norton & Company, 1992), 232.

22. Sidney Shar[p], "*Sapho* in Weak, Distorted Form," *World*, February 6, 1900.

23. "Jury Soon Acquits Miss Nethersole," *New York Times*, April 6, 1900, 7.

24. "*Sapho* in Police Court," *New York Times*, February 24, 1900, 6.

25. Victor Turner, *From Ritual To Theatre: the Human Seriousness of Play* (New York: Performing Arts Journal Publishing, 1982).

26. Kim Marra, "Lesbian Scholar/Gay Subject: Turn-of-the-Century Inversions," *Theatre Topics*, 13.2 (September 2003), 235–46, at 240–241.

27. Reilly, "A Forgotten 'Fallen Woman,'" 115.

28. The *New York Evening Journal* ("Shame's the Limit," February 6, 1900) maintained the curtain rose and fell five times, while the *Telegraph* reported it was five minutes.

29. Owen Davis quoted in "As Society Is, So Is the Stage, That's Owen Davis's View of It," by Lucius Beebe, *New York Herald Tribune*. Owen Davis clipping file, Shubert Archive.

30. "Stairway Scene in Sapho as Staged in a Police Court," *New York Herald*, February 28, 1900, 8.

31. "Court Cuts Short the *Sapho* Trial," *New York Times*, April 5, 1900, 7.

32. "*Sapho* at Wallack's," *New York Times*, February 6, 1900, 6.

33. "At the Play and With the Players," *New York Times*, February 11, 1900, 16.

34. William Winter quoted in *Victorian Actors and Actresses in Review: A Dictionary of Contemporary Views of Representative British and American Actors and Actresses, 1837–1901*, compiled and edited by Donald Mullin (Westport, CT: Greenwood Press, 1983), 353.

35. "Court Cuts Short," 7.

36. "Wallack's – Sapho," *New York Dramatic Mirror*, February 10, 1900, 16.

37. "Miss Olga Nethersole as *Sapho*," *The Sketch*, January 31, 1900, 74.

38. Review of *Sapho, New York Sun*.
39. Shar[p], "*Sapho* in Weak, Distorted Form."
40. "Miss Nethersole Files Suit," *New York Times*, May 4, 1900, 7.
41. Olga Nethersole, "Sex Dramas To-Day and Yesterday," *Green Book Magazine*, 11 (January 1914), 33.
42. Reilly, "A Forgotten 'Fallen Woman,'" 109.
43. Charles Burnham, "Stage Indecency – Then and Now: A Play That Made Our Daddies Blush Could Be Read in Sunday-School Today," *Theatre Magazine* (September 1925), 16.
44. Unidentified clipping. *Sapho* clipping file, Museum of the City of New York.
45. Burnham, "Stage Indecency," 25.
46. Review of *Camille, New York World*, February 19, 1899.
47. "Olga Nethersole Arrives," 7.
48. "Nethersole's New Play Not Wicked," *New York Press*, February 6, 1900.
49. Ibid.
50. W. O. Inglis quoted in "Stairway Scene in Sapho as Staged in a Police Court," *New York Herald*, February 28, 1900, 8.
51. "Wallack's – *Sapho*," 16.
52. "Stairway Scene," 8.
53. Tracy Davis, "The Spectacle of Absent Costume: Nudity on the Victorian Stage," *New Theatre Quarterly*, 5 (1989), 321.
54. Tracy Davis, "Sexual Language in Victorian Society and Theatre," *American Journal of Semiotics*, 6 (1989), 33–49; at 35.
55. W. O. Inglis quoted in "Stairway Scene," 8.
56. "Court Cuts Short the *Sapho* Trial," 7.
57. "Stairway Scene," 8.
58. "Court Cuts Short," 6.
59. "Stairway Scene," 8.
60. "Court Cuts Short," 7.
61. Ibid.
62. Ibid.
63. Reilly, "A Forgotten 'Fallen Woman,'" 120.
64. "Stairway Scene," 8.
65. Ibid.
66. "*Sapho* in Police Court," 7.
67. Nethersole, "My Struggles to Succeed," 195.
68. Ibid., 195.
69. Lavinia Hart, "Olga Nethersole," *Cosmopolitan*, 31 (May 1901), 24.
70. Olga Nethersole, Letter to Margaret and Clement Scott, November 12, 1899. Clipping in The Adelphi File, 1902, The Theatre Museum, London.
71. Review of *Sapho, New York Sun*.
72. "Olga Nethersole's Holy Work," *New York Tribune*, February 6, 1900.
73. "Miss Nethersole Defends *Sapho*," *New York Herald*, February 7, 1900.
74. James Metcalfe, "Review of *Sapho*," *Life Magazine*, December 13, 1900, 752–53.
75. "The Return of Miss Nethersole and Mr. Hawtrey," *Tatler*, May 7, 1902.
76. "*Sapho* Stopped by the Police," *New York Times*, March 6, 1900, 1.

77. "Miss Nethersole Appeals Her Case," *New York Herald*, March 6, 1900.
78. Ibid.
79. Ibid.
80. "*The Profligate* Revived," *New York Times*, March 18, 1900, 11.
81. Ibid.
82. "Jury Soon Acquits," 7.
83. "Miss Nethersole's Trial," otherwise unidentified clipping. The Adelphi File, 1902, The Theatre Museum, London.
84. "Jury Soon Acquits," 7.
85. Olga Nethersole, "I Thank the Women," otherwise unidentified clipping. *Sapho* clipping file, Billy Rose Theatre Collection.
86. "Jury Soon Acquits," 7.
87. "*Sapho* Gets an Ovation," *New York Times*, April 8, 1900, 7.
88. Ibid.
89. Ibid.
90. Unidentified clipping. *Sapho* clipping file, Museum of the City of New York.
91. "Jury Soon Acquits," 7.
92. "*Sapho* Engagement Closed," *New York Times*, May 30, 1900, 7.

3 *The Easiest Way* and the actress-as-whore myth

1. "The Easiest Way," *Theatre Magazine*, 9 (March 1909), 81–84.
2. Owen Davis, *My First Fifty Years in the Theatre* (Boston: Walter H. Baker Co, 1950), 154–55.
3. See "*The Easiest Way*: A Modern American Tragedy," *Dramatist*, 4 (July 1913), 39; and Emma Goldman, "*The Easiest Way*: An Appreciation," *Mother Earth*, 4 (May 1909), 86–92.
4. "Miss Starr Triumphs in *The Easiest Way*," *New York Times*, January 20, 1909, 9.
5. Eugene Walter, *The Easiest Way*, in *Best Plays of the Early American Theatre: From the Beginning to 1916*, edited by John Gassner, (New York: Crown Publishing, 1978), 616–76. Subsequent citations will occur parenthetically within the chapter.
6. James Metcalfe, "The Freedom of the Press," *Life Magazine*, February 4, 1909, 166.
7. Committee of Fourteen, *The Social Evil In New York City: A Study of Law Enforcement by the Research Committee of the Committee of Fourteen* (New York: Andrew H. Kellog Company, 1910), 93.
8. Ibid., 174.
9. Channing Pollock, "Two Big Plays and Some Little Ones," *Green Book Album* (April 1909), 875–877, at 875.
10. Committee of Fourteen, *The Social Evil In New York City*, 93.
11. Brenda Murphy, *American Realism and American Drama, 1880–1940* (London: Cambridge University Press, 1987).
12. Charlton Andrews, *The Drama Today* (Philadelphia: J. B. Lippincott Company, 1913), 87.

13. See Emma Goldman, "The Traffic in Women," (1917; reprint, *The Traffic in Women and Other Essays*, Washington, NJ: Times Change Press, 1970), 179; and Gayle Rubin, "The Traffic in Women: Notes on the 'Political Economy of Sex,'" *Toward an Anthropology of Women*, edited by Rayna R. Reiter (New York: Monthly Review Press, 1975), 157–210.

14. "A Strong Drama at the Stuyvesant," *New York Dramatic Mirror*, January 30, 1909, 3.

15. William Winter, "New Play at the Stuyvesant," otherwise unidentified clipping. *The Easiest Way* clipping file, Billy Rose Theatre Collection.

16. "Notes," *Craftsman*, 15 (1909), 739–741, at 740.

17. Alan Dale, "Eugene Walter's 'The Easiest Way,'" *New York American*, January 20, 1909.

18. "Two Plays of Low Life," *Saturday Review*, February 24, 1912, 236.

19. Ronald Wainscott, "Plays and Playwrights: 1896–1915," *Cambridge History of American Theatre, Volume 2: 1870–1945*, edited by Don B. Wilmeth and Christopher Bigsby (Cambridge, Cambridge University Press, 1999), 272.

20. Eve Kosofsky Sedgwick, *Between Men: English Literature and Male Homosocial Desire* (New York: Columbia University Press, 1985), 21.

21. Ibid., 26.

22. "Notes," 739.

23. Frances Lamont Peirce, "Eugene Walter: an American Dramatic Realist," *The Drama*, 21 (February 1916), 121.

24. Dale, "Eugene Walter's 'The Easiest Way,'" 185.

25. Curtis Lublin, "The Theater," *Town and Country*, January 29, 1909, 17.

26. Dale, "Eugene Walter's 'The Easiest Way.'"

27. Walter quoted in "'The Easiest Way' – Eugene Walter's Moving Portrayal of a Woman's Frailty," *Current Literature*, 51 (July 1911), 73–81, at 73.

28. Matinee Girl, "Touching Many Subjects, Her Ruminations Are Both Grave and Gay," *New York Dramatic Mirror*, January 30, 1909, 4.

29. Wainscott, "Plays and Playwrights," 271.

30. See Allen Churchill, *The Great White Way: A Re-Creation of Broadway's Golden Era of Theatrical Entertainment* (New York: E. P. Dutton & Co., 1962), 254. See also George Rector, *The Girl From Rector's* (New York: Doubleday, Page & Company, 1927).

31. Paul M. Potter, "The Girl From Rector's," unpublished play, Billy Rose Theatre Collection, 1.31.

32. Dale, "Eugene Walter's 'The Easiest Way.'"

33. "A Strong Drama at the Stuyvesant," 3; "The Easiest Way," *Theatre Magazine*, 82.

34. Dale, "Eugene Walter's 'The Easiest Way.'"

35. William Winter, *The Life of David Belasco*, 2 vols. (New York: Moffat, Yard & Company, 1918), vol 1, 456.

36. David Belasco, *The Theatre Through the Stage Door* (New York: Harper & Brothers, 1919), 110.

37. Thorstein Veblen, *Theory of the Leisure Class: An Economic Study of Institutions* (1899; reprint, New York: New American Library, 1953), 126.

38. George Kneeland, *Commercialized Prostitution in New York City* (1913; reprint, Montclair, NJ: Patterson Smith, 1969), 103.

39. Ruth Rosen, *The Lost Sisterhood: Prostitution in America, 1900–1918* (Baltimore: Johns Hopkins University Press, 1982), 156.

40. Ibid., 147.

41. "Notes," 739.

42. Goldman, "*The Easiest Way*: An Appreciation," 91.

43. "*The Easiest Way*," *Bookman*, 54 (Nov. 1921), 230.

44. "News of the Theatre," *Evening Sun*, March 3, 1911.

45. Metcalfe, "The Freedom of the Press," 168.

46. "Pointers on *The Easiest Way*," *Munsey's Magazine*, 41 (January 1909), 878.

47. "Frances Starr – the Cinderella of the Stage," *Theatre Magazine*, 7 (February 1907), 50–51.

48. "Eugene Walter, Dramatist," *New York Dramatic Mirror*, February 12, 1910, 7.

49. Churchill, *The Great White Way*, 159.

50. Pollock, "Two Plays and Some Little Ones," 876.

51. Ashton Stevens, *Evening Journal*, otherwise unidentified article. Quoted in "The Belasco News," undated press release.

52. Louis V. Defoe, untitled review of *The Easiest Way* that appeared in the *World*. Quoted in "The Belasco News," undated press release.

53. Winter, "New Play at the Stuyvesant."

54. Belasco, *The Theatre Through Its Stage Door*, 22.

55. Matinee Girl, "Touching Many Subjects," 4.

56. "Reviews of New Plays," *New York Dramatic Mirror*, January 30, 1909, 3.

57. David Belasco quoted in Matinee Girl, "Touching Many Subjects," 4.

58. Ward Morehouse, *Matinee Tomorrow: Fifty Years of our Theatre* (New York: Whittlesey, 1949), 91.

59. Ludwig Lewisohn, "The Native Theater," *Nation*, October 5, 1921, 381.

60. Pollock, "The Easiest Way," 875–877.

61. "The Belasco News," undated press release.

62. "*The Easiest Way*," *Munsey's Magazine*, 41 (July 1909), 578.

63. Alan Dale, untitled review of *The Easiest Way*. Quoted in "The Belasco News," undated press release.

64. "Pointers on 'The Easiest Way,'" 878.

65. Lise-Lone Marker, *David Belasco: Naturalism in the American Theatre* (Princeton: Princeton University Press, 1975), 169, 172.

66. Ethan Mordden, *The American Theatre* (New York: Oxford University Press, 1981), 42.

67. Belasco, *The Theatre Through Its Stage Door*, 77.

68. Travis Bogard, Richard Moody, and Walter J. Meserve, *The Revels History of Drama in English, vol. VIII, American Drama* (London: Methuen & Co. Ltd., 1977), 113.

69. Marker, *David Belasco*, 169.

70. Ibid.

71. "Pointers on 'The Easiest Way,'" 878.

72. Frances Starr quoted in Ward Morehouse, *Matinee Tomorrow*, 90.

73. Elin Diamond, *Unmaking Mimesis: Essays on Feminism and Theater* (London: Routledge, 1997), 5.
74. Lewisohn, "The Native Theater," 381.
75. Frances Hackett, "After the Play," *New Republic*, 28 (28 September 1921), 138.

Part II Working girls

1. Willa Sibert Cather, "Plays of Real Life," *McClure's Magazine*, 40 (March 1913), 69.
2. Laura Hapke, *Tale of the Working Girl: Wage-Earning Women in American Literature 1890–1925* (New York: Twayne Publishers, 1992).
3. To avoid confusion between Mary Shaw and Bernard Shaw, who are not related, I will use Shaw when referring to the former and Bernard Shaw when referring to the later.

4 The shop girl: Working-girl dramas

1. Laura Hapke, *Tale of the Working Girl: Wage-Earning Women in American Literature 1890–1925* (New York: Twayne Publishers, 1992), 2. See also Annie Marion MacLean, *Wage-Earning Women* (1901; reprint, New York: Arno Press, 1974).
2. For representations of working women and the association with prostitution on the British stage, see chapter 5 in Katharine Cockin, *Women and Theatre in the Age of Suffrage: The Pioneer Players, 1911–1925* (New York: Palgrave, 2001).
3. See Dorothy S. Pam, "Exploitation, Independence, and Solidarity: The Changing Role of American Working Women as Reflected in the Working-Girl Melodrama, 1870–1910," Ph.D. dissertation, New York University, 1980.
4. John A. Degen, "The Evolution of *The Shop Girl* and the Birth of 'Musical Comedy,'" *Theatre History Studies*, 7 (1987), 40–50, at 47. See also W. Macqueen-Pope, *Gaiety: Theatre of Enchantment* (London: W. H. Allen, 1949), 318.
5. George Edwardes quoted in *The Sketch*, November 28, 1894.
6. Peter Bailey, "'Naughty but Nice': Musical Comedy and the Rhetoric of the Girl, 1892–1914," *The Edwardian Theatre: Essays on Performance and the Stage*, edited by Michael R. Booth and Joel H. Kaplan (Cambridge: Cambridge University Press, 1996), 40.
7. H. J. W. Dam and Ivan Caryll (with additional numbers by Adrian Ross and Lionel Monckton), *The Shop Girl* (London: Hopwood & Crew, 1895), 3–4.
8. Ibid., 41.
9. Ibid., 28–29.
10. George Cooper and Charles E. Pratt, "The Shop Girls of New York" (Brooklyn: H. Franklin Jones, 1895).
11. Review of *Only a Shop Girl*, *New York Times*, September 1, 1903, 3.
12. Edward S. Jolly, Winifred Wilde, and Al La Rue, *Only a Shop Girl* (Chicago: Chas. K. Harris, 1903).
13. "Heaven Will Protect the Working Girl," lyrics by Edgar Smith, music by A. Baldwin Sloane, 1909.

14. Mary Rankin Cranston, "The Girl Behind the Counter," *World To-Day*, 10 (March 1906), 271.

15. Joel H. Kaplan and Sheila Stowell, *Theatre and Fashion: Oscar Wilde to the Suffragettes* (Cambridge: Cambridge University Press, 1994): 103–104. See also: 5, 6, and 130–32.

16. "Teaching the Girl Behind the Counter," *Technical World Magazine*, 17 (June 1912), 391.

17. Susan Porter Benson, *Counter Cultures: Saleswomen, Managers, and Customers in American Department Stores, 1890–1940* (Chicago: University of Illinois Press, 1986), 7.

18. Bailey, " 'Naughty but Nice,' " 50.

19. The lyrics are from Edwardes's version of *The Girl From Kay's*, as quoted in Bailey, " 'Naughty but Nice,' " 50.

20. Review of *The Girl Behind the Counter, Life Magazine*, October 17, 1907, 460–61.

21. Leon Berg, Monroe H. Rosenfeld, and Ballard MacDonald, *The Girl Behind the Counter is the Girl I Love* (New York: Jos. W. Stern & Co., 1909).

22. Jacob A Riis, *How the Other Half Lives: Studies Among the Tenements of New York* (1890; reprint, New York: Dover Publications, 1971), 234.

23. Ibid., 242.

24. Linda Elaine Hess, "Girl Behind the Counter: the Image of the Department Store Sales Girl in Popular Magazines 1890–1920," master's thesis, Ohio State University, 1986, 4.

25. Sue Ainslie Clark and Edith Wyatt, "Working-Girls' Budgets: A Series of Articles Based Upon Individual Stories of Self-Supporting Girls," *McClure's Magazine*, 35 (October 1910), 595.

26. Ibid., 610.

27. Benson, *Counter Cultures*, 135.

28. "The Store Girl's Wage," *Literary Digest*, 47 (9 August 1913), 199–200.

29. Ruth M. Alexander, *The "Girl Problem": Female Sexual Delinquency in New York, 1900–1930* (Ithaca: Cornell University Press, 1995), 12.

30. *Diana of Dobson's* ran for just 17 performances at the Savoy Theatre in New York.

31. Charles Klein, *Maggie Pepper* (New York: Grosset & Dunlap, 1911).

32. Stephen Crane, *Maggie, a Girl of the Streets (a Story of New York)*, edited by Thomas A. Gullason (1893; reprint, New York: W. W. Norton & Company, 1979). The actress playing *Maggie Pepper* was Rose Stahl, known for her performance of another fallen figure in *The Chorus Lady* (1906).

33. Channing Pollock, Review of *Maggie Pepper, The Green Book Album* (November 1911), 997–98. Reprinted in Anthony Slide, ed., *Selected Theatre Criticism Volume 1: 1900–1919* (Metuchen, NJ: Scarecrow Press, Inc., 1985), 160–62.

34. James Metcalfe, Review of *Maggie Pepper, Life Magazine*, September 14, 1911, 430–31.

35. "The Stage Society Offers Two Plays," *New York Times*, November 10, 1913, 9. A copy of *By-Products* can be found in the Special Collections at the University of Chicago. The manuscript lists no author or date, but I am confident that it is Patterson's play.

36. John Reed, *Moondown: A Play in One Act*, in *The Masses*, 4 (September 1913), 8–9. Another copy with a different ending can be found in the Library of Congress Manuscript Division.
37. "Little Plays Again at the Bandbox," *New York Times*, March 29, 1915.
38. Reed, *Moondown*, 8.
39. "Little Plays Again."
40. Barbara Meil Hobson, *Uneasy Virtue: the Politics of Prostitution and the American Reform Tradition* (New York: Basic Books, Inc., 1987), 109.

5 The girl shop: *Mrs Warren's Profession*

1. Max Beerbohm, "Mr. Shaw's Profession," *Saturday Review*, May 14, 1898, 651–52, and May 21, 1898, 69. The critiques were assembled and reprinted in the *Shaw Review*. See "Mr. Shaw's Profession", *Shaw Review*, 5.1 (January 1962), 5–9.
2. Mary Shaw, "My 'Immoral' Play," *McClure's Magazine*, 38 (1912), 687.
3. Not until July 7, 1906 – some seven months later – was the matter of "indecency" resolved in the case of *Mrs Warren's Profession*. The New York Court of Special Sessions decided in favor of Daly and manager Samuel Gumpertz. The play would not surface again for two years in New York.
4. "The Limit of Stage Indecency," *New York Herald*, October 31, 1905. Reprinted in Montrose J. Moses and John Mason Brown, eds., *The American Theatre As Seen By Its Critics, 1752–1934* (New York: Norton, 1934), 163–66.
5. James Huneker, "Bernard Shaw and Woman," *Harper's Bazaar*, 39 (June 1905), 538.
6. Martin Meisel, *Shaw and the Nineteenth Century Theatre* (Princeton: Princeton University Press, 1963), 141.
7. George Bernard Shaw, "*Mrs Warren's Profession*: Mr. Bernard Shaw's Reply," *Morning Leader*, November 7, 1905.
8. "Comstock Won't See Bernard Shaw's Play," *New York Times*, October 26, 1905, 9.
9. George Bernard Shaw, *Mrs Warren's Profession: A Play* (1898; reprint, in *Plays Unpleasant*, Harmondsworth: Penguin, 1983), 181. Subsequent citations will occur within the text.
10. Emma Goldman, *The Social Significance of Modern Drama* (1914; reprint, New York: Applause Theatre Books, 1987), 97.
11. For more about Vivie as a New Woman, see J. Ellen Gainor, *Shaw's Daughters: Dramatic and Narrative Constructions of Gender* (Ann Arbor: University of Michigan Press, 1991).
12. Fannie Fair, "Arnold Daly Talks of the Shaw Heroines," *New York Telegram*, October 26, 1905.
13. Constance A. Barnicoat, "Mr. Bernard Shaw's Counterfeit Presentment of Women," *Fortnightly Review*, 79 (March 1906), 519.
14. Quoted in Ruth Rosen, *The Lost Sisterhood: Prostitution in America, 1900–1918* (Baltimore: Johns Hopkins University Press, 1982), 91.
15. See Sabah A. Salih, "The *New York Times* and Arnold Day's Production of *Mrs Warren's Profession*," *Independent Shavian*, 26.3 (1988), 57–60; and Jean

Westrum White, "Shaw on the New York Stage," Ph.D. dissertation, New York University, 1965, 100–107.

16. See Morris L. Ernst and Alan U. Schwartz, *Censorship: The Search for the Obscene* (New York: The MacMillan Company, 1964), 29–33; John H. Houchin, *Censorship of the American Theatre in the Twentieth Century* (Cambridge: Cambridge University Press, 2003); and Nicola Beisel, *Imperiled Innocents: Anthony Comstock and Family Reproduction in Victorian America* (Princeton: Princeton University Press, 1997), 196–98.

17. "Comstock at It Again," *New York Times*, October 25, 1905, 1.

18. "Daly's New Shaw Play Barred in New Haven," *New York Times*, October 29, 1905, 3.

19. Shaw, "My 'Immoral' Play," 685.

20. Review of *Mrs Warren's Profession*, *New York Herald*. Reprinted as "Critics' Verdict Hostile," *New York Times*, October 31, 1905, 9.

21. Unidentified Clipping. *Mrs Warren's Profession* clipping file, Billy Rose Theatre Collection.

22. "Shaw's Play Unfit; the Critics Unanimous," *New York Times*, October 31, 1905, 9.

23. Ibid.

24. Barnard Hewitt, *Theatre U.S.A. 1665 to 1957* (New York: McGraw-Hill, 1959), 293.

25. Judith Butler, *Bodies That Matter: On the Discursive Limits of "Sex"* (New York: Routledge, 1993), 13.

26. "Daly's New Shaw Play Barred in New Haven," *New York Times*, October 29, 1905, 1.

27. Butler, *Bodies*, 12.

28. "The Limit of Stage Indecency."

29. Shaw, "My 'Immoral' Play," 689.

30. Ibid., 689–90.

31. "Pencil on Shaw's Play," *New York Times*, October 30, 1905, 9.

32. Review from the *New Haven Register*. Quoted in "Daly's New Shaw Play Barred in New Haven," 1.

33. "Shaw to Comstock: You Can't Scare Me," *New York Times*, October 27, 1905, 9.

34. "Pencil on Shaw's Play," 9.

35. Ibid.

36. Shaw, "My 'Immoral' Play," 688.

37. Ibid.

38. "Tones Down Shaw Play," *Evening World*, October 30, 1905.

39. Charles A. Berst, "Propaganda and Art in *Mrs Warren's Profession*," *ELH*, 33.3 (September 1966), 390–404.

40. Maureen Montgomery, *Displaying Women: Spectacles of Leisure in Edith Wharton's New York* (New York: Routledge, 1998), 120.

41. William McAdoo, *Guarding a Great City* (New York: Harper and Brothers, 1906), 74.

42. "Shaw's Play Unfit," 9.

43. "Daly May Take Shaw Play Off, Many Believe," *New York Telegram*, October 31, 1905.

44. "Shaw's Play Unfit," 9.

45. Unidentified clipping, Billy Rose Theatre Collection.
46. "Dr. Adler Calls Shaw a Literary Anarchist," *New York Times*, November 6, 1905, 6.
47. "Shaw's Play Stopped; The Manager Arrested," *New York Times*, November 1, 1905, 1.
48. "The Shackles on Dramatic Inspiration," *New York Times*, October 1, 1905, 9.
49. *New Haven Register*. Reprinted in "Daly's New Shaw Play Barred in New Haven," 1.
50. William McAdoo quoted in "Is Bernard Shaw a Menace to Morals?" *Current Literature*, 39 (November 1905), 551–52.
51. "M'Adoo Talk on Virtue Stirs Y.M.C.A. Men," *New York Times*, October 9, 1905, 4.
52. Ibid.
53. Ibid.
54. Unidentified clipping, Billy Rose Theatre Collection.
55. See Claudia D. Johnson, "That Guilty Third Tier: Prostitution in Nineteenth-Century American Theatre," *American Quarterly*, 27.5 (December 1975), 575–84. See also Bank, *Theatre Culture in America*, 122–138.
56. Bruce A. McConachie, *Melodramatic Formations: American Theatre and Society, 1820–1870* (Iowa City: University of Iowa Press, 1992), 73.
57. Bank, *Theatre Culture in America*, 133.
58. Montgomery, *Displaying Women*, 120.
59. Rosemarie K. Bank, "Hustlers in the House: the Bowery Theatre as a Mode of Historical Information," in *The American Stage: Social and Economic Issues from the Colonial Period to the Present*, edited by Ron Engle and Tice L. Miller (Cambridge: Cambridge University Press, 1993), 47–64.
60. See the Committee of Fourteen files, New York Public Library Special Collections.
61. Alfred Kreymborg, *Edna: The Girl of the Street* (New York: Guido Bruno, 1919), 12.
62. Robert G. Allen, *Horrible Prettiness: Burlesque and American Culture* (Chapel Hill: University of North Carolina Press, 1991), 76.
63. Kathy Peiss, *Cheap Amusements: Working Women and Leisure in Turn-of-the-Century New York* (Philadelphia: Temple University Press, 1986), 6.
64. Shaw, "My 'Immoral' Play," 687.
65. John D. Irving's dissertation on Mary Shaw is one of the few sources that examines the gender bias in the reception of the play. See Irving, "Mary Shaw: Actress, Activist, Suffragette, 1854–1929," Ph.D. dissertation, Columbia University, 1978: 94; Randy Kapelke also addresses gender politics, but offers spotty analysis throughout the essay. See Kapelke, "Preventing Censorship: the Audience's Role in *Sapho* (1900) and *Mrs Warren's Profession* (1905)," *Theatre History Studies*, 18 (June 1998), 117–133.
66. Shaw, "My 'Immoral' Play," 692.
67. See Dan H. Laurence, ed., *Bernard Shaw's Collected Letters 1898–1910*, 2 vols. (New York: Dodd, Mead and Company, 1972), vol. 2, 398.
68. Ibid., 464.

69. George E. Wellwarth, "Mrs. Warren Comes to America, or the Blue-Noses, the Politicians and the Procurers," *The Shaw Review*, 2.8 (May 1959), 8–16.
70. Shaw as quoted in "Tones Down Shaw Play."
71. "Ten Commandments Before Shaw – M'Adoo," *New York Times*, November 3, 1905, 6.
72. "Daly May Take Shaw Play Off."
73. See Robert A. Schanke, "Mary Shaw: A Fighting Champion," in *Women in American Theatre*, edited by Helen Krich Chinoy and Linda Walsh Jenkins (New York: Theatre Communications Group, 1987), 98–107. See also Ellen Donkin's biographical summary in *Notable Women in the American Theatre: A Biographical Dictionary*, edited by Alice M. Robinson, Vera Mowry Roberts, and Milly S. Barranger (New York: Greenwood Press, 1989), 784–89.
74. Gainor, *Shaw's Daughters*, 33.
75. Quoted in Shaw, "My 'Immoral' Play," 684.
76. Donkin, "Mary Shaw," 787.
77. Shaw, "My 'Immoral' Play," 692.
78. Ibid.

Part III Opium dens and urban brothels: Staging the white slave

1. Ernest A. Bell, ed., *Fighting the Traffic in Young Girls: or, War on the White Slave Trade* (Chicago: Illinois Vigilance Association, 1910).
2. The White Slave Traffic Act was also known as the 1910 Mann Act. An international conference regarding white slavery was held in Paris in 1902. All participating countries committed to trying to stop the international traffic in women. The United States signed the International Suppression of White Slavery Accord in 1908.
3. Clifford G. Roe and B. S. Steadwell, *Horrors of the White Slave Trade* (New York: [no publisher given], 1911), unpaginated page preceding introduction.
4. "Is White Slavery Nothing More Than a Myth?" *Current Opinion*, 55 (November 1913), 348.
5. Peter Landesman, "The Girls Next Door," *New York Times Magazine*, January 25, 2004, 30.
6. See letters to the editor in the *New York Times Magazine* on February 8, 15, and 22, 2004. The editor's reply appeared in *New York Times Magazine*, February 15, 2004, 3.

6 White slave plays in Progressive Era theatre

1. James Metcalfe, "Here We Are Again, Mr. Merryman," *Life Magazine*, September 4, 1913, 390–91.
2. "Little Lost Sister," *Book News Monthly*, 32 (January 1914), 256.
3. M. Joan McDermott and Sarah J. Blackstone, "White Slavery Plays of the 1910s: Fear of Victimization and the Social Control of Sexuality," *Theatre History Studies*, 16 (1996), 141–155.

4. Mark Thomas Connelly, *The Response to Prostitution in the Progressive Era* (Chapel Hill: University of North Carolina Press, 1980), 117.
5. Upton Sinclair, *The Jungle* (New York: Doubleday, Page, and Co., 1906).
6. Emma Goldman, "The Traffic in Women," in *The Traffic in Women and Other Essays* (1917; reprint, Washington, N J: Times Change Press, 1970), 20.
7. See Egal Feldman's "Prostitution, the Alien Woman and the Progressive Imagination, 1910–1915," *American Quarterly*, 29 (1967), 192–206.
8. Joseph Le Brandt, "Escaped From the Harem," unpublished play, Sherman Theatre Collection, 1890, 2A–3A.
9. Joseph Byron Totten, "The House of Bondage," unpublished play, Ohio State University, 1913, 1.11, 2.2.
10. For a brief history of the term white slave, see David J. Langum, *Crossing Over the Line: Legislating Morality and the Mann Act* (Chicago: University of Chicago Press, 1994), 56. See also Connelly, *The Response to Prostitution*, and Ruth Rosen, *The Lost Sisterhood: Prostitution in America, 1900–1918* (Baltimore and London: Johns Hopkins University Press, 1982). Both Connelly and Rosen trace the history of the term as it applies to sexual slavery.
11. Committee of Fifteen, *The Social Evil In New York City: A Study of Law Enforcement by the Research Committee of the Committee of Fifteen* (New York: G. P. Putnam & Sons, 1902).
12. Nell Nelson (pseudonym), *The White Slave Girls of Chicago: Nell Nelson's Startling Disclosures of the Cruelties and Iniquities Practiced in the Workshops and Factories of a Great City* (Chicago, Barkley Pub. Co., 1888), 17, 33.
13. Kathleen Barry, *Female Sexual Slavery*, rev. edn. (New York: New York University Press, 1979), 32.
14. See, for example, Barry, *Female Sexual Slavery*, and Connelly, *The Response to Prostitution*. See also Timothy J. Gilfoyle, *City of Eros: New York City, Prostitution, and the Commercialization of Sex, 1790–1920* (New York: W. W. Norton & Company).
15. Clifford G. Roe, *The Girl Who Disappeared* (Chicago: American Bureau of Moral Education, 1914), 69.
16. Rosen, *The Lost Sisterhood*, 133.
17. Clifford G. Roe quoted in Bell, *Fighting the Traffic*, 139.
18. Ibid., 141.
19. Bell, *Fighting the Traffic*, 77.
20. Michel Foucault, *The History of Sexuality, Volume I: An Introduction*, translated by Robert Hurley (New York: Vintage Books, 1990), 18.
21. *Report of the Commission for the Investigation of the White Slave Traffic, So Called.* [Massachusetts] House [Document] No. 2281 (Boston: Wright & Potter Printing Company, 1914), 22.
22. Theodore Roosevelt, "White Slave Traffic Worse Than Murder, Says Roosevelt," *New York Tribune*, September 7, 1913, 3.
23. McDermott and Blackstone, "White Slavery Plays," 153.
24. Quoted in Gilfoyle, *City of Eros*, 264.
25. George J. Kneeland, *Commercialized Prostitution in New York City* (1913; reprint, Montclair, NJ: Patterson Smith, 1969).

26. "Is White Slavery Nothing More Than A Myth?" 348.
27. Parke F. Hanley, "New York the Cleanest of Cities,"*New York Sun*, July 8, 1917, 1.
28. Goldman, "The Traffic in Women," 19.
29. *Madeleine: An Autobiography* (1919; reprint, New York: Persea Books, 1986), 321. Madeleine's book was the first of its kind to be published in the United States.
30. Rosen, *The Lost Sisterhood*, 133.
31. Connelly, *The Response to Prostitution*, 133.
32. Mary de Young, "Help, I'm Being Held Captive! The White Slave Fairy Tale of the Progressive Era," *Journal of American Culture*, 6.1 (Spring 1983), 96–99, at 96.
33. Barry, *Female Sexual Slavery*, 7.
34. Julia O'Connell Davidson, *Prostitution, Power and Freedom* (Ann Arbor: University of Michigan Press, 1998), 16.
35. O'Connell Davidson, *Prostitution, Power and Freedom*, 18.
36. David James Burrell, *The Lure of the City: A Book for Young Men* (New York and London: Funk & Wagnalls Company, 1908), 11–12.
37. Connelly, *The Response to Prostitution*, 115.
38. Edwin W. Sims quoted in Bell, *Fighting the Traffic*, 106.
39. Florence Mabel Dedrick, "Our Sister of the Street," in Bell, *Fighting the Traffic*, 105.
40. Charles Washburn, *Come into My Parlor: a Biography of the Aristocratic Everleigh Sisters of Chicago* (1934; reprint, New York: Arno Press, 1974), 243.
41. Unidentified clipping. *Little Lost Sister* clipping file, Billy Rose Theatre Collection.
42. "*Little Lost Sister* Well Acted At Walnut," *Cincinnati Commercial Tribune*, September 28, 1914.
43. Elizabeth Robins, "My Little Sister," *McClure's Magazine*, 40 (December 1912), 121–45; and *McClure's Magazine*, 41 (January 1913), 252–60. Robins's dramatic adaptation can be found in the Elizabeth Robins Papers, which are housed at Fales Library, New York University. See also Angela V. John, *Elizabeth Robins: Staging a Life, 1862–1952* (London: Routledge, 1995), 189–92.
44. "White Slave Play of Some Grim Power," *New York Times*, August 15, 1913, 7.
45. Stanley Olmsted, "Underworld Play at N.Y. Theatre," *New York Telegraph*, November 17, 1913.
46. Ibid.
47. "The Traffic," *Los Angeles Rounder*, August 9, 1913.
48. Whitney Collins, "The Girl Without a Chance," unpublished play, University of Chicago Library, 1914, 4.7. There are, as far as I can tell, two copies of this manuscript: one in the University of Chicago Library and the other in the Sherman Theatre Collection at the University of Southern Illinois at Carbondale. My citations are from the Sherman Theatre Collection's copy.
49. Roe, *Horrors of the White Slave Trade*.
50. Publicity flier from the Shubert Archive.
51. Channing Pollock, *Green Book Magazine*, 18 (July 1917), 14.
52. Arthur Hornblow, "Mr. Hornblow Goes to the Play," *Theatre Magazine*, 25 (June 1917), 342.
53. "The Theatre," *New York Sun*, April 13, 1917.
54. "The Knife," *Nation*, April 19, 1917, 104.

55. See Dave Williams, ed., *The Chinese Other, 1850–1925: An Anthology of Plays* (Lanham, NY: University Press of America, 1997), x. See also Edward Ziter, *The Orient on the Victorian Stage* (Cambridge: Cambridge University Press, 2003).
56. Edward Said, *Orientalism* (New York: Vintage Books, 1978).
57. "New Star – Dealers in White Women," *New York Dramatic Mirror*, September 3, 1904.
58. Joseph Jarrow, *The Queen of Chinatown*, in Williams, ed., *The Chinese Other*, 177.
59. Billy Getthore, "Slaves of the Opium Ring, The Opium Smugglers of 'Frisco or The Crimes of a Beautiful Opium Fiend," unpublished play, University of Chicago Library, 5-B. This title is also attributed to John Oliver in 1908.
60. Walter Montague, "The Slave Girl: 20 Minutes in Frisco's Chinatown," unpublished play, Sherman Theatre Collection, 1913, 3.
61. Roe, *Fighting the Traffic in Young Girls*, 108.
62. Gerald Bordman, *American Theatre: A Chronicle of Comedy and Drama, 1869–1914* (New York: Oxford University Press, 1994), 94.
63. "*East is West*," *Theatre Magazine*, 29 (February 1919), 78.
64. "*East is West*," *Dramatic Mirror of Motion Pictures and the Stage*, January 11, 1919, 47.
65. "*East is West*," *Theatre Magazine*, 78.
66. "*East is West* at the Lyric," *Illustrated London News*, June 26, 1920, 1114.
67. Ziter, *The Orient on the Victorian Stage*, 70.
68. Kremer, "Slaves of the Orient," unpublished play. An undated copy of the typescript is in the Billy Rose Theatre Collection. Another copy is in the Sherman Theatre Collection.
69. "Star – Slaves of the Orient," *New York Dramatic Mirror*, otherwise unidentified clipping. *Slaves of the Orient* clipping file, Billy Rose Theatre Collection.
70. Unidentified clipping. *Slaves of the Orient* clipping file, Billy Rose Theatre Collection.
71. Kremer, "Slaves of the Orient," I.9E.
72. Ibid., IV.5E.
73. Ziter, *The Orient on the Victorian Stage*, 75.
74. "Star – Slaves of the Orient."
75. Unidentified publicity flier from Laurence Senelick's private collection.

7 Brothel anyone? Laundering the 1913–14 white slave season

1. Charles Darnton, "*The Fight* Tries Desperately to Be Sensational," September 3, 1913. *The Fight* clipping file, Museum of the City of New York.
2. James S. Metcalfe, "That Dear Old Sociological Fund," *Life Magazine*, January 29, 1914, 190.
3. "Police Stop Two Plays," *Theatre Magazine*, 18 (September 1913), 116.
4. "The White Slave Plays," *New York Dramatic Mirror*, September 10, 1913, 10.
5. "The Author of *The Lure*," *Theatre Magazine*, 18 (October 1913), 125.
6. Studies showed that in order to survive, working women needed to make a weekly wage of nine dollars by the 1910s. However, women in factories and department stores had an average weekly income of $6.67. See Ruth Rosen, *The Lost Sisterhood: Prostitution in America, 1900–1918* (Baltimore: Johns Hopkins

University Press, 1982), 137–68. See also the chapter on New York workers in Annie Marion MacLean's *Wage-Earning Women* (1910; reprint, New York: Arno Press, 1974).

7. George Scarborough, "The Lure," unpublished play, 1913, 1.15. The version I am using is the uncensored, four-act script found at the Shubert Archive. Subsequent citations will appear parenthetically.

8. M. Joan McDermott and Sarah J. Blackstone, "White Slavery Plays of the 1910s: Fear of Victimization and the Social Control of Sexuality," *Theatre History Studies*, 16 (1996), 141–156.

9. Alfred Henry Lewis, "The Diary of a New York Policeman," *McClure's Magazine*, 40 (1913), 287.

10. Parke F. Hanley, "New York the Cleanest of Cities," *New York Sun*, July 8, 1917, 1.

11. Unidentified clipping. Billy Rose Theatre Collection.

12. "Police May Close *Fight* and *Lure*," *New York Times*, September 7, 1913, 3.

13. Ibid.

14. Review of *The Lure, New York Dramatic Mirror*, August 20, 1913, 6.

15. "Defend Social Evil Play," *New York Times*, October 13, 1913, 9.

16. Nethersole quoted in ibid.

17. "Mrs. Pankhurst's Most Quiet Day," *New York Times*, October 23, 1913, 7.

18. Eugene S. Lucas, Letter, *New York Times*, September 12, 1913, 10.

19. "Mrs. Pankhurst's Most Quiet Day," 7.

20. "Women and Stage Indecency," Editorial, *New York Times*, September 12, 1913, 10.

21. "White Slave Plays," *New York Dramatic Mirror*, September 10, 1913, 10.

22. Bayard Veiller, *The Fun I've Had* (New York: Reynal and Hitchcock, 1941), 213.

23. Ibid., 216. *The Fight* ran for 80 performances beginning on September 2, 1913.

24. "*The Fight* Good Drama in Bad Taste," *New York Sun*, September 3, 1913.

25. "A Successful Playwright's Hardships," *Stage*, 50 (November 1913), 297.

26. "*The Fight* is Full of Thrills," *Morning Telegram*, September 3, 1913.

27. "*The Fight* Acted at Hudson Theatre," *New York Times*, September 3, 1913, 9.

28. "The Fight," *New York Tribune*, September 3, 1913.

29. "*The Fight* Good Drama in Bad Taste."

30. Clayton Hamilton, "Timely Topics in the Theatre," *Bookman*, 38 (October 1913), 133.

31. "Vicious Scene Mars Next Veiller Play *The Fight*," September 3, 1913. *The Fight* clipping file, Museum of the City of New York.

32. "*The Fight* More Exciting Than *Within the Law*," *New York Press*, September 3, 1913.

33. "Women Approve *The Fight*," *New York Times*, October 15, 1913, 11.

34. See "Women as Play Censors," *New York Times*, October 8, 1913, 11; and "Women Approve *The Fight*," 11.

35. "Women to Run Theatre," *New York Times*, October 23, 1913, 11.

36. Unidentified clipping. *The Fight* clipping file, Museum of the City of New York.

37. "*The Fight* Good Drama in Bad Taste."

38. "The Fight is Full of Thrills."

39. Hamilton, "Timely Topics in the Theatre," 133. Witter Bynner portrayed this scene remarkably similarly and Veiller may have borrowed from it. See Witter Bynner,

A Book of Plays (New York: Alfred A. Knopf, 1922). *Tiger* also appeared in *Forum Magazine*, 49 (May 1913), 522–47.

40. "*The Fight* Has Great Popular Appeal," *New York Globe*, September 3, 1913.
41. "White Slave Plays," 10.
42. "Police View Two Plays," *New York Times*, September 5, 1913, 9.
43. Unidentified clipping. *The Fight* clipping file, Museum of the City of New York.
44. "*The Fight* Has Great Popular Appeal."
45. "Police Censorship," Editorial, *New York Dramatic Mirror*, December 17, 1913, 8.
46. "Waldo's Censors Watch Two Plays of Underworld," *World*, September 5, 1913.
47. "Managers of Vice Plays Are Summoned to Court," *World*, September 7, 1913.
48. "White Slave Plays," 10.
49. "Muensterberg Vigorously Denounces Red Light Drama," *New York Times*, September 14, 1913, IV, 4.
50. "Offending Plays," otherwise unidentified clipping. *The Lure* clipping file, Museum of the City of New York.
51. Unidentified editorial from the *New York Herald* quoted in ibid.
52. "Waldo's Censors."
53. "Police Stop Two Plays," *Theatre Magazine*, 18 (September 1913), 116.
54. "Decency and the Stage," Editorial, *New York Times*, September 7, 1913, 12.
55. "Brutally Realistic Presentation of an Unsavory Phase of Life in The Lure," otherwise unidentified clipping. *The Lure* clipping file, Shubert Archive.
56. See Charles Washburn, *Come Into My Parlor: a Biography of the Aristocratic Everleigh Sisters of Chicago* (1934; reprint, New York: Arno Press, 1974), 201–212.
57. Shubert's press release was reprinted in the *Morning Telegraph* as "*Lure* Managers Will Appear in Court To-Day," *Morning Telegraph*, September 8, 1913.
58. David Belasco quoted in "No Excuse for Vicious Red-Light Play On the Stage, Declares David Belasco," *Evening World*, September 6, 1913.
59. Ibid.
60. Ibid.
61. "White Slave Plays," 10.
62. Unidentified clipping. Billy Rose Theatre Collection.
63. "White Slave Play of Some Grim Power," 7.
64. "Police Stop Two Plays," 116.
65. "Laundering of *The Lure*," *Dress & Vanity Fair*, November 1913, 36.
66. "Defend Social Evil Play," 9.
67. "Immoral, Gross, Revolting, Judge Calls *The Lure*," *World*, September 9, 1913.
68. "*The Fight* Good Drama in Bad Taste."
69. "*The Fight* is Full of Thrills."
70. "Immoral, Gross, Revolting, Judge Calls *The Lure*."
71. "Rising Tide of Realism in the American Drama," *Current Opinion*, 55 (October 1913), 250–251.
72. Peter Brooks, "The Mark of the Beast: Prostitution, Melodrama, and Narrative," in *Melodrama*, edited by Daniel Gerould (New York: New York Literary Forum, 1980), 135.
73. "Immoral, Gross, Revolting, Judge Calls *The Lure*."
74. Veiller, *The Fun I've Had*, 214.
75. "*The Fight* is Full of Thrills."

76. Veiller, *The Fun I've Had*, 214.
77. "*The Fight* is Full of Thrills."
78. Channing Pollock, "The Fight," *Green Book Magazine*, 10 (November 1913), 764.
79. According to the *New York Tribune, The Fight* had been previously produced as *When All Has Been Said*. See "The Fight at Long Branch," *New York Tribune*, August 26, 1913.
80. Veiller, *The Fun I've Had*, 215.
81. "Police Stop Two Plays," 116.
82. "A Successful Playwright's Hardships," *Stage*, 50 (November 1913), 297.
83. "White Slave Plays," 10.
84. The uncensored version of *The Fight* consists of actors' "sides," and can be found in the New York Public Library's Billy Rose Theatre Collection. The numbering I use refers to the pagination for each character by using the first initial of the character's name, the act number, and the page number of his or her part. For example "J 1.18" refers to Jane's part, act 1, page 18.
85. "*The Fight*," *New York Dramatic Mirror*, September 10, 1913, 6.
86. Darnton, "*The Fight* Tries Desperately to Be Sensational."
87. Wendell Phillips Dodge, "The Story of *The Lure*, a Play by George Scarborough," *Leslie's Weekly*, September 25, 1913, 299.
88. Djuna Barnes, "The Tireless Rachel Crothers," *Theatre Guild Magazine*, 8 (May 1931), 17–18.
89. Other women playwrights who wrote about prostitution during the 1913–14 season are: Elizabeth Robins with *My Little Sister* (which was never produced) and Rachael Marshall, who co-wrote *The Traffic* with Oliver D. Bailey.
90. "The Process of Dry-Cleaning," *Munsey's Magazine*, 51 (February 1914), 124.
91. "*Ourselves*," *Everybody's Magazine*, 30 (February 1914), 264.
92. "Another Drama of Social Problem," *New York Herald*, November 14, 1913.
93. Crothers was supposed to deliver the script to the Shuberts by March 1, 1913. However, the contract was amended in April, and again in September 1913, suggesting revisions were made. Contract Files, Group II, #317.E, Shubert Archive, December 18, 1912.
94. "Reformatory Girls See Morals Drama," *New York City Tribune*, December 3, 1913.
95. "Dramatic Outlook in New York Brighter," *Louisville Courier*, November 23, 1913.
96. See Contract Files, Group II, #317.E, Shubert Archive.
97. Committee of Fifteen, *The Social Evil with Special Reference to Conditions Existing in the City of New York* (New York: G. P. Putnam's Sons, 1902).
98. "J. J. Shubert to Rachel Crothers," October 13, 1913. Correspondence File 1208 (Rachel Crothers), Shubert Archive.
99. "A Triumph for Rachel Crothers," *Bulletin*, November 17, 1913. See also "Rachel Crothers to Manager of Providence Opera House," November 15, 1913. Correspondence File 1208 (Rachel Crothers), Shubert Archive.
100. "*Ourselves* Deals with That Old Dual Morality," *Telegram*, November 14, 1913.
101. "White Slave Still a Theatrical Asset," otherwise unidentified clipping. *Ourselves* clipping file, Shubert Archive.
102. "A Triumph for Rachel Crothers."
103. "White Slave Still a Theatrical Asset."

104. *"Ourselves* As Seen By a Woman," *Morning Sun*, November 14, 1913.
105. Unidentified clipping. Rachel Crothers clipping file, Shubert Archive.
106. *"Ourselves* as Seen by a Woman."
107. "Rachel Crothers: Taken from the *Woman's Journal* May 1931," otherwise unidentified clipping. Rachel Crothers clipping file, Shubert Archive.
108. The citations refer to a manuscript copy of *Ourselves* that can be found at the Annenberg Rare Book and Manuscript Library at the University of Pennsylvania. Another copy exists in the Shubert Archive.
109. See Ruth Rosen's introduction to *The Maimie Papers*, edited by Ruth Rosen and Sue Davidson (Old Westbury, NY: The Feminist Press, 1977), xiv. See also Rosen, *The Lost Sisterhood*, 68.
110. "Girls Need 'Big Sisters,'" *New York Tribune*, November 17, 1913.
111. Norman Hapgood, "Stage Notes," *Harpers Weekly*, 58 (6 December 1913), 13.
112. Alan Dale, *"Ourselves*: A Feminine View of White Slavery, Says Dale," otherwise unidentified clipping. Illinois Public Library.
113. *"Ourselves," New York Dramatic Mirror*, November 19, 1913, 7.
114. Dale, *"Ourselves*: A Feminine View."
115. "Reformatory Girls See Morals Drama."
116. Ibid.
117. Crothers quoted in "Girls Need 'Big Sisters.'"
118. Bide Dudley, *"Ourselves* Based on Sex Question," *Morning Telegraph*, November 14, 1913.
119. Ruth M. Alexander, *The "Girl Problem": Female Sexual Delinquency in New York, 1900–1930* (Ithaca: Cornell University Press, 1995).
120. Crothers quoted in "Girls Need 'Big Sisters.'"
121. Vanderheyden Fyels, "Dramatic Outlook in New York Brighter," *Louisville Courier Journal*, November 23, 1913.
122. Brenda Murphy, "Feminism and the Marketplace: the Career of Rachel Crothers," in *The Cambridge Companion to American Women Playwrights*, edited by Brenda Murphy (Cambridge: Cambridge University Press, 1999), 88.
123. Colette Lindroth and James Lindroth, eds., *Rachel Crothers: A Research and Production Sourcebook* (Westport, CT: Greenwood Press, 1995).
124. Lois Gotlieb, *Rachel Crothers* (Boston: Twayne Publishers, 1979), 69.
125. *"Ourselves," New York Dramatic Mirror*, 6.
126. "Another Drama of Social Problem," *New York Herald*, November 14, 1913.
127. *"Ourselves* Deals with That Old Dual Morality."
128. Dale, *"Ourselves*: a Feminine View of White Slavery."
129. *"Ourselves* Deals with That Old Dual Morality."
130. *"Ourselves* Based on Sex Question," *Morning Telegraph*, November 14, 1913.
131. Dorris Abramson, "Rachel Crothers: Broadway Feminist," in *Modern American Drama: the Female Canon*, edited by June Schlueter (Madison: Associated University Press, 1990), 57.
132. Charles Darnton, *"Ourselves*: a Play That Goes Wrong," otherwise unidentified clipping. *Ourselves* clipping file, Shubert Archive.
133. A.R., "What is the Drama League Driving At?" *New York City Tribune*, December 6, 1913.

134. Review of *Ourselves, New York City Review*, December 6, 1913.
135. Review of *Ourselves, Baltimore News*, December 10, 1913.
136. "The Process of Drycleaning," *Munsey's Magazine*, 51 (February 1914), 124.
137. The author erroneously calls Bedford "Bradford." See "*Ourselves* at Bradford," *New York City Tribune*, December 7, 1913.
138. "*Ourselves* at Bradford."
139. Ibid.
140. Ibid.
141. "Escaping a House of Bondage," *Munsey's Magazine*, 51 (April 1914), 583.
142. "Police Censorship," 8.
143. "Arrest of Actress Stops a Vice Play," *New York Times*, December 10, 1913, 1.
144. Channing Pollock, *The Footlights Fore and Aft* (Boston: R. G. Badger, 1911), 366.
145. Mari Kathleen Fielder, "The Spooners," in *Notable Women in the American Theatre: A Bibliographical Dictionary*, edited by Alice Robinson, Vera Mowry Roberts and Milly S. Barranger (Westport, CT: Greenwood Press, 1989), 819–20.
146. Burns Mantle and Garrison P. Sherwood erroneously list *The House of Bondage* as premiering at the Longacre Theatre on January 19, 1914. This was the date it reopened after it had been censored. It premiered on December 8, 1913 at the Cecil Spooner Theatre in the Bronx. See Mantle and Sherwood, eds., *The Best Plays of 1899–1909 and the Year Book of the Drama in America* (Philadelphia: The Blakiston Company, 1944), 520.
147. "Police Censorship," 8.
148. Ibid.
149. Ibid.
150. "Hold Cecil Spooner," *New York Times*, December 11, 1913, 8.
151. Unidentified clipping. *The House of Bondage* clipping file, Billy Rose Theatre Collection.
152. "Hold Cecil Spooner," 8.
153. "*The House of Bondage*," *New York Dramatic Mirror*, December 17, 1913, 7.
154. "Hold Cecil Spooner," 8.
155. Ibid.
156. "*The House of Bondage*," *New York Dramatic Mirror*, 7.
157. Alan Dale, "Dale Views *House of Bondage*," otherwise unidentified clipping. Billy Rose Theatre Collection.
158. "*The House of Bondage*," *New York Dramatic Mirror*, 7.
159. Unidentified clipping. Billy Rose Theatre Collection.
160. Unidentified clipping. *The House of Bondage* clipping file, Billy Rose Theatre Collection.
161. Dale, "Dale Views *House of Bondage*."
162. "House of Bondage at the Longacre," *Commercial Advertiser*, otherwise unidentified clipping. *The House of Bondage* clipping file, Billy Rose Theatre Collection.
163. Unidentified clipping. *The House of Bondage* clipping file, Billy Rose Theatre Collection.
164. Unidentified clipping. *The House of Bondage* clipping file, Billy Rose Theatre Collection.
165. Metcalfe, "That Dear Old Sociological Fund," 190.

166. "Escaping a House of Bondage," 583.
167. McDermott and Blackstone, "White Slavery Plays," 141.

8 *Damaged Goods*: Sex hysteria and the *prostitute fatale*

1. "Excerpts, Opinions, Etc. of *Damaged Goods*," unidentified pamphlet. *Damaged Goods* clipping file, Billy Rose Theatre Collection.
2. *Damaged Goods* was first staged privately under the auspices of the Sociological Fund of the *Medical Review of Reviews* on March 14 and 17, 1913 at the Fulton Theatre.
3. "Excerpts, Opinions."
4. Unidentified clipping. *Damaged Goods* clipping file, Billy Rose Theatre Collection.
5. Ibid.
6. "Excerpts, Opinions."
7. *Damaged Goods* was first rehearsed at the Théâtre Antoine in Paris in November 1901, but was forbidden by the French censor until 1905.
8. "Sex O'Clock in America," *Current Opinion*, 55. 2 (August 1913), 113–14.
9. Ibid., 113.
10. Jane Addams, *A New Conscience and An Ancient Evil* (New York: The MacMillan Company, 1912).
11. George Bernard Shaw, "Introduction" in *Three Plays by Brieux*, by Eugène Brieux, translated by John Pollock (New York: Brentano's, 1907), xlvi.
12. "Brieux," *New Republic*, November 21, 1914, 20.
13. Allan M. Brandt, *No Magic Bullet: A Social History of Venereal Disease in the United States Since 1880* (Oxford: Oxford University Press, 1987), 47. Though I critique Brandt on this point, I am indebted to his research.
14. Ibid., 48.
15. Michel Foucault, *The History of Sexuality. Volume I: An Introduction*, translated by Robert Hurley (New York: Vintage Books, 1990), 35.
16. Review of *Damaged Goods*, *New York American*. Quoted in the *New York Dramatic Mirror*, March 19, 1913.
17. "Brieux Play Acted," *New York Times*, March 15, 1913, 13.
18. See Teresa de Lauretis, *Technologies of Gender: Essays on Theory, Film and Fiction* (Bloomington, IN: Indiana University Press, 1987).
19. See Alfred Fournier, *Syphilis and Marriage: Lectures Delivered at the St. Louis Hospital, Paris*, translated by Prince A. Morrow (New York: D. Appelton, 1882).
20. The French text's dedication to Fournier is missing from the American version translated by John Pollock.
21. Eugène Brieux, *Damaged Goods*, in *Three Plays by Brieux*, translated by John Pollock (New York: Brentano's Books, 1907), 187. Subsequent references will be included parenthetically in the text.
22. In the French text George is literally referred to as "*l'Avarié*," or the syphilitic.
23. Edwin E. Slosson, "A Dramatist Who Means Something," *New York Independent*, April 3, 1913, 752.
24. Brandt, *No Magic Bullet*, 12–13.
25. "Excerpts, Opinions."

26. Brandt, *No Magic Bullet*, 9.
27. Prince A. Morrow, *Social Diseases and Marriage, Social Prophylaxis* (New York: Lea Brothers & Co., 1904), iii.
28. Prince A. Morrow, "The Teaching of Sex Hygiene," *Good Housekeeping*, March 1912, 405.
29. "Prizes of Cash Bring Out Chelsea Section's Babies," *New York Times*, August 3, 1912.
30. William Dean Howells, "The Plays of Eugène Brieux," *North American Review*, (March 1915), 201, 402–11, quoted in Brenda Murphy, *A Realist in the American Theatre: Selected Drama Criticism of William Dean Howells* (Athens: Ohio University Press, 1992), 169.
31. Prince A. Morrow, "The Sanitary and Moral Prophylaxis of Venereal Diseases," *Journal of the American Medical Association*, 44 (March 1905), 675.
32. Edward L. Bernays, "When it Struck Sex O'Clock on Broadway," *Variety*, otherwise unidentified clipping. *Damaged Goods* clipping file, Museum of the City of New York.
33. Brieux, *Damaged Goods*, 186.
34. "Excerpts, Opinions."
35. Review of *Damaged Goods*, *New York Dramatic Mirror*, April 23, 1913, 7.
36. Slosson, "A Dramatist Who Means Something," 752.
37. Review of *Damaged Goods*, *New York American*. Reprinted in the *New York Dramatic Mirror*, March 19, 1913.
38. Review of *Damaged Goods*, *New York Dramatic Mirror*, March 19, 1913.
39. Undated flier for *Damaged Goods*. *Damaged Goods* clipping file, Billy Rose Theatre Collection.
40. "Excerpts, Opinions."
41. Quoted in Brandt, *No Magic Bullet*, 16.
42. Albert H. Burr, "The Guarantee of Safety in the Marriage Contract," *Journal of the American Medical Association*, 47 (December 1906), 1887–88.
43. Bernarr MacFadden, *Womanhood and Marriage: Fifty-three Lessons in Sex Hygiene Exclusively for Women* (New York: Physical Culture Publishing Corporation, 1918), ix.
44. Review of *Damaged Goods*, *New York Times*, 13.
45. Review of *Damaged Goods*, *New York Dramatic Mirror*, April 23, 1913, 7.
46. Benjamin M. Woodbridge, "Eugene Brieux," *Dial* (January 17, 1918), 67.
47. Quoted in "The First Nighter," *New York Dramatic Mirror*, March 19, 1913.
48. H. E. Stearns, "Damaged Goods: A Discussion," *New York Dramatic Mirror*, March 26, 1913, 5.
49. Review of *Damaged Goods*, *Life Magazine*, March 27, 1913, 628.
50. Review of *Damaged Goods*, *New York Times*, 13.
51. Review of *Damaged Goods*, *New York American*. Reprinted in the *New York Dramatic Mirror*, March 19, 1913.
52. Unidentified promotional flier. *Damaged Goods* clipping file, Billy Rose Theatre Collection.
53. Quoted in ibid.
54. Unidentified clipping. *Damaged Goods* clipping file, Billy Rose Theatre Collection.
55. Mrs. Annie Klein, "A Prominent Christian Scientist," otherwise unidentified clipping. *Damaged Goods* clipping file, Billy Rose Theatre Collection.

56. "The Drama as an Instrument of Reform," *Dial*, February 1, 1915, 73.
57. Kneeland's study of Bedford prostitutes revealed that most prostitutes worked as domestics before they turned to prostitution. See George J. Kneeland, *Commercialized Prostitution in New York City* (1913; reprint, Montclair, NJ: Patterson Smith, 1969), 222.
58. Ruth Rosen, *The Lost Sisterhood: Prostitution in America, 1900–1918*. (Baltimore: Johns Hopkins University Press, 1982), 35.
59. Slosson, "A Dramatist Who Means Something," 752.
60. Brandt, *No Magic Bullet*, 5.
61. Sander L. Gilman, *Disease and Representation: Images of Illness from Madness to AIDS* (Ithaca, NY: Cornell University Press, 1988), 1.
62. Quoted in Brandt, *No Magic Bullet*, 23.
63. Morrow, *Social Diseases and Marriage*, 343.
64. "Patient Zero" was the name given to a Canadian airline steward who allegedly slept with over 2,000 men while knowing he was infected with AIDS. Epidemiologists have subsequently disputed whether Patient Zero ever existed.
65. Gilman, *Disease and Representation*, 248–262.
66. Review of *Damaged Goods*, *New York Dramatic Mirror*, December 10, 1913, 15.
67. See Kevin Brownlow, *Behind the Mask of Innocence: Sex, Violence, Prejudice, Crime: Films of Social Conscience in the Silent Era* (New York: Knopf, 1990), 60; and Annette Kuhn, *Cinema, Censorship and Sexuality, 1909–1925* (London and New York: Routledge, 1988), 49–74 and 140–50.
68. William F. Snow and Wilbur A. Sawyer, "Venereal Disease Control in the Army," *Journal of the American Medical Association*, 71 (August 1918), 456.
69. Rosen, *The Lost Sisterhood*, 33.
70. Timothy J. Gilfoyle, *City of Eros: New York City, Prostitution, and the Commercialization of Sex 1790–1920* (New York: W. W. Norton & Company, 1992), 609.
71. Quoted in Brandt, *No Magic Bullet*, 67.
72. Quoted in Mark Thomas Connelly, *The Response to Prostitution in the Progressive Era* (Chapel Hill: University of North Carolina Press, 1980), 140.
73. Quoted in Brandt, *No Magic Bullet*, 101.
74. Gilfoyle, *City of Eros*, 314.

9 The repentant courtesan in *"Anna Christie"* and the lesbian prostitute in *The God of Vengeance*

1. Thanks to Zander Brietzke for pointing out these titles to me. See also Gary Vena's "The Role of the Prostitute in the Plays of Eugene O'Neill," *Drama Critique*, 10 (Fall 1967), 129–37; and Arthur and Barbara Gelb, *O'Neill* (New York: Harper and Row, 1962), 129, 152, 161, 166.
2. Gelb, *O'Neill*, 126.
3. James Agate, "Variations on an Air," *Saturday Review*, April 21, 1923, 532.
4. "'Anna Christie': Mr. Eugene O'Neill's Fine Play," *Daily Mail*, April 11, 1923.
5. Francis Hackett, "After the Play," *New Republic*, November 30, 1921, 26.

6. Timothy J. Gilfoyle, *City of Eros: New York City, Prostitution, and the Commercialization of Sex, 1790–1920* (New York: W.W. Norton & Company, 1992), 315.
7. Sheila Hickey Garvey, "Anna Christie and the 'Fallen Woman Genre,'" *Eugene O'Neill Review*, 19 (1995), 67–80, at 68.
8. Gelb, *O'Neill*, 127.
9. Zander Brietzke, "Tragic Vision and the Happy Ending in *'Anna Christie,'*" *Eugene O'Neill Review*, 24:1–2 (Spring-Fall 2000), 3–60, at 44.
10. Andrew Parker and Eve Kosofsky Sedgwick, eds., *Performativity and Performance* (New York: Routledge, 1995), 11.
11. Barbara Meil Hobson, *Uneasy Virtue: The Politics of Prostitution and the American Reform Tradition* (New York: Basic Books, Inc., 1987).
12. Travis Bogard, *Contour in Time: The Plays of Eugene O'Neill*, rev. edn. (New York: Oxford University Press, 1988), 151–152.
13. Ibid.
14. Abbreviations refer to the following edition: Eugene O'Neill, *Complete Plays*, 3 vols., edited by Travis Bogard (New York: The Library of America, 1988). All subsequent citations will occur parenthetically.
15. "'Anna Christie' Has Its Premiere at Vanderbilt," November 2, 1921, otherwise unidentified clipping. "*Anna Christie*" clipping file, Museum of the City of New York.
16. Ibid.
17. Ann C. Hall, "Gawd, You'd Think I Was a Piece of Furniture: O'Neill's *'Anna Christie,'*" in *Staging the Rage: the Web of Misogyny in Modern Drama*, edited by Katherine H. Burkman and Judith Roof (Cranbury, NJ: Associated University Press, 1998), 171–182, at 177.
18. Barbara Voglino, *"Perverse Mind": Eugene O'Neill's Struggle With Closure* (Cranbury: Associated University Press, 1999), 37.
19. Maida Castellun, "Eugene O'Neill's *'Anna Christie'* is Thrilling Drama, Perfectly Acted With a Bad Ending," *New York Call*, November 4, 1921.
20. Percy Hammond, Review of *"Anna Christie," New York Tribune*, November 3, 1921.
21. Ernest Boyd, Review of *"Anna Christie," Freeman*, December 7, 1921, 304.
22. Hall, "Gawd," 172.
23. Brenda Murphy, *American Realism and American Drama, 1880–1940* (Cambridge: Cambridge University Press, 1987), 119.
24. Alexander Woollcott, "Second Thoughts on First Nights," *New York Times*, November 13, 1921, VI: 1.
25. C.S., "The Theatre," *Dial*, 71 (December 1921), 725.
26. "*Anna Christie* Has Its Premiere."
27. Robert C. Benchley, "Drama," *Life Magazine*, November 24, 1921, 18.
28. Castellun, "Eugene O'Neill's *'Anna Christie.'*"
29. G. H. Mair, "Anna Christie Success," *Evening Standard*, November 4, 1923.
30. When the play appeared in an abbreviated version in *Hearst*'s a month earlier, it included the last act.
31. Agate, "Variations on an Air," 532.
32. Hackett, "After the Play," 26.

33. "Eugene O'Neill's 'Anna Christie' is Thrilling Drama Perfectly Acted With a Bad Ending," *New York Call*, November 4, 1921.
34. Walter Prichard Eaton, "The Function of Criticism," *The Freeman*, January 11, 1922, 425.
35. Bogard, *Contour in Time*, 153.
36. Boyd, Review of *"Anna Christie,"* 304.
37. Pauline Lord, "My Anna Christie," *Metropolitan Magazine*, 55 (June 1922), 37.
38. Castellun, "Eugene O'Neill's *'Anna Christie.'*"
39. Woollcott quoted in John Houchin, *The Critical Response to Eugene O'Neill* (Westport, CT: Greenwood Press, 1993), 30.
40. Lesley Ferris, *Acting Women: Images of Women in Theatre* (Hampshire and London: Macmillan Education Ltd., 1990), 79–95, at 92.
41. Vena, "The Role of the Prostitute," 133.
42. "Anna Christie," *Variety*, November 11, 1921.
43. Agate, "Variations on an Air," 533.
44. Voglino, *"Perverse Mind,"* 38. O'Neill felt that audiences misunderstood the reconciliation between Anna and Mat, seeing it as a happy ending, rather than as the bleaker ending he intended.
45. O'Neill quoted in Gelb, *O'Neill*, 481.
46. Dorris Nelson, "O'Neill's Women," *Eugene O'Neill Newsletter*, 6 (Summer/Fall 1982), 3–7, at 3.
47. O'Neill quoted in Gelb, *O'Neill*, 508.
48. "Anna Christie," *Variety*, November 11, 1921.
49. Agate, "Variations on an Air," 532.
50. Ronald Wainscott, "Notable American Stage Productions," in *The Cambridge Companion to Eugene O'Neill*, edited by Michael Manheim (Cambridge: Cambridge University Press, 1998), 101.
51. Robert Allerton Parker, "An American Dramatist Developing," *Independent and the Weekly Review*, December 2, 1921, 236.
52. Benchley, "Drama," 18.
53. Kenneth Macgowan, Review of *"Anna Christie,"* *Vogue Magazine*, otherwise unidentified clipping. *"Anna Christie"* clipping file, Museum of the City of New York.
54. Sydney W. Carroll, Review of *"Anna Christie,"* *Sunday Times*, April 15, 1923.
55. May Herschel Clarke, "The Creator of 'Anna Christie': The Picture Show Meets Pauline Lord," *Picture Show*, April 8, 1923, 20.
56. Lord quoted in Clarke, "The Creator of 'Anna Christie,'" 20.
57. Lord, "My Anna Christie," 36.
58. Gelb, *O'Neill*, 476–477.
59. Nelda K. Balch, "Pauline Lord," in *Notable Women in American Theatre*, edited by Alice M. Robinson, Vera Mowry Roberts, and Milly S. Barranger (Westport, CT: Greenwood Press, 1989), 558–560, at 558. See also Gelb, *O'Neill*, 477.
60. Lord quoted in "Her Big Effort: How Miss Lord Tried to Overcome English Coldness," *Evening Standard*, November 4, 1923.
61. E. A. Baughan, "Triumph of Acting," *Daily News*, April 14, 1923.
62. Margaret Loftus Ranald, *The Eugene O'Neill Companion* (Westport, CT: Greenwood Press, 1984), 390.

63. Here I refer to Laura Mulvey's term that describes how women are objectified through a voyeuristic male gaze. See Mulvey, "Visual Pleasure and Narrative Cinema," *Screen*, 16:3 (Autumn 1975), 6–15.
64. Lord, "My Anna Christie," 37.
65. Balch, "Pauline Lord," 560.
66. Lord quoted in Clarke, "The Creator of 'Anna Christie,'" 20.
67. Ibid.
68. Brietzke, "Tragic Vision," 57.
69. Benchley, "Drama," 18.
70. Harry Weinberger, producer of the play, and the twelve cast members, were found guilty of giving immoral performances on May 23, 1923. See "*God of Vengeance* Players Convicted," *New York Times*, May 24, 1923, 1. Weinberger, and lead actor Schildkraut, appealed to the Appellate Division of the Supreme Court, but lost. Charges were reversed on January 21, 1925, and a new trial ordered. See "Actors Win on Appeal," *New York Times*, January 22, 1925, 23. In April the Assistant District Attorney dropped all charges. See "Court Frees Actors in *God of Vengeance*," *New York Times*, April 4, 1923, 25.
71. *Gott fun Nekoma* was translated in 1918 by Isaac Goldberg. See Sholom Asch, *The God of Vengeance*, translated by Isaac Goldberg (Boston: Stratford Co., 1918).
72. Alisa Solomon, *Re-Dressing the Canon: Essays on Theatre and Gender* (London: Routledge, 1997), 112.
73. See John Houchin, *Censorship in the American Theatre in the Twentieth Century* (Cambridge, Cambridge University Press, 2003), 82–87; Solomon, *Re-Dressing the Canon*, 111–119; see also Harley Erdman, "Jewish Anxiety in 'Days of Judgment': Community Conflict Anti-Semitism, and the *God of Vengeance* Obscenity Case," *Theatre Survey*, 40.1 (May 1999), 51–74.
74. Curtin Kaier, *We Can Always Call Them Bulgarians: The Emergence of Lesbians and Gay Men on the American Stage* (Boston: Alyson Publications, 1987), 25–42, at 25.
75. Solomon, *Re-Dressing the Canon*, 115–116.
76. Asch, *The God of Vengeance*, 62–63.
77. Kaier, *We Can Always Call Them Bulgarians*, 26.
78. Asch, *The God of Vengeance*, 93–94.
79. Ibid., 95.
80. Solomon, *Re-Dressing the Canon*, 117.
81. Houchin, *Censorship*, 82.
82. Erdman, "Jewish Anxiety," 56.
83. Heywood Broun, "The New Play," *World*, December 21, 1922, 13.
84. Ibid.
85. "'God of Vengeance' Players Convicted," 3.

Bibliography

Abramson, Doris. "Rachel Crothers: Broadway Feminist." In *Modern American Drama: the Female Canon*. Ed. June Schlueter. Madison: Associated University Press, 1990.

"Acting Redeems Play of Sordid Life." *New York Times* November 18, 1918: 15.

Acton, William. *Prostitution*. 1857. Reprint, New York: Rederick A. Praeger, 1969.

The Functions and Disorders of Reproductive Organs. 1867. Reprint, *The Sexuality Debates*. Ed. Sheila Jeffreys. New York: Routledge & Kegan Paul, 1987.

"Actors Win on Appeal." *New York Times* January 22, 1925: 23.

Addams, Jane. *A New Conscience And An Ancient Evil*. New York: The MacMillan Company, 1912.

Agate, James. "Variations on an Air." *Saturday Review* April 21, 1923: 532.

Alexander, Ruth M. *The "Girl Problem": Female Sexual Delinquency in New York, 1900–1930*. Ithaca: Cornell University Press, 1995.

"All About Her." *Toledo Blade* October 16, 1913.

Allen, Robert C. *Horrible Prettiness: Burlesque and American Culture*. Chapel Hill: University of North Carolina Press, 1991.

Anderson, Amanda. *Tainted Souls and Painted Faces: the Rhetoric of Fallenness in Victorian Culture*. Ithaca: Cornell University Press, 1993.

"The Prostitute's Artful Guise." *diacritics* (Summer/Fall 1991): 102–22.

Anderson, Eric. "Prostitution and Social Justice: Chicago, 1910–1915." *Social Service Review* 48 (1974): 203–228.

Andrews, Charlton. *The Drama Today*. Philadelphia: J. B. Lippincott Company, 1913.

"*Anna Christie*." Dir. Clarence Brown. Screenplay by Frances Marion. With Greta Garbo and Charles Bickford. MGM, 1930.

"*Anna Christie*." *Variety* November 11, 1921.

"'*Anna Christie*' Has Its Premiere at Vanderbilt." November 2, 1921. Otherwise unidentified clipping. "*Anna Christie*" clipping file, Museum of the City of New York.

"*Anna Christie*, Mr. Eugene O'Neill's Fine Play." *Daily Mail* April 11, 1923.

"*Anna Christie* (Play of the Month)." *Hearst's* 41 (March 1922): 45–7; 56–7.

"Annie, Get my Prettiest Dress." *The Playbill*. New York: New York Theatre Program Corp, 1938.

"Another Drama of Social Problem." *New York Herald* November 14, 1913.

"*Any Night* Acted at the Princess." *Chicago Post* March 21, 1914.

Appleton, Robert. *Violet: The American Sappho*. Boston: Franklin Publishing Company, 1894.

Aron, Cindy Sondik. "Introduction." In *The Long Day: the Story of a New York Working Girl.* 1905. Reprint, Charlottesville: University Press of Virginia, 1990: ix–xxxvii.

Asch, Sholom. *The God of Vengeance.* Trans. Isaac Goldberg. Boston: Stratford Co., 1918.

"At the Play and With the Players." *New York Times* February 11, 1900: 16.

Auster, Albert. *Actresses and Suffragists: Women in the American Theater, 1890–1920.* New York: Praeger Publishers, 1984.

Austin, J. L. *How To Do Things With Words.* Eds. J. O. Urmson and Marina Sbisà. Cambridge: Harvard University Press, 1962.

"The Author of *The Lure.*" *Theatre Magazine* 18 (October 1913): 124.

Bailey, Peter. "'Naughty but Nice': Musical Comedy and the Rhetoric of the Girl, 1892–1914." In *The Edwardian Theatre: Essays on Performance and the Stage.* Eds. Michael R. Booth and Joel H. Kaplan. Cambridge: Cambridge University Press, 1996.

Balch, Nelda K. "Pauline Lord." In *Notable Women in American Theatre.* Eds. Alice M. Robinson, Vera Mowry Roberts, and Milly S. Barranger. Westport, CT: Greenwood Press, 1989: 558–560.

Bank, Rosemarie K. "Hustlers in the House: the Bowery Theatre as a Mode of Historical Information." In *The American Stage: Social and Economic Issues from the Colonial Period to the Present.* Eds. Ron Engle and Tice L. Miller. Cambridge: Cambridge University Press, 1993: 47–64.

Theatre Culture in America, 1825–1860. Cambridge: Cambridge University Press, 1997.

Bantock, Leedham, Arthur Anderson, and Howard Talbot. *The Girl Behind the Counter.* London: Chappell & Co., 1906.

Barnes, Djuna. "The Tireless Rachel Crothers." *Theatre Guild Magazine* 8 (May 1931): 17–18.

Barnes, Eric Wollencott. *The High Room: a Biography of Edward Sheldon.* London: W. H. Allen, 1957.

Barnicoat, Constance A. "Mr. Bernard Shaw's Counterfeit Presentment of Women." *Fortnightly Review* 79 (March 1906): 519.

Barry, Kathleen. *Female Sexual Slavery.* Englewood Cliffs, NJ: Prentice-Hall Inc., 1979.

Baudelaire, Charles. "Allegory." In *Les Fleurs du Mal.* Trans. Richard Howard. Boston: Godine, 1982.

My Heart Laid Bare and Other Prose Writings. Trans. Norman Cameron. Ed. Peter Quennell. London: Soho Book Company, 1986.

Baudrillard, Jean. "Simulacra and Simulations." In *Selected Writings.* Ed. Mark Poster. Stanford: Stanford University Press, 1988.

Baughan, E. A. "Triumph of Acting." *Daily News* April 14, 1923.

Beebe, Lucius. "As Society Is, So Is the Stage, That's Owen Davis's View of It." *New York Herald Tribune.* Otherwise unidentified clipping. Owen Davis clipping file, Shubert Archive.

Beerbohm, Max. "Mr. Shaw's Profession." *Saturday Review* May 14, 1898: 651–52 and May 21, 1898: 69.

Beisel, Nicola. *Imperiled Innocents: Anthony Comstock and Family Reproduction in Victorian America.* Princeton: Princeton University Press, 1997.

Belasco, David. "Zaza." Unpublished play. New York Public Library, 1898.

The Theatre Through Its Stage Door. New York: Harper & Brothers, 1919.

"Belasco and Mrs. Carter End Their 25-Year Feud." *New York Telegram* April 10, 1931.

"Belasco 'Find' Made Real Hit." *Philadelphia Record* January 25, 1925.

Bell, Archie. "Celebrated Actress, Once a Cleveland School Girl, Tells Why She has Played the 'Bad Women of the Stage.'" April 13, 1913. Otherwise unidentified clipping.

Bell, Ernest A., ed. *Fighting the Traffic in Young Girls: or, War on the White Slave Trade.* Chicago: Illinois Vigilance Association, 1910.

Bell, Hillary. "Genius the Word for Mrs. Carter." *New York Herald* January 10, 1899.

"This Much Is Sure: Last Night's Audience Was Fashionable and Applauded Vociferously." *New York Herald* January 11, 1899.

Bell, Shannon. *Reading, Writing, and Rewriting the Prostitute Body.* Bloomington, IN: Indiana University Press, 1994.

Benchley, Robert C. "Drama." *Life Magazine* November 24, 1921: 18.

Benjamin, Walter. "Central Park." *New German Critique* 34 (Winter 1985): 32–58.

Benson, Susan Porter. *Counter Cultures: Saleswomen, Managers, and Customers in American Department Stores, 1890–1940.* Chicago: University of Illinois Press, 1986.

Bentley, Irene. "Chorus Girl to Leading Lady." *Theatre Magazine* 7 (September 1901): 16–17.

Berg, Leon, Monroe H. Rosenfeld, and Ballard MacDonald. *The Girl Behind the Counter is the Girl I Love.* New York: Jos. W. Stern & Co., 1909.

Berger, John. *Ways of Seeing.* New York: Penguin, 1972.

"Bernard Shaw on American Women." 1907. Reprint, *The Independent Shavian* 10 (Winter 1971/72): 1–5.

Bernays, Edward L. *Biography of an Idea: Memoirs of Public Relations Counsel.* New York: Simon and Schuster, 1965.

"When it Struck Sex O'Clock on Broadway." *Variety.* Otherwise unidentified clipping. *Damaged Goods* clipping file, Museum of the City of New York.

Berst, Charles A. "Propaganda and Art in *Mrs. Warren's Profession.*" *ELH* 33.3 (September 1966): 390–404.

Berton, Pierre and Charles Simon. *Zaza.* Paris: Librairie Charpentier et Fasquelle, 1904.

Blackwell, Alice Stone. Letter. *Survey* 25 (December 10, 1910): 436–37.

Bogard, Travis. *Contour in Time: the Plays of Eugene O'Neil.* Rev. edn. New York: Oxford University Press, 1988.

Bogard, Travis, Richard Moody, and Walter J. Meserve. *The Revels History of Drama in English.* London: Methuen & Co. Ltd., 1977. Vol. VIII.

Bordman, Gerald. *American Theatre: a Chronicle of Comedy and Drama, 1914–1930.* New York: Oxford University Press, 1995.

Bowlby, Rachel. *Just Looking: Consumer Culture in Dreiser, Gissing and Zola.* New York: Methuen, 1985.

Boyd, Ernest. "*Anna Christie.*" *Freeman* December 7, 1921: 304.

Brandt, Allan M. *No Magic Bullet: A Social History of Venereal Disease in the United States Since 1880.* New York: Oxford University Press, 1987.

Breslow, M. M. Letter. *New York Times* January 20, 1909: 8.

Brietzke, Zander. "Tragic Vision and the Happy Ending in '*Anna Christie.*'" *Eugene O'Neill Review* 24: 1–2 (Spring/Fall 2000): 3–60.

"Brieux." *The New Republic* November 21, 1914: 19–20.

Brieux, Eugène. *Damaged Goods*. In *Three Plays by Brieux*. Trans. John Pollock. New York: Brentano's Books, 1907.

Théâtre complet de Brieux. Paris: Librairie Stock, 1923.

"Brieux's New Sociological Sermon in Three Acts." *Current Opinion* 54 (April 1913): 296–97.

"Brieux Play Acted." *New York Times* March 15, 1913: 13.

Bronson, Howard. *The Autobiography of a Play*. New York: Columbia University, 1914.

Brooks, Peter. "The Mark of the Beast: Prostitution, Melodrama, and Narrative." In *Melodrama*. Ed. Daniel Gerould. New York: New York Literary Forum, 1980.

Broun, Heywood. "The New Play." *World* December 21, 1922: 13.

Brown, T. Allston. *A History of the New York Stage From 1732 to 1901*. New York: Benjamin Blom, Inc., 1903.

Brownlow, Kevin. *Behind the Mask of Innocence: Sex, Violence, Prejudice, Crime: Films of Social Conscience in the Silent Era*. New York: Knopf, 1990.

Buci-Glucksmann, Christine. "Catastrophic Utopia: the Feminine as Allegory of the Modern." In *The Making of the Modern Body: Sexuality and Society in the Nineteenth Century*. Eds. Catherine Gallagher and Thomas Laquer. Berkeley: University of California Press, 1987.

Buck-Morss, Susan. "The Flâneur, the Sandwichman, and the Whore: the Politics of Loitering." *New German Critique* 39 (Fall 1986): 99–140.

The Dialectics of Seeing: Walter Benjamin and the Arcades Project. Cambridge, MA: MIT Press, 1989.

Buckley, Peter G. "Introduction." In *Inventing Times Square: Commerce and Culture at the Crossroads of the World*. Ed. William R. Taylor. New York: Russell Sage Foundation, 1991.

Burnham, Charles. "Stage Indecency – Then and Now. A Play That Made Our Daddies Blush Could Be Read in Sunday-school Today." *Theatre Magazine* 42 (September 1925): 16, 56.

Burr, Albert H. "The Guarantee of Safety in the Marriage Contract." *Journal of American Medical Association* 47 (1906): 1887–88.

Burrell, David James. *The Lure of the City: A Book for Young Men*. New York: Funk & Wagnalls Company, 1908.

Butler, Judith. *Gender Trouble: Feminism and the Subversion of Identity*. New York: Routledge, 1990.

Bodies That Matter: On the Discursive Limits of "Sex." New York: Routledge, 1993.

Butsch, Richard. *The Making of American Audiences: From Stage to Television, 1750–1990*. Cambridge: Cambridge University Press, 2000.

Bynner, Witter. *Tiger*. In *A Book of Plays*. New York: Alfred A. Knopf, 1922.

Tiger. In *Forum Magazine* 49 (May 1913): 522–47.

Callis, Ann Everal. "Olga Nethersole and the *Sapho* Scandal." Master's thesis, Ohio State University, 1974.

Campbell, Bartley. *The White Slave*. In *The White Slave and Other Plays*. Ed. Napier Wilt. Princeton: Princeton University Press, 1941.

Camille. Dir. George Cukor. Screenplay by Frances Marion. With Greta Garbo, Robert Taylor, and Lionel Barrymore. MGM 1936.

"Camille." *New York Spirit of the Times* November 13, 1894.

"Camille." *Theatre Magazine* 4 (May 1904): 109.

Carlson, Marvin. *Places of Performance: The Semiotics of Theatre Architecture*. Ithaca: Cornell University Press, 1989.

  The Haunted Stage: the Theatre as Memory Machine. Ann Arbor: University of Michigan Press, 2001.

Carroll, Sydney W. "Anna Christie." *Sunday Times* April 15, 1923.

Carter, Mrs. Leslie. "Mrs. Leslie Carter Discusses *Zaza* and Morality." *Broadway Magazine* (December 1899): 183.

  "What My Career Means to Me." Otherwise unidentified clipping. Mrs. Leslie Carter folder, C & L Brown Collection, Billy Rose Theatre Collection.

Case, Sue-Ellen. "Performing Lesbian in the Space of Technology: Part II." *Theatre Journal* 47 (1995): 329–343.

Castellun, Maida. "Eugene O'Neill's *Anna Christie* is Thrilling Drama, Perfectly Acted With a Bad Ending." *New York Call* November 4, 1921.

Cather, Willa Sibert. "Plays of Real Life." *McClure's Magazine* 40 (March 1913): 69.

de Certeau, Michel. *The Practice of Everyday Life*. Trans. Steven Rendall. Berkeley: University of California Press, 1988.

Chapman, John and Garrison P. Sherwood, eds. *The Best Plays of 1894–1899*. New York: Dodd, Mead and Company, 1955.

Chapman, Mary Megan. "Living Pictures: Women and the Tableaux Vivants in Nineteenth-Century American Fiction and Culture." Ph.D. dissertation. Cornell University, 1992.

Chauncey, George. *Gay New York: the Making of the Gay Male World, 1890–1940*. London: Flamingo Original, 1994.

Chicago Vice Commission. *The Social Evil in Chicago*. 1911. Reprint, New York: Arno Press, 1970.

Churchill, Allen. *The Great White Way: A Re-Creation of Broadway's Golden Era of Theatrical Entertainment*. New York: E. P. Dutton & Co., 1962.

Clark, Sue Ainslie and Edit Wyatt. "Working-Girls' Budgets: a Series of Articles Based Upon Individual Stories of Self-Supporting Girls." *McClure's Magazine* (October 1910): 595–614.

Clarke, May Herschel. "The Creator of 'Anna Christie:' The Picture Show Meets Pauline Lord." *Picture Show* April 8, 1923: 20.

"Clergy are Impressed with Play's Moving Power." *New York North Side News* December 6, 1908.

Cockin, Katharine. *Women and Theatre in the Age of Suffrage: The Pioneer Players, 1911–1925*. New York: Palgrave, 2001.

Collins, Charles W. "White Slave Drama." *Inter Ocean* November 24, 1913.

Collins, Whitney. "The Girl Without a Chance." Unpublished play. University of Chicago Library, 1914.

Committee of Fifteen. *The Social Evil with Special Reference to Conditions Existing in the City of New York*. New York: G. P. Putnam's Sons, 1902.

Committee of Fourteen. *The Social Evil In New York City: A Study of Law Enforcement by the Research Committee of the Committee of Fourteen*. New York: Andrew H. Kellog Company, 1910.

"Comstock At it Again." *New York Times* October 25, 1905: 1.

"Comstock Vs. Shaw." *New York Times* October 26, 1905: 8.

"Comstock Won't See Bernard Shaw's Play." *New York Times* October 26, 1905: 9.

Connelly, Mark Thomas. *The Response to Prostitution in the Progressive Era*. Chapel Hill: University of North Carolina Press, 1980.

Cooper, George and Charles E. Pratt. "The Shop Girls of New York." Brooklyn: H. Franklin Jones, 1895.

Corbett, Mary Jean. *Representing Femininity: Middle Class Subjectivity in Victorian and Edwardian Women's Autobiographies*. Oxford: Oxford University Press, 1992.

Corbin, John. "The Two *Zazas* – French Drama and American Melodrama." *New York Times* November 27, 1904: IV, 1.

"The Drama of the Slums." *Saturday Evening Post* March 20, 1909: 15.

"Court Cuts Short the *Sapho* Trial." *New York Times* April 5, 1900: 7.

"Court Frees Actors in *God of Vengeance*." *New York Times* April 4, 1923: 25.

Crane, Stephen. *Maggie: A Girl of the Streets (a Story of New York)*. Ed. Thomas A. Gullason. 1893. Reprint, New York: W. W. Norton & Company, 1979.

Cranston, Mary Rankin. "The Girl Behind the Counter." *World To-Day* 10 (March 1906): 271.

"Critics' Verdict Hostile." *New York Times* October 31, 1905: 9.

Crothers, Rachel. "Ourselves." Unpublished play. Shubert Archive, 1913.

C. S. "The Theatre." *Dial* 71 (December 1921): 725.

Dale, Alan. "An Opinion of Mrs. Leslie Carter's Performance." *New York American* January 10, 1899.

"A Chronicle of New Plays." *The Cosmopolitan* (April 1909): 569–72.

"Eugene Walter's *The Easiest Way*." *The New York American* January 20, 1909.

"Dale Views *House of Bondage*." Otherwise unidentified clipping. *The House of Bondage* clipping file, Billy Rose Theatre Collection.

"*The Fight* Tries Desperately to Be Sensational." *Evening World* September 3, 1913.

"*Ourselves*: A Feminine View of White Slavery Says Dale." Otherwise unidentified clipping. Illinois Public Library.

"Daly May Take Shaw Play Off, Many Believe." *New York Telegram* October 31, 1905.

"Daly's New Shaw Play Barred in New Haven." *New York Times* October 29, 1905: 3.

Dam, H. J. W. and Ivan Caryll (with additional numbers by Adrian Ross and Lionel Monckton). *The Shop Girl*. London: Hopwood & Crew, 1895.

"Damaged Goods." *New York Dramatic Mirror* April 23, 1913: 7.

Dangerfield, Fred. "The Girl Behind the Counter." *Play Pictorial* 8 (1906): 30–31.

Darnton, Charles. "*Ourselves*: a Play That Goes Wrong." Otherwise unidentified clipping. *Ourselves* clipping file, Shubert Archive.

Daudet, Alphonse. *Sappho*. Trans. Hamish Hamilton. 1884. Reprint, London: Soho Book Company, 1987.

Daudet, Alphonse and Adlophe Belot. *Sappho: A Play in Five Acts*. Trans. Elizabeth Beall Gint. New York: F. Rullman, 1895.

Davies, W. E. Letter. *New York Times* February 24, 1900: 7.

Davis, Owen. *My First Fifty Years in the Theatre*. Boston: Walter H. Baker Co., 1950.

Davis, Tracy. "Does the Theatre Make for Good?: Actresses' Purity and Temptation in the Victorian Era." *Queens Quarterly* 93 (Spring 1986): 33–49.

"Questions for a Feminist Methodology in Theatre History." In *Interpreting the Theatrical Past*. Eds. Thomas Postlewait and Bruce McConachie. Iowa City: University of Iowa Press, 1989.
"Sexual Language in Victorian Society and Theatre." *American Journal of Semiotics* 6 (1989): 33–49.
"The Actress in Victorian Pornography." *Theatre Journal* 41 (1989): 294–315.
Actresses as Working Women: Their Social Identity in Victorian Culture. London: Routledge, 1991.
"Spectacles of Women and Conduits of Ideology." *Nineteenth Century Theatre* 19 (Summer 1991): 52–66.
"Decency and the Stage." Editorial. *New York Times* September 7, 1913: 12.
Degen, John A. "The Evolution of *The Shop Girl* and the Birth of 'Musical Comedy.'" *Theatre History Studies* 7 (1987): 42.
de Lauretis, Teresa. *Technologies of Gender: Essays on Theory, Film, and Fiction*. Bloomington: Indiana University Press, 1987.
Department of Justice. "White Slave Traffic Act." Washington, 1910.
de Young, Mary. "Help, I'm Being Held Captive! The White Slave Fairy Tale of the Progressive Era," *Journal of American Culture* 6.1 (Spring 1983): 96–99.
Diamond, Elin. *Unmaking Mimesis: Essays on Feminism and Theater*. London: Routledge, 1997.
Dithmar, Edward A. "Sapho." *New York Times* February 25, 1900: 16.
Dixon, Jane. "Put Motherhood Above All, with Work and Love on One Plane, Says Mrs. Carter." *Evening Telegram* November 6, 1921.
Dodge, Wendell Phillips. "The Story of *The Lure*, a Play by George Scarborough." *Leslie's Weekly* September 25, 1913: 299.
Dolan, Jill. *The Feminist Spectator as Critic*. Ann Arbor: University of Michigan Press, 1988.
Donkin, Ellen. "Mary Shaw." In *Notable Women in the American Theatre: A Biographical Dictionary*. Eds. Alice M. Robinson, Vera Mowry Roberts, and Milly S. Barranger. New York: Greenwood Press, 1989.
"Dr. Adler Calls Shaw a Literary Anarchist." *New York Times* November 6, 1905: 6.
"Drama." *Harper's Weekly* January 21, 1899.
"Drama." *Nation* January 21, 1909: 72.
"Drama as an Instrument of Reform." Editorial. *Dial* 58 (February 1915): 73.
"Drama of the Month." *Metropolitan Magazine* 29 (January 1909): 452.
"Dramatic Outlook in New York Brighter." *Louisville Courier* November 23, 1913.
Dreiser, Theodore. *Sister Carrie*. 1900. Reprint, New York: Literary Classics of the United States, 1987.
Dudley, Bide. "*Ourselves* Based on Sex Question." *Morning Telegraph* November 14, 1913.
Dumas *fils*, Alexandre. *Camille*. 1852. Trans. Edith Reynolds and Nigel Playfair. New York: Hill and Wang, 1957.
"The Easiest Way." *Munsey's Magazine* 41 (July 1909): 578.
"The Easiest Way." *Theatre Magazine* 9 (March 1909): 81–84.
"*The Easiest Way*." *Bookman* 54 (November 1921): 230.
"*The Easiest Way*: A Modern American Tragedy." *Dramatist* 4 (July 1913): 39.
"*The Easiest Way*: Eugene Walter's Moving Portrayal of A Woman's Frailty." *Current Literature* 51 (July 1911): 73–81.

"East is West." *Dramatic Mirror of Motion Pictures and the Stage* 80 (January 11, 1919): 47.

"East is West at the Lyric." *Illustrated London News* June 26, 1920: 1114.

Eaton, Walter Prichard. "The Function of Criticism." *Freeman* January 11, 1922: 425.

Edwardes, George. *The Sketch* November 28, 1894.

Ellington, George. *The Women of New York; or, the Under-World of the Great City.* 1869. Reprint, New York: Arno Press, 1972.

Eltis, Sos. "The Fallen Woman on Stage: Maidens, Magdalens, and the Emancipated Female." In *The Cambridge Companion to Victorian and Edwardian Theatre*. Ed. Kerry Powell. Cambridge: Cambridge University Press, 2004.

Erdman, Harley. "Jewish Anxiety in 'Days of Judgment': Community Conflict Anti-Semitism, and the *God of Vengeance* Obscenity Case." *Theatre Survey* 40.1 (May 1999): 51–74.

Ernst, Morris L. and Alan U. Schwartz. *Censorship: The Search for the Obscene*. New York: Macmillan, 1964.

"Escaping a House of Bondage." *Munsey's Magazine* 51 (April 1914): 583.

"Eugene Walter, Dramatist." *New York Dramatic Mirror* February 12, 1910: 7.

"The Evolution of a Star of the Stage." Otherwise unidentified clipping. Mrs. Leslie Carter clipping file, Shubert Archive.

"Excerpts, Opinions, Etc., of *Damaged Goods.*" 1913. Otherwise unidentified pamphlet. *Damaged Goods* clipping file, Billy Rose Theatre Collection.

Fair, Fannie. "Arnold Daly Talks of the Shaw Heroines." *New York Telegram* October 26, 1905.

"Farewell American Tour of Sarah Bernhardt, Season 1905–06." Playbill. New York: F. Rullman, likely 1906.

Faxon, Fredrick Winthrop, Mary E. Bates, and Anne C. Sutherland, eds. *Cumulated Dramatic Index 1909–1949*. 2 vols. Boston: G. K. Hall & Company, 1965.

Feldman, Egal. "Prostitution, the Alien Woman and the Progressive Imagination, 1910–1915." *American Quarterly* 29 (1967): 192–206.

Ferris, Lesley. *Acting Women: Images of Women in Theatre*. Hampshire and London: Macmillan Education Ltd., 1990.

Fielder, Mari Kathleen. "The Spooners." In *Notable Women in the American Theatre: A Bibliographical Dictionary*. Eds. Alice Robinson, Vera Mowry Roberts, and Milly S. Barranger. Westport, CT: Greenwood Press, 1989.

"The Fight." *New York Dramatic Mirror* September 10, 1913: 6.

"The Fight." *Theatre Magazine* 18 (September 1913): 111–12.

"The Fight Acted at Hudson Theatre." *New York Times* September 3, 1913: 9.

"'The Fight' at Long Branch." *New York Tribune* August 26, 1913.

"The Fight Good Drama in Bad Taste." *New York Sun* September 3, 1913.

"The Fight Has Great Popular Appeal." *New York Globe* September 3, 1913.

"The Fight is Full of Thrills." *Morning Telegram* September 3, 1913.

"The Fight More Exciting Than *Within the Law.*" *New York Press* September 3, 1913.

"The First Lady with the Camelias." *The Theatre* 1.8 (October 1901): 14–16.

Fitch, Clyde. "Sapho." Unpublished play. New York Public Library, 1900.

Letter to Minnie Gerson. May 14, 1898. *Clyde Fitch and His Letters*. Eds. Montrose J. Moses and Virginia Gerson. Boston: Little Brown & Company, 1924.

Flexner, Abraham. *Prostitution in Europe*. New York: Century, 1914.

Forbes, James. *The Chorus Girl*. In *The Famous Mrs. Fair and Other Plays*. Intro. Walter Prichard Eaton. 1906. Reprint, New York: George H. Doran Company, 1920.
The Show Shop. In *The Famous Mrs. Fair and Other Plays*. Intro. Walter Prichard Eaton. 1914. Reprint, New York: George H. Doran Company, 1920.
Foucault, Michel. *The History of Sexuality: Volume I, An Introduction*. Trans. Robert Hurley. New York: Vintage Books, 1990.
Fournier, Alfred. *Syphilis and Marriage: Lectures Delivered at the St. Louis Hospital, Paris*. Trans. Prince A. Morrow. New York: D. Appelton, 1882.
"Frances Starr – the Cinderella of the Stage." *Theatre Magazine* 7 (February 1907): 50–51.
"From the Sewers Up." *Life Magazine* September 18, 1913: 476.
"G.B.S. and New York." *The New Age* May 23, 1907. Reprinted in *The Independent Shavian* 9 (1971): 37–38.
Gainor, J. Ellen. *Shaw's Daughters: Dramatic and Narrative Constructions of Gender*. Ann Arbor: University of Michigan Press, 1991.
Garvey, Sheila Hickey. "Anna Christie and the 'Fallen Woman Genre.'" *Eugene O'Neill Review* 19 (1995): 67–80.
Gassner, John, ed. *Best Plays of the Early American Theatre: From the Beginning to 1916*. New York: Crown, 1967.
Gelb, Arthur and Barbara Gelb. *O'Neill*. New York: Harper and Row, 1960.
Getthore, Billy. "Slaves of the Opium Ring, The Opium Smugglers of 'Frisco or The Crimes of a Beautiful Opium Fiend." Unpublished play. University of Chicago Library.
Gilfoyle, Timothy J. *City of Eros: New York City, Prostitution, and the Commercialization of Sex, 1790–1920*. New York: W. W. Norton & Company, 1992.
"Policing of Sexuality." In *Inventing Times Square: Commerce and Culture at the Crossroads of the World, 1880–1939*. Ed. William R. Taylor. New York: Russell Sage Foundation, 1991.
Gilman, Sander L. "Sexology, Psychoanalysis, and Degeneration: From a Theory of Race to a Race to Theory." In *Degeneration: The Dark Side of Progress*. Eds. J. Edward Chamberlain and Sander Gilman. New York: Columbia University Press, 1985.
Disease and Representation: Images of Illness from Madness to AIDS. Ithaca: Cornell University Press, 1988.
"The Girl Behind the Counter." *Life Magazine* October 17, 1907: 460–61.
"Girls Need 'Big Sisters.'" *New York Tribune* November 17, 1913.
"'God of Vengeance' Players Convicted." *New York Times* May 24, 1923: 3.
Goldman, Emma. "*The Easiest Way*: An Appreciation." *Mother Earth* 4 (1909): 86–92.
The Social Significance of Modern Drama. 1914. Reprint, New York: Applause Theatre Books, 1987.
"The Traffic in Women." In *The Traffic in Women and Other Essays*. 1917. Reprint, Washington, NJ: Times Change Press, 1970.
Gotlieb, Lois. *Rachel Crothers*. Boston: Twayne Publishers, 1979.
"Grand Jury to See 'Lure' and 'Fight.'" *New York Times* September 10, 1913: 1.
Grecco, Stephen. "Vivie Warren's Profession: a new Look at *Mrs. Warren's Profession*." *Shaw Review* 10.3 (September 1967): 93–97.
Griffin, Susan. *The Book of Courtesans: A Catalogue of Their Virtues*. New York: Broadway Books, 2001.

Hackett, Francis. "After the Play." *New Republic* September 28, 1921: 138–39.

"After the Play." *New Republic* November 30, 1921: 26.

Hall, Ann C. "Gawd, You'd Think I Was a Piece of Furniture: O'Neill's *Anna Christie.*" In *Staging the Rage: the Web of Misogyny in Modern Drama.* Eds. Katherine H. Burkman and Judith Roof. Cranbury, NJ: Associated University Press, 1998.

Hamilton, Cicely. *Diana of Dobson*'s. In *New Woman Plays.* Eds. Linda Fitzsimmons and Viv Gardner. London: Methuen, 1991.

Hamilton, Clayton. "Timely Topics in the Theatre." *Bookman* 38 (October 1913): 133–34.

Hamilton, James Shelley. "The Sex-Tangled Drama." *Everybody's Magazine* 29 (July 1913): 676–87.

Hammond, Percy. "'*Anna Christie.*'" *New York Tribune* November 3, 1921.

This Atom in the Audience: A Digest of Reviews and Comment by Percy Hammond. New York: The Ferris Printing Company, 1940.

Hanley, Parke F. "New York the Cleanest of Cities." *New York Sun* July 8, 1917: 1.

Hapgood, Norman. *The Stage in America 1897–1900.* New York: The Macmillian Company, 1901.

"Stage Notes." *Harpers Weekly* 58 (December 6, 1913): 12–13.

"Mrs. Leslie Carter in *Zaza.*" *The American Theatre As Seen By its Critics, 1752–1934.* Eds. Montrose Moses and John M. Brown. New York: Norton & Company, 1934.

Hapke, Laura. *Tale of the Working Girl: Wage-Earning Women in American Literature 1890–1925.* New York: Twayne Publishers, 1992.

Hart, Lavinia. "Olga Nethersole." *Cosmopolitan* (May 1901): 15–24.

Haskell, Molly. *From Reverence to Rape: The Treatment of Women in the Movies.* New York: Penguin, 1974.

Hasting, Basil MacDonald. "That Sort." Unpublished play. Library of Congress Manuscript Division, 1914.

Hayward, C. *Dictionary of Courtesans: An Anthology, Sometimes Gay, Sometimes Tragic, of the Celebrated Courtesans of History from Antiquity to the Present Day.* New York: University Books, 1962.

"Heaven Will Protect the Working Girl." Lyrics by Edgar Smith, music by A. Baldwin Sloane, 1909.

Henderson, Archibald. *George Bernard Shaw: Man of the Century.* New York: Appleton-Century-Crofts, Inc., 1956.

Henderson, Lucile Kelling. "Shaw and Woman: a Bibliographical Checklist." *Shaw Review* 17.2 (January 1974): 60–66.

"Her Big Effort. How Miss Lord Tried to Overcome English Coldness." *Evening Standard* November 4, 1923.

"Here is the Plain Story of Zaza. Judge for Yourself as to its Morality." *New York Journal* January 11, 1899.

Herman, W.C. "The Innocence of Youth, or, White Slavers of a Great City." Unpublished play. Sherman Theatre Collection, 1915.

Hess, Linda Elaine. "Girl Behind the Counter: the Image of the Department Store Sales Girl in Popular Magazines 1890–1920." Master's thesis, Ohio State University, 1986.

Hewitt, Barnard. *Theatre U.S.A., 1665 to 1957.* New York: McGraw-Hill, 1959.

Hobson, Barbara Meil. *Uneasy Virtue: The Politics of Prostitution and the American Reform Tradition*. New York: Basic Books, Inc., 1987.

"Hold Cecil Spooner For Her Vice Play." *New York Times* December 11, 1913: 8.

Holland, Clive. *The Lure of Fame*. New York: New Amsterdam Book Company, 1896.

Hornblow, Arthur. "Mr. Hornblow Goes to the Play." *Theatre Magazine* 25 (June 1917): 342.

Houchin, John H. "Depraved Women and Wicked Plays: Olga Nethersole's Production of *Sapho*." *Journal of American Drama and Theatre* 6 (Winter 1994): 40.

Censorship of the American Theatre in the Twentieth Century. Cambridge: Cambridge University Press, 2003.

ed. *The Critical Response to Eugene O'Neill*. Westport, CT: Greenwood Press, 1993.

"*House of Bondage* at the Longacre." *Commercial Advertiser*. Otherwise unidentified clipping. The House of Bondage clipping file, Billy Rose Theatre Collection.

Huneker, James. "Bernard Shaw and Woman." *Harper's Bazaar* 39 (June 1905): 538.

"Immoral, Gross, Revolting, Judge Calls *The Lure*." *World* September 9, 1913.

"Indecent Plays." *New York Times* September 9, 1913: 6.

Irving, John. "Mary Shaw: Actress, Activist, Suffragette, 1854–1929." Ph.D. dissertation, Columbia University, 1978.

"Is Bernard Shaw a Menace to Morals?" *Current Literature* 39 (November 1905): 551–52.

"Is White Slavery Nothing More Than A Myth?" *Current Opinion* (November 1913): 348.

Jacobs, Lea. *The Wages of Sin: Censorship and The Fallen Woman Film, 1928–1942*. Madison: University of Madison Press, 1991.

Janney, Oliver Edward. *The White Slave Traffic in America*. New York: National Vigilance Committee, 1911.

Jarrow, Joseph. *The Queen of Chinatown*. In *The Chinese Other, 1850–1925: An Anthology of Plays*. Ed. Dave Williams. Lanham, NY: University Press of America, 1997.

Jeffreys, Sheila. *The Idea of Prostitution*. Melbourne: Spinifex Press, 1997.

ed. *The Sexuality Debates*. New York: Routledge & Kegan Paul, 1987.

John, Angela V. *Elizabeth Robins: Staging a Life, 1862–1952*. London: Routledge, 1995.

Johnson, Claudia D. "That Guilty Third Tier: Prostitution in Nineteenth-Century American Theaters." *American Quarterly* 27 (1975): 575–84.

Johnston, Mary. "Clause 79." *Survey* December 10, 1910: 435.

Jolly, Edward S., Winifred Wilde, and Al La Rue. *Only a Shop Girl*. Chicago: Chas. K. Harris, 1903.

"Jury Soon Acquits Miss Nethersole." *New York Times* April 6, 1900: 7.

Kaier, Curtin. *We Can Always Call Them Bulgarians: The Emergence of Lesbians and Gay Men on the American Stage*. Boston: Alyson Publications, 1987.

Kapelke, Randy. "Preventing Censorship: the Audience's Role in *Sapho* (1900) and *Mrs. Warren's Profession* (1905)." *Theatre History Studies* 18 (June 1998): 117–133.

Kaplan, E. Ann. *Women and Film: Both Sides of the Camera*. London: Routledge, 1983.

Kaplan, Joel H. and Sheila Stowell. *Theatre and Fashion: Oscar Wilde to the Suffragettes*. Cambridge: Cambridge University Press, 1994.

Kibler, M. Alison. *Rank Ladies: Gender and Cultural Hierarchy in American Vaudeville*. Chapel Hill: University of North Carolina Press, 1999.

Klein, Charles. *Maggie Pepper*. New York: Grosset & Dunlap, 1911.

Kneeland, George J. *Commercialized Prostitution in New York City.* 1913. Reprint, Montclair, NJ: Patterson Smith, 1969.

The Knife. Dir. Robert G. Vignola, 1918.

"The Knife." *Nation* April 19, 1917: 104.

Kornbluth, Martin L. "Two Fallen Women: Paula Tanqueray and Kitty Warren." *The Shavian* 1.14 (February 1959): 15.

Kreymborg, Alfred. *Edna: The Girl of the Street.* New York: Guido Bruno, 1919.

Kuhn, Annette. *Cinema, Censorship and Sexuality, 1909–1925.* London and New York: Routledge, 1988.

Landesman, Peter. "The Girls Next Door." *New York Times Magazine* January 25, 2004, 30.

Langum, David J. *Crossing Over the Line: Legislating Morality and the Mann Act.* Chicago and London: University of Chicago Press, 1994.

Laufe, Abe. *The Wicked Stage: History of Theater Censorship and Harassment in the United States.* New York: Frederick Ungar Publishing Co., 1978.

"Laundering of *The Lure.*" *Dress & Vanity Fair* (November 1913): 36.

Le Brandt, Joseph. "Escaped From the Harem." Unpublished play. Library of Congress.

Leiter, Samuel L., ed. *The Encyclopedia of the New York Stage, 1920–1930.* Westport, CT: Greenwood Press, 1985.

Levine, Lawrence W. *Highbrow/Lowbrow: the Emergence of Cultural Hierarchy in America.* Cambridge, MA: Harvard University Press, 1990.

Lewis, Alfred Henry. "The Diary of a New York Policeman." *McClure's Magazine* 40 (1913): 287.

Lewisohn, Ludwig. "The Native Theater." *Nation* October 5, 1921: 381.

Library of Congress Copyright Office. *Dramatic Compositions Copyrighted in the United States, 1870–1916.* Washington: Government Printing Office, 1918.

Library of Congress Copyright Office. *Motion Pictures, 1912–1939, Cumulative Series.* Washington: Library of Congress, 1951.

"The Limit of Stage Indecency." *New York Herald* October 31, 1905. Reprinted in Montrose J. Moses and John Mason Brown, eds. *The American Theatre As Seen By Its Critics, 1752–1934.* New York: Norton, 1934.

Lindroth, Colette, and James Lindroth, eds. *Rachel Crothers: A Research and Production Sourcebook.* Westport, CT: Greenwood Press, 1995.

"*Little Lost Sister* Well Acted At Walnut." *Cincinnati Commercial Tribune* September 28, 1914.

"Little Plays Again at the Bandbox." *New York Times* March 29, 1915.

Lublin, Curtis. "The Theater." *Town and Country* January 29, 1909: 17.

Lucas, Eugene S. Letter. *New York Times* September 12, 1913: 10.

"Lure." *New York Dramatic Mirror* August 20, 1913: 6.

"*Lure* and *Fight* Lead to Strife." *New York Tribune* September 7, 1913.

"*Lure* Managers Will Appear in Court To-Day." *Morning Telegraph* September 8, 1913.

"*The Lure* Not as Lurid as Its Subject Implies." Unidentified clipping. *The Lure* clipping file, Billy Rose Theatre Collection.

Luter, Gary S. "Sexual Reform on the American Stage in the Progressive Era, 1900–1915." Ph.D. dissertation, University of Florida, 1981.

"M'Adoo Talk on Virtue Stirs Y. M. C. A. Men." *New York Times* October 9, 1905: 4.

MacDonal, Bruce. "*Sapho* Seen By Mr. Devery." *Telegraph* February 6, 1900.

Macfadden, Bernarr. *Womanhood and Marriage*. New York: Physical Culture Corporation, 1918.

MacGowan, Kenneth, "Year's End: December Sees Broadway Littered With Failures – Repertory Again the One Way Out." *Theatre Arts Magazine* 6 (January 1922): 6.

"*Anna Christie*." *Vogue*. Otherwise unidentified clipping. "*Anna Christie*" clipping file, Museum of the City of New York.

Mackay, Constance D'Arcy. *The Little Theatre in the United States*. New York: Henry Hort & Co., 1917.

MacLean, Annie Marion. *Wage-Earning Women*. 1910. Reprint, New York: Arno Press, 1974.

Macqueen-Pope, W. *Gaiety: Theatre of Enchantment*. London: W. H. Allen, 1949.

Madeleine: An Autobiography. 1919. Reprint, New York: Persea Books, 1986.

Mair, G. H. "Anna Christie Success." *Evening Standard* November 4, 1923.

Maltby, Richard. "The Social Evil, The Moral Order and the Melodramatic Imagination, 1890–1915." In *Melodrama: Stage, Picture, Screen*. Eds. Jacky Bratton, Jim Cook and Christine Gledhill. London: British Film Institute, 1994.

"Managers of Vice Plays Are Summoned to Court." *World* September 7, 1913.

Mander, Raymond and Joe Mitchenson. "Mrs. Warren on Stage." Unpublished notes. Clipping file, Mander and Mitchenson Theatre Collection, London.

Mantle, Burns, ed. *The Best Plays of 1920–21 and the Year Book of the Drama in America*. Boston: Small Maynard & Company, 1921.

Mantle, Burns and Garrison P. Sherwood, eds. *The Best Plays of 1899–1909 and the Year Book of the Drama in America*. Philadelphia: The Blakiston Company, 1944.

The Best Plays of 1909–1919 and the Year Book of the Drama in America. New York: Dodd, Mead and Company, 1943.

Marker, Lise-Lone. *David Belasco: Naturalism in the American Theatre*. Princeton: Princeton University Press, 1975.

Marra, Kim. "Lesbian Scholar/Gay Subject: Turn-of-the-Century Inversions." *Theatre Topics* 13.2 (September 2003): 235–46.

"Clyde Fitch." In *American Playwrights, 1880–1945: A Research and Production Sourcebook*. Ed. William M. Demastes. Westport, CT: Greenwood Press, 1995.

Mason, Hamilton. *French Theatre in New York: A List of Plays, 1899–1939*. New York: Columbia University Press, 1940.

Matinee Girl. "Touching Many Subjects, Her Ruminations Are Both Grave and Gay." *New York Dramatic Mirror* January 30, 1909: 4.

Mattus, Martha Elizabeth. "The 'Fallen Woman' in the 'Fin de Siècle' English Drama: 1884–1914." Ph.D. dissertation, Cornell University, 1974.

McAdoo, William. *Guarding a Great City*. New York: Harper and Brothers, 1906.

McConachie, Bruce A. *Melodramatic Formations: American Theatre and Society, 1820–1870*. Iowa City: University of Iowa Press, 1992.

McDermott, M. Joan and Sarah J. Blackstone. "White Slavery Plays of the 1910s: Fear of Victimization and the Social Control of Sexuality." *Theatre History Studies* 16 (1996): 141–155.

McKenzie, Jon. *Perform or Else: From Discipline to Performance*. London: Routledge, 2001.

McLeister, Ira Ford and Mrs. Clara McLeister. *The White Slave and Other Poems.* Akron, OH: [no publisher given], 1909.

Meisel, Martin. *Shaw and the Nineteenth-Century Theater.* New Jersey: Princeton University Press, 1963.

Realizations: Narrative, Pictorial, and Theatrical Arts in Nineteenth-century England. Princeton: Princeton University Press, 1983.

Meserve, Walter J. *An Outline History of American Drama.* Totowa, NJ: Littlefield, Adams & Co., 1965.

Metcalfe, James S. "Sapho." *Life Magazine* December 13, 1900: 752–53.

"The Freedom of the Press." *Life Magazine* February 4, 1909: 166.

"*Maggie Pepper.*" *Life Magazine* September 14, 1911: 430–31.

"Here We Are Again, Mr. Merryman." *Life Magazine* September 4, 1913: 390–91.

"That Dear Old Sociological Fund." *Life Magazine* January 29, 1914: 190.

"Forward!" *Life Magazine* May 10, 1917: 817.

Miller, Jordan Y., ed. *Eugene O'Neill and the American Critic: a Bibliographical Checklist.* Hamden, CT: Archon Books, 1973.

Miller, Tice L. "Plays and Playwrights: Civil War to 1896." In *The Cambridge History of American Theatre.* Eds. Don B. Wilmeth and Cristopher Bibsby. 3 vols. Cambridge: Cambridge University Press, 1999.

Millstone, Amy. "French Feminist Theater and the Subject of Prostitution, 1870–1914." *The Image of the Prostitute in Modern Literature.* Eds. Pierre L. Horn and Mary Beth Pringle. New York: Frederick Ungar Publishing Co., 1984.

"Miss Nethersole Appeals Her Case." *New York Herald* March 6, 1900.

"Miss Nethersole Defends *Sapho.*" *New York Herald* February 7, 1900.

"Miss Nethersole Files Suit." *New York Times* May 4, 1900: 7.

"Miss Nethersole's Trial." Otherwise unidentified clipping. The Adelphi File, 1902, The Theatre Museum, London.

"Miss Starr Triumphs in *The Easiest Way.*" *New York Times* January 20, 1909: 9.

Mizejewski, Linda. *Ziegfeld Girl: Image and Icon in Culture and Cinema.* Durham: Duke University Press, 1999.

Montgomery, Maureen. *Displaying Women: Spectacles of Leisure in Edith Wharton's New York.* New York: Routledge, 1998.

"Moondown." *Boston Transcript* March 30, 1915.

Montague, Walter. "The Slave Girl: 20 Minutes in Frisco's Chinatown." Unpublished play. Sherman Theatre Collection, 1913.

Mordden, Ethan. *The American Theatre.* New York: Oxford University Press, 1981.

Morehouse, Ward. *Matinee Tomorrow: Fifty Years of Our Theater.* New York: Whittlesey, 1949.

Morrow, Prince A. *Social Diseases and Marriage, Social Prophylaxis.* New York: Lea Brothers & Co., 1904.

"The Sanitary and Moral Prophylaxis of Venereal Diseases." *Journal of the American Medical Association* 44 (March 1905): 675.

"The Teaching of Sex Hygiene." *Good Housekeeping* (March 1912): 404–07.

Moses, Montrose J. and John M. Brown, eds. *The American Theatre As Seen By its Critics, 1752–1934.* New York: W. W. Norton and Company, 1934.

Moses, Montrose J. and Virginia Gerson, eds. *Clyde Fitch and His Letters*. Boston: Little Brown & Company, 1924.

"Mrs. Carter and the Auburn Theory." Press release. Mrs. Leslie Carter clipping file, Shubert Archive.

"Mrs. Carter Back in New York." *New York Herald* September 11, 1921.

"Mrs. Carter in *Zaza*." Otherwise unidentified clipping. *Zaza* clipping file, Billy Rose Theatre Collection.

"Mrs. Carter's Latest Portraiture is a Triumph." Otherwise unidentified clipping. *Zaza* clipping file, Billy Rose Theatre Collection.

"Mrs. Fiske Goes to the Slums for a Plot." *Hampton's Magazine* 22 (February 1909): 245.

"Mrs. Leslie Carter Again Ill." *New York Times* March 8, 1900: 7.

"Mrs. Leslie Carter and Her Temperament." Press release. Mrs. Leslie Carter clipping file, Shubert Archive.

"Mrs. Leslie Carter Discusses *Zaza* and Morality." *Broadway Magazine* (December 1899): 183.

"Mrs. Leslie Carter Freed From Debt." October 5, 1899. Otherwise unidentified clipping. Mrs. Leslie Carter clipping file, Billy Rose Theatre Collection.

Mrs. Leslie Carter in Zaza, 1899. Otherwise unidentified booklet. Billy Rose Theatre Collection.

"Mrs. Marie Wilmerding, of the '400' and the Cousin of Cornelius Vanderbilt, Who Wants to Be an Actress, Interviews Mrs. Leslie Carter, ex-Society Woman and Leader of Fashion." *New York Journal* January 22, 1899.

"Mrs. Pankhurst's Most Quiet Day." *New York Times* October 23, 1913: 7.

"Mrs. Warren's Profession." *Theatre Magazine* 27 (April 1918): 218.

"Muensterberg Vigorously Denounces Red Light Drama." *New York Times* September 14, 1913: IV, 4.

Mulvey, Laura. "Visual Pleasure and Narrative Cinema." *Screen* 16:3 (Autumn 1975): 6–15.

Murphy, Brenda. *American Realism and American Drama, 1880–1940*. Cambridge: Cambridge University Press, 1987.

  "Feminism and the Marketplace: the Career of Rachel Crothers." In *The Cambridge Companion to American Women Playwrights*. Ed. Brenda Murphy. Cambridge: Cambridge University Press, 1999.

My Little Sister. Dir. Kenean Buel. Standard Pictures/Fox Film Corporation, 1919.

"My, What a Lovely Spasm of Virtue!" *Life Magazine* February 25, 1909: 260.

Nelson, Doris. "O'Neill's Women." *Eugene O'Neill Newsletter* 6 (Summer/Fall 1982): 307.

Nelson, Nell (pseudonym). *The White Slave Girls of Chicago: Nell Nelson's Startling Disclosures of the Cruelties and Iniquities Practiced in the Workshops and Factories of a Great City*. Chicago, Barkley Pub. Co., 1888.

Nethersole, Olga. "My Struggles to Succeed." *Cosmopolitan* (November 1899): 193–203.

  Letter to Margaret and Clement Scott. November 12, 1899. Otherwise unidentified clipping. The Adelphi File, 1902, The Theatre Museum, London.

  "Sex Dramas To-Day and Yesterday." *Green Book Magazine* 11 (January 1914): 33.

  "I Thank the Women." Otherwise unidentified clipping. *Sapho* clipping file, Billy Rose Theatre Collection.

"Nethersole's New Play Not Wicked." *New York Press* February 6, 1900.
"New Methods of Grappling With the Social Evil." *Current Opinion* (August 1913): 308–09.
"New Star – Dealers in White Women." *New York Dramatic Mirror* September 3, 1904.
"The Newest Camille and Some Famous Ones." *Theatre Magazine* 27 (February 1918): 95.
"News of the Theatre." *Evening Sun* March 3, 1911.
"A Night of New Plays." *New York Times* January 10, 1899: 7.
"No Excuse for Vicious Red-Light Play On the Stage, Declares David Belasco." *Evening World* September 6, 1913.
"No Staircase Scene in the French *Sapho*." *New York Times* November 29, 1904: 6.
"Notes." *Craftsman* 15 (1909): 739–41.
Oberdeck, Kathryn J. *The Evangelist and the Impresario: Religion, Entertainment, and Cultural Politics in America, 1884–1914*. Baltimore: Johns Hopkins University Press, 1999.
O'Connell Davidson, Julia. *Prostitution, Power and Freedom*. Ann Arbor: University of Michigan Press, 1998.
Odell, George C. D. *Annals of the New York Stage: Vol. XV, 1891–94*. New York: Columbia University Press, 1949.
"Olga Nethersole – Actress and Philanthropist." *Theatre Magazine* 7 (July 1907): 194–96.
"Olga Nethersole Arrives." *New York Times* October 2, 1899: 7.
"Olga Nethersole's Holy Work." *New York Tribune* February 6, 1900.
Olmsted, Stanley. "Underworld Play at N.Y. Theatre." *New York Telegraph* November 17, 1913.
"One of the Scenes in *Zaza* Concerning Whose Propriety There Has Been Much Discussion." *New York Journal* January 11, 1899.
O'Neill, Eugene. "*Anna Christie*." *Theatre Magazine* 35 (April 1922): 220–24.
    "*Anna Christie*." 1921. Reprint, New York: Vintage Books, 1995.
    Complete Plays. Ed. Travis Bogard. 3 vols. New York: The Library of America, 1988. Vol I.
"Ourselves." *Everbody's Magazine* 30 (February 1914): 264.
"Ourselves as Seen by a Woman." *Morning Sun* November 14, 1913.
"*Ourselves* at Bradford." *New York City Tribune* December 7, 1913.
"*Ourselves* Based on Sex Question." *Morning Telegraph* November 14, 1913.
"*Ourselves* Deals with That Old Dual Morality." *Telegram* November 14, 1913.
Palmer, John. "Two Plays of Low Life." *Saturday Review* February 24, 1912: 235–36.
Parker, Andrew, and Eve Kosofsky Sedgwick. "Introduction." In *Performativity and Performance*. New York: Routledge, 1995.
Parker, Robert Allerton. "An American Dramatist Developing." *Independent and the Weekly Review* December 2, 1921: 236.
Peirce, Frances Lamont. "Eugene Walter: an American Dramatic Realist." *The Drama* 21 (February 1916): 121.
Peiss, Kathy. *Cheap Amusements: Working Women and Leisure in Turn-of-the-Century New York*. Philadelphia: Temple University Press, 1986.
"Pencil on Shaw's Play." *New York Times* October 30, 1905: 9.
Phelan, Peggy. *Unmarked: the Politics of Performance*. London: Routledge, 1993.

Pierce, Jr., Glenn Quimby. "Arnold Daly's Productions of Plays by Bernard Shaw."
    Ph.D. dissertation, University of Illinois, 1960.
Pinero, Arthur W. *The Profligate.* Boston: Walter H. Baker & Co., 1892.
    Iris. Boston: Walter H. Baker & Co., 1900.
Pivar, David J. *Purity Crusade: Sexual Morality and Social Control, 1868–1900.* Westport,
    CT: Greenwood Press, 1973.
"Plays & Players." *New York Globe* October 27, 1905.
"Plays of Brothel Still Unchecked." *New York Herald* September 6, 1913.
"Pointers on 'The Easiest Way.'" *Munsey's Magazine* 41 (January 1909): 879.
"Police Censorship." Editorial. *New York Dramatic Mirror* September 17, 1913: 8.
"Police Censorship." Editorial. *New York Dramatic Mirror* December 17, 1913: 8.
"Police May Close *Fight* and *Lure*." *New York Times* September 7, 1913: 3.
"Police Stop Two Plays." *Theatre Magazine* 18 (September 1913): 116.
Pollock, Channing. "Two Big Plays and Some Little Ones." *The Green Book Album*
    (April 1909): 875–877.
    The Footlights Fore and Aft. Boston: R.G. Badger, 1911.
    "Maggie Pepper." *Green Book Album* (November 1911): 997–98.
    "The Fight." *Green Book Magazine* 10 (November 1913): 764.
    "End of a Primrose Path." *The Stage* 14 (August 1937): 80.
Potter, Paul M. "The Girl From Rector's." Unpublished play. Billy Rose Theatre
    Collection.
"Princess Theatre Opens With Sensational Play." *New York Globe* March 15, 1913.
Prins, Yopi. *Victorian Sappho.* Princeton: Princeton University Press, 1999.
"Prizes of Cash Bring Out Chelsea Section's Babies." *New York Times* August 3, 1913.
"The Process of Dry-Cleaning." *Munsey's Magazine* 51 (February 1914): 124.
"*The Profligate* Revived." *New York Times* March 18, 1900: 11.
Prostitution in America: Three Investigations, 1902–1914. Reprint of the 2nd rev. edn. of *The
    Social Evil by the Committee of Fifteen.* 1912. Reprint, New York: Arno Press, 1976.
Pullen, Kristin. *Actresses and Whores On Stage and In Society.* Cambridge: Cambridge
    University Press, 2005.
Purdom, C. B. *A Guide to the Plays of Bernard Shaw.* London: Methuen & Co. Ltd., 1955.
Quinn, Michael. "Celebrity and the Semiotics of Acting." *New Theatre Quarterly* 4
    (1990): 154–61.
Rabinovitz, Lauren. *For the Love of Pleasure: Women, Movies and Culture in Turn-of-the
    Century Chicago.* New Brunswick, NJ: Rutgers University Press, 1998.
"The Real Mrs. Carter." Press release. Mrs. Leslie Carter clipping file, Shubert Archive.
Rector, George. *The Girl From Rector's.* New York: Doubleday, Page & Company, 1927.
Reed, Florence. "The Sex Appeal." *Theatre Magazine* 27 (February 1918): 94–95.
Reed, John. *Moondown: A Play in One Act. The Masses* 4 (September 1913): 8–9.
"Reformatory Girls See Morals Drama." *New York City Tribune* December 3, 1913.
Reilly, Joy Harriman. "A Forgotten 'Fallen Woman:' Olga Nethersole's *Sapho*." In *When
    They Weren't Doing Shakespeare.* Eds. Judith L. Fisher and Stephen Watt. Athens:
    University of Georgia Press, 1989.
    "From Wicked Woman of the Stage to New Woman: The Career of Olga Nethersole
    (1870–1951); Actress-Manager, Suffragist, Health Pioneer." Ph.D. dissertation,
    Ohio State University, 1984.

Réjane, Gabriele. *The One Correct Version of My Plays Translated & Printed From My Own Prompt Books*. New York: F. Rullman, 1904.

Report of the Commission for the Investigation of the White Slave Traffic, So Called, [Massachusetts] House [Document] No. 2281. Boston: Wright & Potter Printing Company, 1914.

"The Return of Miss Nethersole and Mr. Hawtrey." *The Tatler* May 7, 1902.

Review of *Sapho*. *New York Sun* February 6, 1900.

"Reviews of New Plays." *New York Dramatic Mirror* January 30, 1909: 3.

Reynolds, Margaret. *The Sappho Companion*. London: Chatto & Windus, 2000.

Rich, Adrienne. "Compulsory Heterosexuality and Lesbian Existence." 1979. Reprinted in *Feminist Frontiers II*. Eds. Laurel Richardson and Verta Taylor. New York: McGraw Hill, 1989.

Rigdon, W., ed. *Notable Names in the American Theatre*. Clifton, NJ: James T. White & Co., 1988.

Riis, Jacob A. *How the Other Half Lives: Studies Among the Tenements of New York*. 1890. Reprint, New York: Dover Publications, 1971.

"Rising Tide of Realism in the American Drama." *Current Opinion* 55 (October 1913): 250–251.

Roach, Joseph. *Cities of the Dead: Circum-Atlantic Performance*. New York: Columbia University Press, 1996.

Robins, Elizabeth. "My Little Sister." *McClure's Magazine* 60.2 (December 1912): 121–45; and *McClure's Magazine* (January 1913): 252–60.

"My Little Sister." Unpublished play. Fales Library, New York University, 1913.

Robinson, Alice M., Vera Mowry Roberts, and Milly S. Barranger, eds. *Notable Women in the American Theatre: A Biographical Dictionary*. New York: Greenwood Press, 1989.

Roe, Clifford G. *The Girl Who Disappeared*. Chicago: American Bureau of Moral Education, 1914.

and B. S. Steadwell. *Horrors of the White Slave Trade*. New York [no publisher given], 1911.

Roosevelt, Theodore. "White Slave Traffic Worse Than Murder, Says Roosevelt." *New York Tribune* September 7, 1913: 3.

Rosen, Ruth. *The Lost Sisterhood: Prostitution in America, 1900–1918*. Baltimore: Johns Hopkins University Press, 1982.

"Introduction." In *The Maimie Papers*. Old Westbury, NY: The Feminist Press, 1977.

Rubin, Gayle. "The Traffic in Women: Notes on the 'Political Economy' of Sex." In *Toward An Anthropology of Women*. Ed. Rayna Reiter. New York: Monthly Review, 1975.

Russell, C. Walcott. "Dens of Frisco." Unpublished play. The Sherman Theatre Collection.

Sachs, Murray. *The Career of Alphonse Daudet*. Cambridge, MA: Harvard University Press, 1965.

Said, Edward. *Orientalism*. New York: Vintage Books, 1978.

Salih, Sabah A. "Bernard Shaw in America: A Study of Shaw's Relations with the American Theater." Ph.D. dissertation, Southern Illinois University, 1988.

Sanger, William. *The History of Prostitution: Its Extent, Causes, and Effect Throughout The World*. 1858. Reprint, New York: Eugenics Publishing Company, 1937.

"Sapho." *New York Sun* February 6, 1900.

"*Sapho* at Wallack's." *New York Times* February 6, 1900: 5.

"The *Sapho* Case." *New York Times* March 8, 1900: 7.

"*Sapho* Engagement Closed." *New York Times* May 30, 1900: 7.

"*Sapho* Gets an Ovation." *New York Times* April 8, 1900: 7.

"*Sapho* in Police Court." *New York Times* February 24, 1900: 7.

"*Sapho* Stopped by the Police." *New York Times* March 6, 1900: 1.

"*Sapho* Taken to Court." *New York Times* February 22, 1900: 3.

Scarborough, George. "The Lure." Unpublished play. Shubert Archive, 1913.

Schanke, Robert A. "Mary Shaw: A Fighting Champion." In *Women in American Theatre*. Ed. Helen Krich Chinoy and Linda Walsh Jenkins. New York: Theatre Communications Group, 1987.

Schneider, Rebecca. *The Explicit Body in Performance*. London: Routledge, 1997.

Sedgwick, Eve Kosofsky. *Between Men: English Literature and Male Homosocial Desire*. New York: Columbia University Press, 1985.

Senelick, Laurence. *Lovesick: Modernist Plays of Same-Sex Love, 1894–1925*. London: Routledge, 1999.

"Sex O'Clock in America." *Current Opinion* 55 (1913): 113–14.

Seymour, Gertrude. "The Health of Soldier and Civilian." *Survey* 40 (1918): 154.

"The Shackles on Dramatic Inspiration." *New York Times* October 1, 1905: 9.

Shakespeare, William. *Macbeth*. In *Complete Works of William Shakespeare*. Ed. William Aldis Wright. Garden City, NY: Garden City Publishing, 1936.

"Shame's the Limit." *New York Evening Journal* February 6, 1900.

Shar[p], Sidney. "*Sapho* in Weak, Distorted Form." *World* February 6, 1900.

Shaw, George Bernard. *Mrs Warren's Profession: A Play*. 1898. Reprinted in George Bernard Shaw, *Plays Unpleasant*. Harmondsworth: Penguin, 1983.

   Collected Letters, 1898–1910. 2 vols. Ed. Dan H. Laurence. New York: Podd, Mead and Company, 1972.

   "Preface to *Damaged Goods*." In *Three Plays by Brieux*. Trans. John Pollock. New York: Brentano's, 1911.

   "*Mrs. Warren's Profession*: Mr. Bernard Shaw's Reply." *Morning Leader* November 7, 1905.

Shaw, Mary. "My 'Immoral' Play." *McClure's Magazine* 38 (1912): 684–94.

"Shaw's Play Stopped; The Manager Arrested." *New York Times* November 1, 1905: 1.

"Shaw's Play Unfit; The Critics Unanimous." *New York Times* October 31, 1905: 8.

Sheldon, Edward, *Salvation Nell*. 1908. In *Best Plays of the Early American Theatre: From the Beginning to 1916*. Ed. John Gassner. New York: Crown Publishers Inc., 1967.

Sherman, Robert L. *Drama Cyclopedia, a Bibliography of Plays and Players*. Chicago: Robert Sherman, 1944.

The Shop Girl. Dir. George D. Baker. 1916.

Showalter, Elaine. *The Female Malady: Women, Madness, and English Culture, 1830–1980*. New York: Penguin Books, 1985.

   Sexual Anarchy: Gender and Culture at the Fin de Siècle. New York: Viking, 1990.

Sinclair, Upton. *The Jungle*. New York: Doubleday, Page, and Co., 1906.

Skinner, Cornelia Otis. *Madame Sarah*. Boston: Houghton Mifflin Company, 1967.

"The Slave Girl: 20 Minutes in Frisco's Chinatown." Unpublished play. The Library of Congress Manuscript Division.

Sloan, Kay. *The Loud Silents: Origins of the Social Problem Film*. Urbana: University of Illinois Press, 1988.

Slosson, Edwin E. "A Dramatist Who Means Something." *Independent* April 3, 1913: 749–52.

Smith, Edgar, and A. Baldwin Sloane. "Heaven Will Protect the Working Girl." 1909.

Smith, Harry B., Victor Herbert, and Stanislaus Stangé. *The Singing Girl*. New York: M. Witmark & Sons, 1899.

Smith, Madeline, and Richard Eaton, eds. *Eugene O'Neill: an Annotated Bibliography*. New York: Garland Publishing, Inc., 1988.

Snow, William F., and Wilbur A. Sawyer. "Venereal Disease Control in the Army." *Journal of American Medical Association* 71 (1918): 456–462.

Social Hygiene 4.2 (1918): 527.

Solomon, Alisa. *Re-Dressing the Canon: Essays on Theatre and Gender*. London: Routledge, 1997.

Solomon, Harry C. *Syphilis of the Innocent: A Study of the Social Effects of Syphilis on the Family and the Community*. Washington: US Interdepartmental Social Hygiene Board, 1922.

Sonnichsen, Natalie. "The Mandrin Club on Doyer Street." Committee of Fourteen files, New York City Public Library Special Collections, Box 96, Folder 1913.

"The Stage Society Offers Two Plays." *New York Times* November 10, 1913, 9.

"Stage Struck Girl." *Theatre Magazine* 22 (November 1915): 249.

Staiger, Janet. *Bad Women: Regulating Sexuality in Early American Cinema*. Minneapolis: University of Minnesota Press, 1995.

"Stairway Scene in *Sapho* as Staged in a Police Court." *New York Herald* February 28, 1900: 8.

Stanton, Stephen S. "Introduction." In *Camille and Other Plays*. New York: Hill and Wang, 1957.

Stearns, H. E. "'Damaged Goods': A Discussion." *New York Dramatic Mirror* March 26, 1913: 5.

Stevens, Ashton. *Evening Journal*. Quoted in "The Belasco News." Undated press release.

"The Store Girl's Wage." *Literary Digest* 47 (August 1913): 199–200.

Strang, Lewis C. *Famous Actresses of The Day in America*. Boston: L. C. Page and Company, 1902.

Famous Prima Donnas. Boston: L. C. Page and Company, 1900.

"A Strong Drama at the Stuyvesant." *New York Dramatic Mirror* January 30, 1909: 3.

"A Successful Playwright's Hardships." *Stage* 50 (November 1913): 297.

Sudermann, Herman. *Magda*. Trans. Charles Edward Amory. 1894. Reprint, New York: Samuel French, 1923.

"Suffragists Approve Lure." *New York Times* September 7, 1913: 3.

"Teaching the Girl Behind the Counter." *Technical World Magazine* 17 (June 1912): 391.

"Ten Commandments Before Shaw – M'Adoo." *New York Times* November 3, 1905: 6.

"The Theatre." *New York Sun* April 13, 1917.

Thompson, Frank. *Lost Films: Important Movies That Disappeared*. Secaucus, NJ: Carol Publication Group, 1996.

Timberlake, Craig. *The Life and Work of David Belasco: The Bishop of Broadway.* New York: Library Publishers, 1954.

"Tones Down Shaw Play." *Evening World* October 30, 1905.

"The Traffic." *Los Angeles Rounder* August 9, 1913.

"A Triumph for Rachel Crothers." *Bulletin* November 17, 1913.

Tullberg, Rita McWilliams. *Women at Cambridge.* Cambridge: Cambridge University Press, 1998.

Tupper, Edith Sessions. "Camille was Bad, Zaza Only a Woman." *New York World* January 15, 1899.

Turner III, Frederick W., ed. *The Portable North American Indian Reader.* New York: Penguin, 1974.

Turner, Victor. *From Ritual To Theatre: the Human Seriousness of Play.* New York: Performing Arts Journal Publishing, 1982.

"Two Plays of Low Life." *Saturday Review* February 24, 1912: 236.

Veblen, Thornstein. *Theory of the Leisure Class: An Economic Study of Institutions.* 1899. Reprint, New York: New American Library, 1953.

Veiller, Bayard. "The Fight." Unpublished play. University of Chicago Library, 1913.

Vena, Gary A. "The Role of the Prostitute in the Plays of Eugene O'Neill." *Drama Critique* 10 (Fall 1967): 129–37.

"Venereal Peril to Our Army." *Journal of American Medical Association* 71 (1917): 734.

Vice Commission of Chicago. *The Social Evil in Chicago.* Chicago: Gunthrop-Warren Printing Company, 1911.

"Vicious Scene Mars Next Veiller Play *The Fight.*" September 3, 1913. Otherwise unidentified clipping. *The Fight* clipping file, Museum of the City of New York.

Victorian Actors and Actresses in Review: A Dictionary of Contemporary Views of Representative British and American Actors and Actresses, 1837–1901. Ed. Donald Mullin. Westport, CT: Greenwood Press, 1983.

"A Vivisection of Sarah Bernhardt's Art." *Current Opinion* 53 (October 1912): 451–52.

Voglino, Barbara. *"Perverse Mind": Eugene O'Neill's Struggle With Closure.* Cranbury: Associated University Press, 1999.

W., K. Letter. *New York Times* February 24, 1900: 7.

Wainscott, Ronald H. *The Emergence of the Modern American Theater, 1914–1929.* New Haven: Yale University Press, 1997.

"Notable American Stage Productions." In *The Cambridge Companion to Eugene O'Neill.* Ed. Michael Manheim. Cambridge: Cambridge University Press, 1998.

"Waiting." *Life Magazine* January 28, 1909: 130–31.

"Waldo's Censors Watch Two Plays of Underworld." *World* September 5, 1913.

Walkowitz, Judith. *Prostitution and Victorian Society: Women, Class, and the State.* Cambridge: Cambridge University Press, 1980.

"Wallack's – Sapho." *New York Dramatic Mirror* February 10, 1900: 16.

Walter, Eugene. *The Easiest Way.* 1909. In *Best Plays of the Early American Theatre: From the Beginning to 1916.* Ed. John Gassner. New York: Crown Publishing, 1978.

and Arthur Hornblower. *The Easiest Way.* New York: G.W. Dillingham Company, 1911.

"The Knife." Unpublished play. Shubert Archive, 1917.

"Was Mrs. Leslie Carter Taught to Act?" Undated press release (likely from 1907). Mrs. Leslie Carter clipping file, Shubert Archive.

Washburn, Charles. *Come into My Parlor: a Biography of the Aristocratic Everleigh Sisters of Chicago.* New York: Knickerbocker Press, 1934.

Wellwarth, George E. "Mrs. Warren Comes to America, or the Blue-Noses, the Politicians and the Procurers." *The Shaw Review* 2.8 (May 1959): 8–16.

Wharton, Edith. *The House of Mirth.* New York: Charles Scribner's Sons, 1903.

   and Clyde Fitch. *The House of Mirth.* 1906. Reprint, ed. Glenn Loney. London: Associated University Presses, 1981.

"What is the Drama League Driving At?" *New York City Tribune* December 6, 1913.

White, Jean Westrum. "Shaw on the New York Stage." Ph.D. dissertation, New York University, 1965.

"White Slave Drama." *Evening World* August 15, 1913.

"White Slave Play of Some Grim Power." *New York Times* August 15, 1913: 7.

"The White Slave Plays." *New York Dramatic Mirror* September 10, 1913: 10.

"White Slave Plays Again on Trial." *New York Times* September 12, 1913: 11.

"Why Stage Modesty Should Prevail in Musical Comedy." *Theatre Magazine* 18 (September 1913): 93.

Williams, Dave, ed. *The Chinese Other, 1850–1925: An Anthology of Plays.* Lanham, NY: University Press of America, 1997.

Williamson, C. N. and A. M. Williamson. *The Shop Girl.* New York: Grosset & Dunlap, 1914.

Wilmeth, Don B. *Staging the Nation: Plays from the American Theater, 1787–1909.* Boston: Bedford Books, 1998.

   "American Theatre History, 1865–1915." In *Theatre in the United States: A Documentary History.* Ed. Barry Witham. Cambridge: Cambridge University Press, 1996. Vol. I.

Winter, William. *The Life of David Belasco.* 2 vols. New York: Moffat, Yard & Company, 1918.

   "Introduction." In *American Stage of Today: Biographies and Photographs of One Hundred Leading Actors and Actresses.* New York: P. F. Collier & Son, 1910.

   "New Play at the Stuyvesant." Otherwise unidentified clipping. Billy Rose Theatre Collection.

"Women and Stage Indecency." Editorial. *New York Times* September 12, 1913: 10.

"Women Approve *The Fight.*" *New York Times* October 15, 1913: 11.

"Women to Run Theatre." *New York Times* October 23, 1913: 11.

Woodbridge, Benjamin M. "Eugène Brieux." *Dial* (January 17, 1918): 67–68.

Woods, Leigh. "Two-a-Day Redemptions and Truncated Camilles: the Vaudeville Repertoire of Sarah Bernhardt." *New Theatre Quarterly* 10 (1994): 11–23.

Woollcott, Alexander. *Mrs. Fiske, Her Views on Actors, Acting, and the Problems of Production.* 1917. Reprint, New York: B. Bloom, 1968.

   "Second Thoughts on First Nights." *New York Times* November 13, 1921: VI, 1.

   "The Yellow Dramatist." *Outlook* 81 (November 1905): 701.

"Zaza." *New York Telegram* January 3, 1899.

"Zaza." *Sketch* April 18, 1900: 550.

"Zaza." *Stage* 16 (December 1938): 28–29.

"Zaza." *Life Magazine* January 9, 1939: 37–39.
"*Zaza* at the Garrick." *New York Times* September 12, 1899: 6.
"*Zaza* Imported From Paris and Adapted by David Belasco." *New York Times* January 10, 1899: 7.

Archives

Billy Rose Theatre Collection, New York Library for the Performing and Visual Arts at Lincoln Centre.
Fales Library, New York University.
Museum of the City of New York, New York City.
New York Public Library Special Collections, New York City.
Raymond Mander & Joe Mitchenson Theatre Collection, London.
Sherman Theatre Collection, University of Southern Illinois, Carbondale.
Shubert Archive, New York City.
Theatre Museum, London.

Index